MW00908639

FUNCTIONS

To generate a random number _____

To extract a substring starting from the left-most character _____

To extract a substring starting from the right-most character _____

To extract an arbitrary substring _____

To search for one string in another _____

COMMANDS

To delete a line from a program _____

To end a session _____

To clear the work area _____

To save a program in secondary storage _____

To retrieve a program from secondary storage _____

To erase a program from secondary storage _____

To show the names of the programs you have saved _____

SIGN-ON PROCEDURE _____

BASIC
for students:
with applications

MICHAEL TROMBETTA

Queensborough Community College

Bayside, N.Y.

ADDISON-WESLEY PUBLISHING COMPANY

Reading, Massachusetts · Menlo Park, California

London · Amsterdam · Don Mills, Ontario · Sydney

To my parents,
Rose and Louis Trombetta

Library of Congress Cataloging in Publication Data

Trombetta, Michael.
   BASIC for students: with applications

   Includes index.
   1. Basic (Computer program language)—Problems,
exercises, etc. I. Title.
HF5548.5.B3T76   001.64'24   80-15605
ISBN 0-201-07611-X

Reprinted with corrections, April 1982

ISBN 0-201-07611-X
   EFGHIJK-AL-898765432

preface

It is said that when authors of BASIC textbooks die, Saint Peter stops them at the pearly gates and does not let them pass unless they can give a satisfactory answer to his question, "Why did you have to write still another BASIC textbook?" When my turn comes to answer that question, I will say that I wrote this book because in eight years of teaching BASIC and reviewing textbooks I never found one that my students could read and understand.

Many authors who have been programming for years forget how enormously difficult programming can be for novices. I decided to write a book that would be so accessible to students that, if a student missed a lecture, I could simply tell the student which pages to read, and he or she would be able to make up a good part of the missed lecture.

Some of the techniques used to help make the book understandable to students are

1. Each chapter begins with a short discussion of the objectives of the chapter and a list of vocabulary words that will be defined in the chapter. (All the vocabulary words are also defined in the Glossary.) Each chapter ends with a summary of the most important points covered in the chapter.

2. Students have as much difficulty developing an algorithm for a problem as they have understanding BASIC syntax. Therefore every illustrated problem is solved by carefully developing an algorithm and then writing the program. This problem-solving technique is formalized in a nine-point procedure (the procedure is shown on the inside back cover) that serves as a guide for students when they solve their problems.

3. Starting in the first chapter BASIC statements are introduced in the context of complete programs, so that students learn not only the syntax of the statement but also how the statement is used in a program.

4. Since the only way to learn to program is actually to program, almost every section ends with a series of programming exercises. This series of programming exercises starts with a problem that is virtually a restatement of the example problem in the section, which every student should be able to program, and progresses through problems of increasing difficulty. The variety of problems available means that weaker students need not be overwhelmed by problems they cannot solve and stronger students need not be bored by problems they find too simple. A "Solutions Manual" is available from the publisher for adoptors.

5. Almost all the examples and exercises involve either simple business applications, such as calculating gross pay or utility bills, or personal affairs, such as calculating students' grades or average gas mileage, all of which students can immediately understand. When more complicated applications, such as calculating a depreciation table, are discussed, the application is thoroughly explained. Furthermore the only mathematics required to understand the examples and solve the exercises is a knowledge of elementary algebraic notation.

6. The clearest way to show students exactly what a program does is by tracing it. Therefore programs are traced not only in Chapter 1 but whenever new concepts—such as the IF statement, accumulators, FOR-NEXT loops, and arrays—are introduced.

7. Since students generally make errors the first time they enter their programs, debugging is introduced in Chapter 1. Every instructor has had a student, overjoyed at finally getting the computer to produce some output, submit a program that is totally wrong. Therefore I have emphasized the crucial necessity of checking computer-produced answers against hand-calculated answers to ensure that a program is free of logic errors.

8. Flowcharts are used to develop programs. I know that the conventional wisdom holds that the use of pseudocode is superior to the use of flowcharts. Maybe this is so for those of us who have been programming for years, but my experience has convinced me that students understand complicated logic much better when it is explained with flowcharts rather than pseudocode. A welcome indication that the antiflowchart bias within this profession may be

fading is that in their new book* Linger, Mills, and Witt, who are leaders in the "programming revolution," use flowcharts extensively. In fact, flowcharts display complicated logic so clearly that they have been introduced into new areas. It would be ironic if we were to stop using flowcharts in teaching programming at the very moment when people in other disciplines are discovering their usefulness.

9. Topics that cause students difficulty are covered very throughly and carefully. Students always have a lot of trouble with the IF statement, so the first program using an IF statement is explained in 10 pages using three flowcharts and five program listing. Only arrays tend to cause as much trouble as the IF statement, so the bubble sort is explained in 9 pages using three flowcharts. (There are no program listings because writing the program is a student assignment.)

That this book moves carefully and slowly does not mean it does not travel far. Some "advanced" topics are discussed; they include compound conditions, a report with subtotals, and a binary search. In addition, since file processing is at the heart of business data processing, Chapter 7 contains an extensive discussion of file processing.

Although the text emphasizes good programming practices in the use of indentation, documentation, and subroutines in the more complicated programs in the second half of the book, the magic words "structured programming" do not appear. It is obvious that programs should be written in a structured manner, *if the language has the necessary constructs*. These constructs include a multiline IF-THEN-ELSE statement and a DO-WHILE loop. Since most BASICs available today do not have either construct, writing structured programs requires the language to be used in a confusing and unnatural way. In the process the advantages of structured programming—that programs are easier to develop, understand, and maintain—are completely lost. An ANSI (American National Standards Institute) committee under the direction of Thomas Kurtz is currently developing a standard for BASIC that includes a multiline IF-THEN-ELSE and a DO-WHILE loop. When that standard is published and when the BASIC it describes is widely implemented, then it will be possible and desirable to write structured programs in BASIC.

One of the annoying difficulties faced by authors, instructors, and students of BASIC is the variety of BASIC dialects available. To help

* Richard Linger, Harlan Mills, and Bernard Witt, *Structured Programming, Theory and Practice* (Reading, Mass.: Addison-Wesley Publishing Company, 1979).

students find their way through this variety, the inside front cover has been designed to permit the student to write how his or her particular version of BASIC implements those features of the language that have not been standardized. The book can therefore be made to reflect the idiosyncrasies of any version of BASIC. I hope that by the time the second edition of this book appears Professor Kurtz's committee will have done its good work, and we will have one BASIC language.

There is sufficient material in the book for a semester-length course. The first six chapters must be covered in order, but Chapters 7 and 8 may be covered in any order. If less than a full semester is available, some topics will have to be omitted or assigned as independent student study. To aid the instructor in selecting topics to omit, I have indicated with asterisks and footnotes those sections and subsections that serve to deepen the student's understanding but that do not contain material specifically discussed in later sections. I would, however, particularly urge instructors not to omit Chapter 8 simply because it is the last chapter; it does contain material that is important and fun.

I would like to thank my colleagues, Charles Fromme and John Zipfel, who taught from a preliminary version of this book and who made suggestions for improving it. Throughout my teaching career I have had many discussions with Melchiore La Sala of Queensborough Community College and Gary Popkin of New York City Community College about the strategy for teaching computer programming. The ideas developed during those conversations are part of every page of this book. Edward McNally made sure that the computing equipment I needed was available when I needed it, and for that I am grateful. Debra Osnowitz transformed my manuscript into this book with patience, skill, and "grace under pressure," which are greatly appreciated. Finally I would like to thank my wife Angela, who kept the kids occupied during the many hours I was writing this book.

contents

introduction

OBJECTIVES

In this chapter you will learn

- A systematic procedure for solving problems using a computer
- How to draw a simple flowchart
- The rules for the BASIC statement END
- The rules for simplified versions of the BASIC statements

    1. LET
    2. PRINT

- How to detect and correct errors
- The commands

    1. RUN
    2. LIST
    3. BYE (or OFF)

    In addition you should learn the meanings of the following words:

Algorithm	Central processing unit (CPU)
Command	Compiler
Conversational computing	Debugging
Expression	Flowchart
Input unit	Logic error
On-line	Output unit—CRT and hard copy
Primary storage unit	Program
Secondary storage unit	Sign-on
Syntax error	Terminal
Timesharing	Tracing
Variable	

INTRODUCTION TO COMPUTERS AND BASIC

Everyone knows that these days computers are widely used. They are used to prepare our paychecks and our bills and to guide rocket ships to the moon. What most people do not know is that by itself a computer cannot solve any problems. Computers do not know anything about overtime pay or income tax withholding or going to the moon. Before a computer can be used to solve a problem a person must tell it exactly what to do. We tell a computer what to do by giving it a set of instructions to follow. This set of instructions is called a **program.** The objective of this book it so teach you how to write programs.

Components of a Computer System

The best way to learn how to write programs is actually to write and execute them, and for that you will need a computer. There is now a wide variety of computers you might use. At one extreme, you might use a personal computer, such as the TRS-80 shown in Fig. 1.1, which costs less than one thousand dollars and which you can pick up and carry with you. At the other extreme, you might use a large computer that costs millions of dollars and occupies a whole floor in an office building. Or you might use a computer in between the two extremes.

Fig. 1.1. Radio Shack TRS-80 personal computer. (Courtesy of Tandy Corp.)

Despite these differences in size and cost, all computer systems have the same five basic components shown in Fig. 1.2.

The **input unit** sends data and instructions from the outside world (that is, from you and me) into the computer. A typical input unit has a typewriterlike keyboard on which the users type their data and instructions. The keyboard is clearly visible in Fig. 1.1.

The **output unit** sends the computer's answers from the computer to the outside world. In a typical output unit the computer's answers are displayed on a televisionlike screen. This kind of output unit is called a **cathode ray tube,** or **CRT** for short. The CRT is clearly visible in Fig. 1.1. In other output units the computer's answers are printed on paper. This kind of output unit is called a **hard-copy** unit. The term "hard copy" refers to the printed results, which provide a permanent copy of the computer's answers.

The input and output units are often combined in one device called a **terminal.** A terminal is any device that can be used to enter data and instructions into a computer and get answers back. A CRT terminal is shown in Fig. 1.3, and a hard-copy terminal is shown in Fig. 1.4.

A large computer can have up to several hundred terminals connected to it. The computer is often at a remote site, and the terminals are connected to it with telephone lines. Each user has his or her own terminal, and all of these terminals can be used at the same time. The computer works on the first user's problem for a very short time, then on the second user's problem, and so on until all the users have been serviced. It then goes back to the first user and starts the cycle over

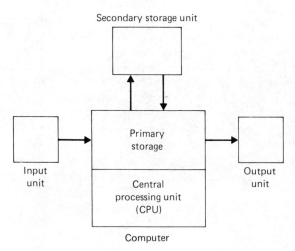

Fig. 1.2. The major components of a computer system.

Fig. 1.3. A CRT terminal. (Courtesy Hazeltine Corporation.)

again. We call this method of using a computer **timesharing.** Because the computer is so fast, each user has the impression of being the only one using the computer.

Look again at the computer components shown in Fig. 1.2. The computer itself consists of two units: the **central processing unit** and the **primary storage unit.** The central processing unit, which is usually abbreviated CPU, is the place where the computer does arithmetic. The primary storage unit is the place where the data and instructions with which the computer is working are stored.

When we are finished using the computer and the next user enters his or her data and instructions, our data and instructions are erased from primary storage. This means that if we want to solve the same problem at a later time, we must retype all the data and instructions. Doing that is clearly a bother, and so we use the last component of the computer system, the **secondary storage unit,** to help us. We can have

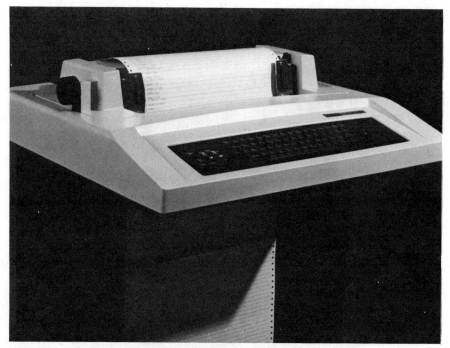

Fig. 1.4. A hard-copy terminal. (Courtesy of Digital Equipment Corporation.)

the computer save our data and instructions on a secondary storage device, and our data and instructions will be stored there as long as we like. When we want to use those data and instructions again, we need only tell the computer to get them from the secondary storage device. In personal computers, cassette recorders are often used as secondary storage devices. The cassette recorder is clearly visible in Fig. 1.1. In larger computer systems, magnetic disks are used for secondary storage. Typically the user never even sees them.

Computer Languages

If we want to use a computer to solve a problem, we must write a program. Since we want the computer to follow the program, the program must be written in a language the computer understands. Modern computers understand many languages. Perhaps you have heard of some of them: COBOL, FORTRAN, RPG, and PL/I. In this book you will learn the BASIC language (the name stands for Beginner's All-purpose Symbolic Instruction Code).

Actually, computers do not really understand BASIC, COBOL, or the other languages. The only language computers really understand is machine language. Machine language is fine for computers, but it is very difficult (some people would say impossible) for people. To permit people to use BASIC, a special program called a BASIC **compiler** is used to translate BASIC instructions into machine language. Similarly, a COBOL compiler translates COBOL instructions into machine language, and other compilers translate instructions in other languages. In some computer systems the program that translates BASIC instructions into machine language is called an interpreter. Although a compiler and an interpreter are not the same, for our purposes we can consider an interpreter and a compiler to be equivalent.

Each computer has its own machine language, which is different from the machine language of other computers, so each computer needs its own BASIC compiler. When a computer is purchased, the manufacturer usually supplies a BASIC compiler, which will translate BASIC instructions into that computer's machine language.

Versions of BASIC

Unfortunately, different manufacturers have implemented slightly different versions of BASIC. This means that a BASIC program written for one computer sometimes does not work properly on a different computer. To end this undesirable situation, the American National Standards Institute has developed rules for "standard" BASIC. Many manufacturers have already made, or are in the process of making, their versions of BASIC agree with standard BASIC.

Fortunately, most BASIC statements are the same in all versions of BASIC. In fact, until we get to Chapters 7 and 8, the differences between different versions of BASIC will be minor. The text will warn you whenever we discuss a feature of BASIC that differs among different versions of BASIC. Your instructor will tell you how the feature is used in your version of BASIC. The inside front cover of this book is designed so that you have space to write how the features that are different in different versions of BASIC are used in your version of BASIC.

BASIC is a relatively simple language and is easy to learn. At the same time it is powerful enough to use to solve complicated problems. Another nice feature of BASIC is that it is designed to permit "interactive" or "**conversational computing.**" This means that the computer gives you answers immediately. Other languages are designed to be used in a "batch" manner. In batch computing, a program and data are submitted in a batch to the computer. It may take from several minutes to several hours for the computer to give you answers. A student can learn more in a few minutes of interactive computing than in a few hours of batch computing.

A PAYROLL PROBLEM

Let's use a computer to solve the following problem. Assume that an employee's rate of pay is $4 per hour, and she worked 30 hours. Calculate and print her gross pay. We will develop a systematic procedure for solving problems on a computer, which you should always use in solving a problem.

Variable Names

The first step of our systematic procedure is to pick names for the variables in our problem. A **variable** is any quantity in a problem whose value may change. Although it is true that in this problem the rate of pay and hours worked are fixed at $4 per hour and 30 hours, respectively, next week the employee might work 40 hours or get a raise to $5 per hour. If either rate of pay or hours worked changes, gross pay will also change. Therefore the variables in this problem are rate of pay, hours worked, and gross pay.

BASIC has two kinds of variables: numeric or ordinary variables whose values are numbers, and string variables whose values are letters or combinations of letters and numbers. In this chapter we will use only numeric variables. You will learn about string variables in Chapter 2.

In picking names for the variables we learn our first BASIC rule:

> The name of a numeric variable must consist of a single letter or a single letter followed by a single digit.[1]

This means that A, Q, Z7, and P1 are legal names, but that HOURS, GP, and 4E are illegal. (Do you understand why these last three names are illegal?) We must pick names for the three variables in our problem: rate of pay, hours worked, and gross pay. We could choose any legal names we like for these variables–A, B, and C, for example–but it is a good idea to use names that will help us remember what they stand for. So we will use the following variable names:

Rate of pay	R
Hours worked	H
Gross pay	G

---

1. A few BASICs allow longer names. Write the rules for your version of BASIC on the inside front cover of this book.

Algorithm and Hand-calculated Answer

The second step of our procedure is to develop a plan to solve the problem. In fancy language we call the plan to solve a problem an **algorithm.** An algorithm is a series of steps a computer can follow to solve a problem. For this relatively simple problem the algorithm is straightforward:

1. Assign 4 to the variable R.

2. Assign 30 to the variable H.

3. Multiply the variables R and H, and assign the product to the variable G.

4. Print the value of the variable G.

The third step in our systematic procedure is to calculate the answer to our problem. I can almost hear you say, "I thought we were going to use a computer to solve this problem." That is true, but the only way we can be sure that the computer's solution is correct is to compare it with the solution we calculated using paper and pencil (and maybe a hand calculator). You might argue that if we calculate the answer to our problem by hand we do not need a computer. At this point in your study of BASIC that is a good argument, but in Chapter 2 you will see why computers are useful, even though we must calculate the answer to our problem by hand. For our payroll problem we can easily calculate that the gross pay should be $4 per hour times 30 hours, which is $120.

Flowcharts

The fourth step in our systematic procedure is to draw a **flowchart.** A flowchart is a picture of an algorithm that shows the logical structure of the algorithm very clearly. A flowchart for our payroll algorithm is shown in Fig. 1.5.

Notice that we used three different symbols in our flowchart. The oval is used to show the beginning and the end of the flowchart. It is called the terminal symbol. As Fig. 1.5 shows, the beginning of the flowchart is shown by an oval with the word START in it, and the end of the flowchart is shown by an oval with the word END in it. The purpose of the terminal symbols is to make it easy for a reader of a complicated flowchart to locate quickly the beginning and end of the flowchart.

A rectangle is used to show an arithmetic step. It is called the process symbol. A step like R = 4 is considered a very simple form of an arithmetic step. Finally, a parallelogram is used to show the step in which the computer will print an answer. In Chapter 2 you will learn

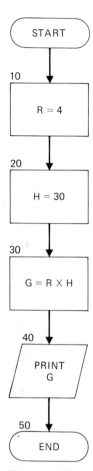

Fig. 1.5. Flowchart for a payroll problem.

that a parallelogram is also used for the step in which the computer reads in data. The parallelogram is therefore called the input/output symbol. A few other symbols used in drawing flowcharts will be introduced as we need them. The meaning of the numbers 10, 20, and so on, will be explained later.

The BASIC Program

The fifth step in our systematic procedure is to translate our flowchart into a BASIC program. A BASIC program consists of a set of BASIC statements that the computer is to follow to solve our problem. The following BASIC program, which is based on our flowchart, contains three different kinds of BASIC statements: the LET statement, the PRINT statement, and the END statement. The words LET, PRINT, and END, which begin each statement, are called BASIC key words. Every BASIC statement begins with a key word. Our BASIC program is as follows:

```
10 LET R = 4
20 LET H = 30
30 LET G = R * H
40 PRINT G
50 END
```

Let's examine this BASIC program in detail. You will notice that every line begins with a line number. This is another BASIC rule:

Every line in a BASIC program begins with a line number.

Line numbers can be any integer from 1 to some large number like 9999, or in some versions of BASIC even as high as 99999. In any event, the upper limit is so high that we never have to worry about it. Although the statements in the example could have had the line numbers 1, 2, 3, 4, and 5, there are advantages to numbering by tens that will be explained later.

The numbers 10, 20, 30, 40, and 50 on the flowchart in Fig. 1.5 correspond to the line numbers used in the program. This correspondence between the flowchart and the program helps us to write the program once the flowchart is drawn. You might think that this program is so straightforward that it could have been written directly from the algorithm without the help of the flowchart. That might be true in this case, but, as we get into more complicated problems, the flowchart will be essential, and at that time you will appreciate the experience of drawing simple flowcharts.

Besides line numbers, our program uses two numbers, a 4 in line 10 and a 30 in line 20. We know that the 4 stands for $4 per hour, but we write it as the number 4, without the dollar sign. The computer always uses "pure" numbers, without any units. It really does not know whether the 4 stands for $4 per hour or 4 radishes or 4 rabbits. This is just more evidence that the computer does not know anything about the problem we are solving, but simply follows our instructions.

Whenever you have to use a number in a BASIC program, you can just write it the way you would in everyday life. There are just two exceptions to this rule. First, always use decimals, not fractions. So if someone is paid $4 1/2 per hour, we would write the pay as 4.5 or 4.50, not 4 1/2. Second, never use commas in numbers larger than 999. If a plane flies 4,352 miles, we write the number in BASIC as 4352, without the comma between the 4 and the 3.

When the BASIC compiler translates a program into machine language, it assigns locations in the computer's primary storage unit where the computer will "remember" the value of each variable used in the program. We can think of these storage locations as little boxes that contain the value of each variable. The important fact to remember about these boxes is that they can hold only one number at a time. When a BASIC statement causes a new number to be put in a box, the old number is erased. For our program the compiler will set up an R box, an H box, and a G box.

The LET Statement

The LET statement is used when we want the computer to calculate a value. In our program, lines 10, 20, and 30 are examples of LET statements. The format[2] of the LET statement is

LET variable = expression

The LET statement starts with the keyword LET. LET is followed by a variable name, which is followed by an equal sign. On the right side of the equal sign is an **expression.** What is an expression? An expression is the part of the LET statement where we ask the computer to calculate a value. When the computer executes a LET statement, it first does the arithmetic we asked it to do in the expression. When the arithmetic is done, the computer is left with a number. It then puts that number in the storage location, or the box, for the variable on the left side of the equal sign.

Let's see how this procedure applies to the three LET statements in our program. In line 10, the expression is particularly simple; it is just the number 4. Since the computer does not have to do any arithmetic to convert the expression into a number (it already is a number), it skips the arithmetic step and puts the number 4 into the R box. Line 20 is equally simple, and the computer puts the number 30 into the H box.

The expression in line 30 is more complicated. In the first place it contains an asterisk. In BASIC we use an asterisk when we want the computer to multiply. We cannot use the usual × for multiplication, since the compiler would not know whether it stood for multiplication or a variable named "X." You will be happy to know, however, that for the other arithmetic operations the usual symbols are used. So when we want to add, we use a +; to subtract we use a −; and to divide we use

2. For reference the formats of all the BASIC statements discussed in the book are shown on the inside back cover.

a /. Now that you know an asterisk means multiply, you can understand the expression in line 30. The computer will take the number in the R box (which is 4) and multiply it by the number in the H box (which is 30). When it gets the answer (which is 120), it will put it into the G box. When the computer uses a number from a box to evaluate an expression, it does not change the number. So after line 30 is executed, the R box still contains the number 4, and the H box still contains the number 30.

Now that we have examined several LET statements, we can define an expression more precisely. An expression is a combination of variables, numbers, and arithmetic operational symbols that can be evaluated to produce a number. The number calculated is assigned to the variable on the left side of the equal sign.

Expressions can be much more complicated than those we have used so far. I will tell you the rules for more complicated expressions when you need them, but for now, you only need to know that expressions can mix variables and numbers. For example, the LET statement

LET H = M / 60

means to divide the number in the M box by 60 and to put the answer in the H box.

It is important to realize that the equal sign in a LET statement is not the same as the equal sign in an algebraic equation. For example, in a later chapter we will use the following LET statement:

LET C = C + 1

As an algebraic equation, $c = c + 1$, this makes no sense. Nothing is equal to itself plus 1. As a BASIC statement, however, it means to take the number in the C box, add 1 to it, and put the answer back in the C box.

The format of the LET statement says that the variable must be on the left side of the equal sign, and the expression must be on the right side. This means that the following two LET statements are wrong:

LET 4 = R

LET R * H = G

Do you see why they are wrong? The first says to take the number in the R box and put it in the 4 box, but there is no 4 box! Boxes are set up just for variables, not for a constant like 4. Similarly, the second example says to take the number in the G box and put it in the R * H box. We have an R box and an H box, but no R * H box.

You should understand the difference between the following two LET statements:

LET A = B

LET B = A

Both of these are legal LET statements, but they have very different effects. Suppose that initially we have a 1 in the A box and a 2 in the B box. Do you know what will be in the A and B boxes after the first LET statement is executed? When we want to understand what happens when the computer executes a statement, it is helpful to set up boxes on paper for each variable, corresponding to the boxes the compiler has set up in the computer's primary storage unit. In this case we start with the following situation:

A   B

1   2

The first LET statement says to take the number in the B box and put it in the A box. After that statement is executed, we have the following situation:

A   B

X̸   2

2

Since these boxes can only hold one number at a time, the 1 that was in the A box is erased and replaced by a 2, so that there is a 2 in both boxes. Notice that nothing happens to the 2 in the B box.

Suppose we return to the original situation, with a 1 in the A box and a 2 in the B box. What will be in the A and B boxes after the second LET statement is executed? I hope you figured out that there will be a 1 in both boxes.

Some BASICs allow you to omit the key word LET from a LET statement. They are smart enough to analyze the form

variable = expression

and figure out that you meant a LET statement. All the LET statements in this book will contain the word LET, but you should ask your instructor whether your BASIC allows you to omit the LET. If it does, you should indicate this on the inside front cover, and, of course, you do not have to type it.

The PRINT and END Statements

A PRINT statement is shown in line 40. Line 40 simply tells the computer to print the number in the G box. Of course, if your output unit is a CRT, nothing is actually printed; the number in the G box is displayed on the screen. The format of the PRINT statement is

PRINT variable, variable, variable

and you can list as many variables as you want. For example, line 40 could have been

40 PRINT R, H, G

This statement tells the computer to print the numbers in the R box, the H box, and the G box, in that order. You must follow the form shown exactly. Notice the comma between the R and the H and the comma between the H and the G, but not after the G. We will have a lot more to say about the PRINT statement in later chapters.

An END statement is shown in line 50. The END statement is the simplest statement of all. It simply tells the BASIC compiler that it has come to the end of your program. The rule is

The END statement must be the last statement in every BASIC program.

Exercise

1.1 Indicate which of the following LET statements contain errors. Rewrite the incorrect statements correctly.

a) LET A = 1,000
b) LET Q = P / R
c) LET X1 = -17
d) LET R * T = D
e) LET AP = F + G
f) LET P = $400.00

ENTERING AND EXECUTING A PROGRAM

Now that we have written our BASIC program, we are ready for the sixth step in our systematic procedure, which is entering the program into a computer. But first you must establish contact with the computer. Exactly how you do that depends on the computer system you are using. If you are using a personal computer, you establish contact by simply turning it on. You are then ready to start entering your program. If you are using a terminal system, establishing contact with the computer is a little more complicated. You must first connect the terminal to the central computer. In some terminal systems, you connect the terminal to the central computer by simply turning a switch. In other cases, you must use a telephone to call the computer. The actual steps you must follow to connect your terminal to your computer vary so much from one computer system to another that specific rules would not be worthwhile.

Your instructor will have to tell you the exact steps to be followed at your installation. Write these instructions on the inside front cover of this book.

Sign-on

When the terminal is connected to the computer, we say the terminal is **on-line.** After you get your terminal on-line, you must **sign-on** to the computer. The purpose of the sign-on procedure is to identify yourself as a valid user to the computer. The sign-on procedure frequently includes typing an account number so that the computer can charge your account for the time you spend on-line. It is also often necessary for you to indicate that you want to enter a BASIC program.

A typical sign-on procedure is shown in Fig. 1.6. The information entered by the user is underlined. At the end of each line you must hit the RETURN key. The Ⓡ at the end of every line is a reminder that you must end every line by hitting the RETURN key, but of course the RETURN key does not cause anything to be printed. (On some keyboards this key is called the ENTER or SEND key.) Do you see why this is called conversational computing? The computer asks a question, PROJECT NUMBER, ID?, and the user responds.

The exact steps to be followed to sign-on vary so much from one system to another that specific rules would not be worthwhile. Your instructor will tell you exactly how you sign-on at your installation. You should write your sign-on procedure on the inside front cover of this book.

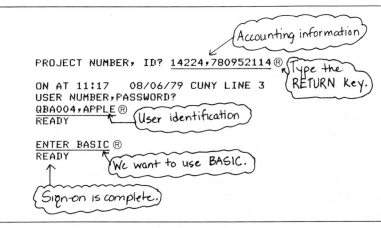

Fig. 1.6. A typical sign-on procedure.

Typing the Program

When your sign-on is complete, most computer systems respond with the message READY, to indicate that you may now begin entering your program. As mentioned earlier, the program is entered by typing it on the input unit's keyboard.

The keyboards on different input units are slightly different, but they all have a separate key for each number. So if you want to type zero, use the number 0 key in the top row of keys, not the key for the letter "O." Similarly, to type the number one, use the number 1 key and not the letter "l."

BASIC uses only capital letters, and most keyboards have only capital letters, so you do not have to hold down the shift key to get capital letters, the way you must with a typewriter. You use the shift key only when you want the special symbols printed on the top of a key. For example, if you want a right parenthesis,), on most keyboards you must hold down the shift key and hit the number 9 key simultaneously. On those keyboards that have both capital and lowercase letters, you get all capital letters by depressing the CAPS ONLY key.

The program is entered by typing it just as we wrote it, one statement on a line. At the end of each line you must press the RETURN key. Figure 1.7 shows how our payroll program was entered into the computer. Again an (R) is written at the end of every line to remind you that you must end every line by hitting the RETURN key.

You might wonder about the spacing you should use when you type the statements. BASIC allows you to use spaces just about any way you

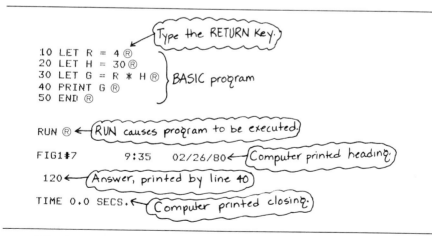

Fig. 1.7. A BASIC program to calculate gross pay.

like. You should, however, use spaces to help make your program easy to read and understand. The use of a space is suggested after a line number, after BASIC keywords like LET and PRINT, and around equal signs and the arithmetic operational symbols $+$, $-$, $*$, and $/$.

Executing the Program

Merely typing the program does not cause anything to happen; the computer does not do the arithmetic you asked, or print any answers. To have the computer execute the program, you must type the **command** RUN. RUN is a command, not a BASIC statement. One difference between commands and BASIC statements is that commands never have line numbers. Another difference is that when you type a command you are giving the computer an order to do something immediately. When you type a BASIC statement, on the other hand, you are just adding another line to the program, and the computer does not execute the statement until later when you type RUN. As you study BASIC, you will learn additional commands.

Figure 1.7 shows what happens when we type RUN. The computer first prints a one line heading, giving the name of the program,[3] the date, and the time. (Not all computers type a heading line, and if they do, the wording may be different.) Next the BASIC compiler translates the program into machine language. Nothing is printed during this step, so we are not even aware that it is happening. When the compilation is complete, the computer executes the program and prints the answer. In this case the answer is 120. Remember that our hand-calculated answer was also 120, so we are satisfied that the program is correct. Finally, the computer tells us it is finished by printing a message telling how much time the computer took to solve the problem. The simple problem in Fig. 1.7 took less than 0.1 seconds. (Different computers may print different closing messages.)

Tracing the Program

It is essential that we understand exactly what happens when the computer executes the program. The best way of doing that is to execute the program, line by line, just as though you were the computer. When we do this, we say we are **tracing** the program. To help in our tracing, we set up boxes on paper for each variable corresponding to the boxes the compiler has set up in the computer's storage unit. This is exactly

---

3. The way in which a program gets a name will be explained in Chapter 2.

what we did earlier when we were following the execution of LET statements.

When the computer executes a program, it always starts with the lowest line number. For the program shown in Fig. 1.7 it starts with line 10. When the computer executes line 10, it puts a 4 in the R box. We should also put a 4 in our R box, as shown in Fig. 1.8(a). After the computer executes line 10, it moves to the next line, which in this case is line 20. When the computer executes line 20, it puts a 30 in the H box, and in Fig. 1.8(b), we put a 30 in our H box. The computer next executes line 30. Line 30 tells the computer to take the number in the R box, which is 4, and multiply it by the number in the H box, which is 30. The answer, which is 120, is put in the G box. We also put a 120 in our G box (Fig. 1.8c). The computer then executes line 40. Line 40 tells the computer to print the number in the G box. Since the number in the G box is 120, line 40 causes a 120 to be printed. Recall that in Fig. 1.7, when the program was executed, the answer printed was 120. By tracing the program, we have been able to see exactly how the computer came to print the answer 120. Tracing is very important because it helps us understand exactly how the computer executes our programs.

Errors

Figure 1.7 shows an ideal situation, in which no errors were made. Unfortunately, when you use the computer, you will make one or more errors most of the time, so it is important to know how to correct them. The seventh step in our systematic procedure is to correct errors. Errors are often called bugs, and the process of correcting errors is called **debugging**.

R	H	G
4	–	–

(a) After executing line 10

R	H	G
4	30	–

(b) After executing line 20

R	H	G
4	30	120

(c) After executing line 30

Fig. 1.8. Tracing the program in Fig. 1.7

The simplest errors are typing errors. If you hit the wrong key, you can backspace to correct the mistake. Some keyboards have a backspace key, while other keyboards require that you hit a special combination of keys. Therefore you can backspace, type the correct character, and continue. (On many hard-copy terminals the print mechanism does not move back, and the correct character does not overstrike the incorrect character. But that does not matter, because the correct character does replace the incorrect character in the computer's storage unit, and that is where it counts.)

Sometimes you will notice a mistake after you have hit the RETURN key. At that point it is too late to use the backspace key, but you can simply retype the line, number and all, correctly. Whenever you retype a line, the new version of that line replaces the old version. You do not have to retype the line immediately. Suppose you type lines 10, 20, and 30, and then notice that you made a mistake in line 10. At that point, after you have typed line 30, you may retype line 10, and the new version of line 10 will replace the old version.

Syntax Errors

You might make a typing error, but not notice it. For example, let's assume you make a mistake and type line 40 as

40 PRITN G

Assume you do not notice this mistake, but finish typing the program, and then type RUN. What will happen? Remember that when you type RUN, the BASIC compiler translates your BASIC statements into machine language.

Since PRITN G is not a legal BASIC statement, the compiler cannot translate line 40 into machine language. We call this kind of error a **syntax error.** You make a syntax error whenever your program contains a statement that is not legal in BASIC. As Fig. 1.9 shows when the compiler discovers a syntax error, it prints the line number of the illegal statement and a brief error message. (The wording of the message may be different in different computers.) Some computers check the syntax of each line as it is entered. In those computers you do not have to wait until you type RUN to discover your syntax errors. The seventh step of our systematic procedure is to correct syntax errors.

Since the computer tells you the line number of the illegal statement, all you have to do to find your mistake is to compare your statement with the correct example shown on the inside back cover of this book. Once you have figured out your mistake, you can replace the illegal

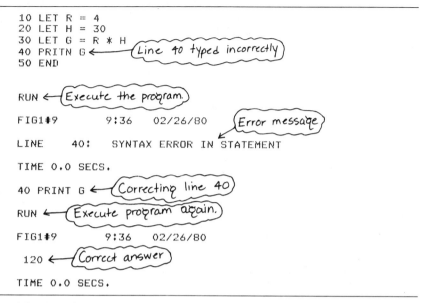

```
10 LET R = 4
20 LET H = 30
30 LET G = R * H
40 PRITN G
50 END
```
(Line 40 typed incorrectly)

RUN (Execute the program.)

FIG1#9   9:36   02/26/80   (Error message)

LINE   40:   SYNTAX ERROR IN STATEMENT

TIME 0.0 SECS.

40 PRINT G (Correcting line 40)

RUN (Execute program again.)

FIG1#9   9:36   02/26/80

120 (Correct answer)

TIME 0.0 SECS.

Fig. 1.9. Correcting a syntax error

line by simply typing it correctly, as we discussed earlier. Notice that you can replace a line by retyping it, even after you have typed RUN. In Fig. 1.9 you can see how the incorrect line 40 was replaced. After you correct your syntax errors, you must type RUN again to have your program executed. If your corrections were correct, your program should execute properly. Figure 1.9 shows the program executed properly after line 40 was corrected.

Logic Errors

Syntax errors are easy to make, but as you have seen, they are also relatively easy to correct. Unfortunately, that is not true of the second kind of error that you can (and will!) make: **logic errors.** A program contains a logic error when it executes but gives the wrong answer. How could this happen? Suppose, for example, that line 30 were incorrectly typed as

30 LET G = R + H

Figure 1.10 shows a program with this incorrect line 30. Notice that the computer does not print any messages about syntax errors. Why not? Because the expression R + H is perfectly legal BASIC! Of course, adding

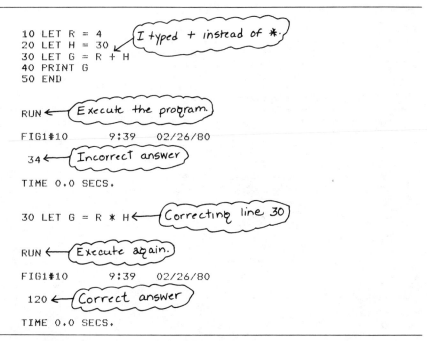

```
10 LET R = 4
20 LET H = 30
30 LET G = R + H
40 PRINT G
50 END
```
I typed + instead of *.

RUN ← *Execute the program.*

FIG1#10   9:39   02/26/80

34 ← *Incorrect answer*

TIME 0.0 SECS.

30 LET G = R * H ← *Correcting line 30*

RUN ← *Execute again.*

FIG1#10   9:39   02/26/80

120 ← *Correct answer*

TIME 0.0 SECS.

Fig. 1.10. Correcting a logic error.

R and H does not make any sense if we are trying to calculate G, but the computer does not know that. If we tell it to add R and H, that is what it will do.

How do we know when our program has a logic error? We know our program contains a logic error if the answer printed by the computer does not agree with the answer we calculated by hand. So the eighth step of our systematic procedure is to compare the computer's answers against the answers we calculated by hand in the third step. In Fig. 1.10 we can see that the computer printed an answer of 34. Since our hand calculation gave an answer of 120, we know our program contains a logic error. This brings us to the ninth and final step of our systematic procedure, to correct logic errors.

How can we find and correct logic errors? Unlike syntax errors, for which the computer told us which line was wrong, logic errors can be anywhere in our program. The best way of discovering logic errors is to trace the program as we discussed earlier. Pretend you are the computer; execute the program line by line, putting numbers into the variable boxes, and you will discover the line that contains the logic error. That line can then be replaced by simply typing it over correctly. Figure 1.10 shows how line 30 was corrected. To have the computer execute your program again, type RUN. Figure 1.10 shows the program finally producing the correct answer, 120.

Exercises

1.2   Trace the following program to determine what the output will be.

    10 LET A = 9

    20 LET B = 5

    30 LET S = A + B

    40 LET D = A − B

    50 PRINT S,D

    60 END

In the following programming assignments you should develop your programs by following our systematic procedure. Make up any numbers you like for the data you need, but be sure to calculate an answer by hand so that you will know when your program is correct.

1.3   Enter the program given in Fig. 1.7 into your computer. Try to make syntax errors so you will see how your computer responds to them, and so you will get experience correcting them. After the program is working, give the employee a raise by making her R equal to $5 an hour.

1.4   Write and execute a program to calculate and print average gas mileage by dividing miles traveled by gas used.

1.5   A delicatessen sells cold cuts by the pound. Write and execute a program to calculate customers' bills by multiplying pounds purchased by price per pound.

1.6   Write and execute a program to calculate and print total calories consumed in a day by adding the calories consumed in breakfast, in lunch, and in dinner. Also calculate and print the difference between total calories consumed and the recommended daily total of 2400 calories.

ADDITIONAL COMMANDS: LIST AND BYE (OR OFF)

There are two additional commands you should know. The command LIST causes the current version of your program to be displayed. You can type LIST whenever you like and as often as you like. LIST should always be used when the computer gives you unexpected output. For example, if the computer indicates you have a syntax error in a particular line that you thought you typed correctly, LIST the program, and you will probably find you made a typing error.

LIST is especially helpful when you are correcting logical errors. Since you will be tracing the program, you should make sure that you and the computer are executing the same program. By typing LIST you will see the version of the program that the computer is executing. As a general rule, you should always LIST your program before you start to correct logical errors.

After you have corrected all your errors, and your program is running successfully, you should LIST and RUN one last time to get a copy of the final correct version of your program and its output to put in your notebook.

If your program is large, you may want to list only part of it. To list part of a program, include the line numbers of the first and last lines you listed as part of the LIST command. For example, the command

LIST 80-120

will cause all the lines in the program starting from 80 up to and including 120 to be listed.

When you have finished using the terminal and want to end the session, you must use the command BYE. (On some systems the corresponding command is OFF.) BYE tells the computer that you are finished and that it should stop charging your account. It also disconnects your terminal from the computer, freeing the communication line you were using for another user. You must also turn the terminal off. (On a personal computer you end the session by simply turning the machine off.)

Exercises

1.7 Define the following terms in your own words:
   a) algorithm
   b) flowchart
   c) logic error
   d) program
   e) syntax error
   f) tracing

SUMMARY

In this chapter you have learned

■   A systematic procedure for solving problems with a computer:

   1. Pick names for the variables in the problem.

2. Develop an algorithm for solving the problem.

3. Calculate answers to the problem by hand.

4. Draw a flowchart.

5. Write a BASIC program.

6. Enter the program into a computer and execute it.

7. Correct syntax errors.

8. Check the computer's answers against the answers calculated by hand in step 3.

9. Correct logic errors.

■ The following flowcharting symbols:

1. The terminal symbol—the oval

2. The process symbol—the rectangle

3. The input/output symbol—the parallelogram

■ The rules for the following BASIC instructions:

1. LET (simplified version)

2. PRINT (simplified version)

3. END

■ The commands to perform the operations

1. Execute the program—RUN

2. List the program—LIST

3. End the session—BYE (or OFF)

■ How to trace a program

writing complete programs

OBJECTIVES

In this chapter you will learn

- How to write programs that process many cases
- How to write complicated expressions
- The rules for the BASIC statements
    1. READ
    2. DATA
    3. GO TO
    4. REM
- Additional rules for the PRINT statement
- The rules governing string variables
- The commands
    1. SCRATCH (or CLEAR or NEW)
    2. SAVE
    3. OLD (or LOAD)
    4. UNSAVE (or PURGE or KILL)

In addition you should learn the meanings of the following terms:

Documenting	Exponentiation
Loop	Round-off error
Rules of precedence	String
String variable	Unconditional branching statement
Uninitialized variable	

The program in Fig. 1.7 calculates gross pay for a particular employee. If we wanted to use that program to calculate gross pay for a different employee, we would have to retype lines 10 and 20 using the new employee's rate of pay and hours worked. Whenever we wanted to calculate gross pay for a different employee, we would have to retype lines 10 and 20. This is obviously very inconvenient, and in this chapter you will learn an easy way to have a computer calculate gross pay for any number of employees.

A PAYROLL PROBLEM WITH MANY EMPLOYEES

Let us develop a program to solve the following problem. We have three employees, whose rates of pay and hours worked are given as

Employee number	Rate of pay	Hours worked
1	4.00	30
2	7.00	25
3	5.00	40

Our problem is to write a program to calculate and print the gross pay for these three employees. Our method follows.

Variable Names

Following our systematic procedure, we first pick variable names. The names we used in Chapter 1 will do quite well here:

Rate of pay	R
Hours worked	H
Gross pay	G

Although we have three employees who have three different rates of pay, we define only one rate of pay variable, R. This one R will be used for all the employees. Similarly, we assign only one H and one G.

Algorithm and Hand-calculated Answer

In the second step of our systematic procedure we develop an algorithm. The algorithm for this problem is similar to the algorithm we used in Chapter 1:

1. Assign values to R and H for the first employee.

2. Calculate G by multiplying R and H.

3. Print R, H, and G.

4. Repeat until all the employees have been processed.

Notice that in step 3 we print R and H as well as G. Since this program will calculate G for three employees, it is helpful to print R and H as well as G so that we can tell which G goes with which R and H.

   Printing R and H also helps us eliminate logic errors. Suppose the computer prints an incorrect value for G. We know we have a logic error, but we do not know where it is. By examining the values printed for R and H we can see whether the proper values were assigned to R and

H. If they were, we know that the logic error must be in the calculation of G. If they were not assigned correctly, the error must be in the statements that assign values to R and H.

In the third step of our systematic procedure we calculate an answer by hand. For employee number 1, G is $4 \times 30 = 120$. That is all we have to do! Even though the computer will calculate G for three employees, we only have to do the hand calculation for one of them. If the computer's answer agrees with our hand-calculated answer for that one employee, we can assume that the program is correct, and we do not have to check the answers for the other employees.

Now you can see why computers are useful even though it is necessary to calculate an answer by hand. The basic idea is that we prove a program is correct by comparing our hand-calculated answer with the computer's answer for one case. If the two answers agree, we know that the program is correct. We can then use that program to calculate two or two thousand or even two million additional cases, and we can be sure that the answers for these additional cases are correct. (In Chapter 3 you will learn that in more complicated problems it is necessary to check more than one case. But the basic idea remains the same: you prove that a program is correct by checking a limited number of cases and then use that program to calculate many additional cases.)

Flowchart

The fourth step of our systematic procedure is to draw a flowchart. A flowchart for our payroll program is shown in Fig. 2.1. We will use a READ statement, shown in box 10, to assign values to R and H. The READ statement is an input statement, and, as you recall from Chapter 1, both input and output steps are drawn using a parallelogram. In step 20 the multiplication of R and H is shown with an asterisk. Since the reason we draw a flowchart is to help us write the BASIC program, we may as well use the same multiplication symbol we will use in the program.

The most important new feature of the flowchart shown in Fig. 2.1 is the flowline that goes from box 30 to box 10. That flowline indicates that, after the computer executes line 30, it should execute line 10. We have established a **loop**. Loops are very important in computer programming because the typical computer programming problem has the following structure:

1. Get the data for a case. (A case might be an employee, a customer, or a student.) This is the input step.

2. Calculate the answer for this case. This is the process step.

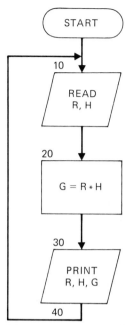

Fig. 2.1. Flowchart for a payroll problem with many employees.

3. Print the answer for this case. This is the output step.

4. Repeat steps 1, 2, and 3 until all the cases have been processed.

Notice that our algorithm involves exactly these four steps. To accomplish step 4 requires a loop, shown by the flowline that goes from box 30 to box 10 in Fig. 2.1. You will meet this basic sequence (input, process, output, repeat) many times throughout this book.

Complicated flowcharts can be difficult to read. One aid in reading them is the arrowheads on the ends of the flowlines. These arrowheads show the direction in which the flowlines run. Because of the loop, this flowchart does not have a logical endpoint, so it does not contain an end terminal symbol. As you will see, however, the progran will contain an END statement.

The fifth step of our systematic procedure is to write a BASIC program. A BASIC program based on the flowchart in Fig. 2.1 is shown in Fig. 2.2.

The new statements in this program are the READ statement in line 10, the GO TO statement in line 40, and the DATA statements in lines 50, 60, and 70. Let's explain these new statements.

```
10 READ R,H
20    LET G = R * H
30    PRINT R,H,G
40 GO TO 10
50 DATA 4,30
60 DATA 7,25
70 DATA 5,40
80 END
```

Answers

```
RUN      R              H                  G

FIG2#2          10:54      08/03/79

    4                      30                    120
    7                      25                    175
    5                      40                    200

LINE    10:    END OF DATA

TIME 0.0 SECS.
```

Fig. 2.2. Program for payroll with three employees.

The READ and DATA Statements

The READ and DATA statements are always used together. When the computer executes the READ statement in line 10, it performs the following steps. (1) It finds a DATA statement. If, as in this case, there is more than one DATA statement, it takes the one with the lowest line number. In this case that is the DATA statement in line 50. (2) It takes the first number from this DATA statement and puts it into the box of the first variable listed in the READ statement, and it takes the second number from the DATA statement and puts it into the box of the second variable listed in the READ statement. In this case it puts the 4 into the R box and the 30 into the H box. (3) The computer then marks the 4 and the 30 as "used," so they will not be used again. If more variables were listed in the READ statement, the computer would continue this process until all the variables had been assigned values. The format of the READ statement is

READ variable, variable, variable

and you can list as many variables as you like. The format of the DATA statement is

DATA value, value, value

and again you can list as many values as you like.

The READ statement is complicated, and its operation will become clearer when we trace this program a little later. For now let's explain what is meant when we say that, when the computer executes a READ statement, it "finds" a DATA statement. This means the computer searches the whole program looking for a DATA statement. We can therefore put the DATA statements anywhere we like. The best place to put the DATA statements is at the end of the program, just before the END statement, as in Fig. 2.2. Placing the DATA statements at the end of the program leaves the part of the program where the actual processing takes places uncluttered, easier to read, and easier to follow.

Notice that the DATA statements do not appear in the flowchart for this problem, Fig. 2.1. DATA statements never appear in a flowchart because they are not part of the logic of the program. After all, when we developed the algorithm and flowchart we were not thinking of the particular numbers that were going to be in the DATA statements. To be useful, our program must work for any values of R and H. For example, if employee number 1 were to get a raise to $5 per hour, we would have to change only the DATA statement in line 50, but the flowchart and the processing section of our program, lines 10 through 40, would still be perfectly correct.

The GO TO Statement

A GO TO statement is shown on line 40. You remember from Chapter 1 that, after the computer executes a particular line, it automatically goes to the next line. In this problem, however, after the computer executes line 30, we want it to execute line 10. The GO TO statement is used when we want to change the order in which the lines are executed. After the computer executes the statement GO TO 10, it will next execute the READ statement in line 10.

The format of the GO TO statement is

GO TO line number

The line number specified can be either higher or lower than the line number of the GO TO itself. For example, both of the following statements are correct:

70 GO TO 40

70 GO TO 110

The GO TO is not represented in the flowchart by a box. Instead it is represented by the flowline that goes from box 30 to box 10.

Statements, like the GO TO, that cause a change in the order in which lines are executed, are called branching statements. We say that the GO TO statement causes the computer to branch to the specified line number. For example, in Fig. 2.2, the GO TO in line 40 causes a branch to line 10. Because a branch occurs every time a GO TO statement is executed, it is called an **unconditional branching statement.** (In Chapter 3 you will learn about a more complicated statement called a conditional branching statement.)

Notice that lines 20 and 30 are indented two spaces. BASIC does not require that these lines be indented, but because the indentation helps show the loop clearly, in this book the lines within a loop will always be indented two spaces. You should also use this convention as an aid.

Tracing the Program

Figure 2.2 shows an execution of our payroll program. For the first employee the computer calculated a gross pay of 120, and, since that was the value we calculated by hand, we can be sure our program is free of logic errors. To be certain we understand how this program works, we will trace it and see whether we can get the same output the computer printed.

To help us trace a program we set up boxes to hold the values of the variables as shown in Fig. 2.3. When we type RUN, the computer starts by executing line 10. When the computer executes line 10, it looks

R	H	G
4	30	–

(a) After executing line 10

R	H	G
4	30	120

(b) After executing line 20

R	H	G
4̸	3̸0̸	120
7	25	

(c) After executing line 10

R	H	G
4̸	3̸0̸	12̸0̸
7	25	175

(d) After executing line 20

Fig. 2.3. Tracing the program in Fig. 2.2.

for a DATA statement, which it finds in line 50. As we said earlier, it puts the 4 into the R box and the 30 into the H box, as shown in Fig. 2.3(a). The computer also marks the 4 and the 30 as having been used. Notice that line 50 is not executed. The computer merely takes the numbers from line 50. It is line 10 that is executed. The computer next executes line 20, which causes it to multiply the number in the R box by the number in the H box and put the answer in the G box. We follow the computer and multiply 4 by 30 and put the answer, 120, in the G box as shown in Fig. 2.3(b). The computer next executes line 30, which causes it to print the numbers in the R, H, and G boxes. Since Fig. 2.3(b) shows that the numbers in the R, H, and G boxes are 4, 30, and 120, we expect a line of output containing these three numbers. Referring to Fig. 2.2, we see that 4, 30, and 120 is exactly what the computer printed for its first line of output. So far, so good, but let's continue tracing.

When the computer executes line 40, it branches to line 10. When it executes line 10, it looks for a DATA statement. It remembers that the two numbers in line 50 have been used, so it goes to the next DATA statement, line 60. It puts the 7 into the R box and the 25 into the H box, as shown in Fig. 2.3(c). But remember that these boxes can only hold one number at a time. When the new numbers are put into these boxes, the old numbers are erased.

To indicate that the old number is erased, I cross it out, as in Fig. 2.3(c). When you trace programs, you should also cross out the old number when a new number is put into a box. Now when the computer executes line 20, it will multiply the 7 in the R box by the 25 in the H box, and put the answer, 175, in the G box. As shown in Fig. 2.3(d), when the computer puts the 175 in the G box, the 120 that was there is erased. When the computer executes line 30, it prints the numbers in the R, H, and G boxes, which in this case are 7, 25, and 175. Referring to Fig. 2.2, we see that this is exactly what the computer printed for its second line of output. I will leave tracing the program for the third employee as an exercise for you. You should be able to figure out how the computer generated its third line of output.

Before we leave Fig. 2.2, I would like to explain the meaning of the message LINE 10 END OF DATA, which you can see at the end of the output. When the computer executes line 10 for the third employee, it uses the 5 and the 40 from line 70 and marks these two numbers as used. After the answers for the third employee are printed, line 40 will cause a branch back to line 10. But now when the computer tries to find a DATA statement, it discovers that they have all been used. When that happens, the computer prints the message LINE 10 END OF DATA and stops executing. Notice that it is the line number of the READ statement that is printed, not of a DATA statement. Whenever the computer tries to execute a READ statement but cannot find an unused DATA statement from which to get values, it will print that message, with the line number of the READ statement that could not be executed. Your system may print a slightly different message, but the meaning is the same.

We have developed this program to calculate and print gross pay for three employees. It should be clear by now, however, that the same program could be used for any number of employees. All we need is a DATA statement with a rate of pay and hours worked for each employee. The computer will keep calculating and printing gross pay for each employee until all the employees have been processed.

More About the DATA Statement

What we have said so far about the DATA statement is correct, but is not the whole story. When the compiler encounters DATA statements in a program, it processes them in numerical order and places the values from each DATA statement in a single data bank. The data bank generated from the DATA statements in the program in Fig. 2.2 is shown in Fig. 2.4. Each time a READ statement is executed, the computer takes the values it needs from the next available numbers in the data bank and marks these values as used, so that they will not be used again.

```
 4
30
 7
25
 5
40
```

Fig. 2.4. Data bank formed from DATA statements in Fig. 2.2.

The fact that READ statement really gets its values from the data bank rather than from the DATA statement, as we said originally, has no effect on the answers generated by the program. The fact that the compiler generates a data bank does, however, have one consequence. All of the sets of DATA statements shown in Fig. 2.5 would give the data

```
50 DATA 4,30          50 DATA 4,30,7,25,5,40      50 DATA 4,30,7
60 DATA 7,25                                      60 DATA 25,5
70 DATA 5,40                                      70 DATA 40

       (a)                      (b)                      (c)
```

Fig. 2.5. Alternative, equivalent DATA statements.

bank shown in Fig. 2.4. This means that any of these sets of DATA statements could have been used in the program in Fig. 2.2 and would have given the same answers.

Since all the sets of DATA statements shown in Fig. 2.5 give the same answers, which is the best set to use in our program? Consider the set shown in Fig. 2.5(a), which is the set we used originally in Fig. 2.2. When we study the program we see that line 10 says READ R, H, and, when we examine the DATA statements, we see that each DATA statement has a value for R and a value for H. This arrangement, where each DATA statement contains exactly the number of values necessary for one execution of a READ statement, is much easier to understand than any of the other sets of DATA statements shown in Fig. 2.5. Because we want our programs to be easy to read and understand, we will adopt this rule:

> Each DATA statement should contain the exact number of values necessary for one execution of the READ statement.

There is only one exception to this rule. If we are reading a single variable, we will permit a DATA statement to have many values. For example, if we want to read sales for each employee, our program will contain the statement READ S. If the sales for three employees are $400, $700, and $200, we will use a DATA statement like DATA 400, 700, 200, instead of a separate DATA statement for each employee. Since only one variable is in the READ statement, a strict application of our rule would require that each DATA statement contain only one value. Since all three values stand for sales, however, there is no chance for confusion if we put all the values in one DATA statement, and so we allow this exception to our rule.

Documenting the Program: The REM Statement

It is good practice to include comments in your program that will be helpful to someone who reads it. This is called **documenting** your program. Figure 2.6 shows how the REM statement can be used to include comments in your program. The format of a REM statement is

REM any comment you like

When the BASIC compiler encounters a REM statement, it knows that that line contains a comment that is not supposed to be translated into machine language, and the compiler completely ignores it.

It is important to understand that REM statements have no effect on the output produced by the program. The program shown in Fig. 2.6

```
1 REM PAYROLL WITH MANY EMPLOYEES      REM statements
2 REM PROGRAMMER M. TROMBETTA          added to program
10 READ R,H
20    LET G = R * H
30    PRINT R,H,G
40 GO TO 10
50 DATA 4,30
60 DATA 7,25
70 DATA 5,40
80 END


RUN

FIG2#6       11:39    08/03/79

    4              30           120
    7              25           175
    5              40           200

LINE   10:   END OF DATA

TIME 0.0 SECS,
```

Fig. 2.6. Documenting a program with REM statements.

produces exactly the same output as the program shown in Fig. 2.2. The only time the REM statements are printed is when you list the program.

You can use as many REM statements as you like, and they may be placed anywhere in the program. Since REM statements are not part of the logic of the program, they are not shown on the flowchart.

Every program you write should contain REM statements at least giving the purpose of the program and your name. You can, in addition, include any other information you think someone reading your program would find helpful. When we develop more complicated programs, we will use REM statements to explain the functions of different parts of the program.

Exercises

2.1 What output will be produced if the following changes are made to the program in Fig. 2.2? Trace the program to determine what the output will be. Before making each new change, assume that the program is restored to its original form.

a) The PRINT statement in line 30 is eliminated.

b) The PRINT statement in line 30 is written as

30 PRINT G, H, R

  c) The GO TO statement in line 40 is eliminated.

  d) The GO TO statement in line 40 is changed to

   40 GO TO 20

  e) The GO TO statement in line 40 is changed to

   40 GO TO 30

  f) The GO TO statement in line 40 is eliminated, and the following new statement is inserted:

   25 GO TO 10

2.2 In this programming assignment you should develop your program by following our systematic procedure. You should print the input data as well as the calculated answers. Your program should be able to process an arbitrary number of cases. Use REM statements to document your program.

   Given a distance driven and gas used for a trip, write a program to calculate and print gas mileage, in miles per gallon, obtained during the trip.

STRING VARIABLES

We have all received computer-prepared bills and checks that had our names printed on them. It must be true then that computers can process data that are letters as well as numbers. Data that consist of letters, or mixed numbers and letters—as in the address "14 Elm Street", or even special symbols like ! # @) %—are called string data or simply **strings.** A variable used to store string data is called a **string variable.**

   A legal name for a string variable is a single letter followed by $. Therefore N$, T$, and A$ are legal names for string variables, but L1$ and $P are not. Notice that although L1 is legal name for an ordinary numeric variable, L1$ is not a legal name for a string variable.[1] When we talk about string variables, we pronounce the $ as the word "string." N$ is called N-string.

   When the BASIC compiler encounters a string variable, it sets up a storage location for it just as it does for numeric variables. The amount of data that can fit in one of these storage locations is measured in characters, where each letter, number, and special symbol counts as one character. Even a blank counts as one character. The number of characters that can fit into the storage location set up for a string variable

---

1. Some versions of BASIC do permit a string variable name to consist of a letter followed by a digit followed by a $. In those versions of BASIC L1$ would be a legal string variable name.

varies from one BASIC system to another. In some versions of BASIC it is only 15 characters, while in others it is several hundred characters. Your instructor will tell you the number of characters a string variable can hold in your version of BASIC, and you should write that number on the inside front cover of this book.

Using String Variables

String variables may be used just like ordinary variables, although, of course, you may not do arithmetic with them. So if A$ stands for an address and we want to assign the string 14 Elm Street to A$, we could use the LET statement

    100 LET A$ = "14 ELM STREET"

Notice that the string 14 ELM STREET must be enclosed in quotation marks. BASIC uses quotation marks to determine the beginning and end of the string, but the quotation marks are not part of the string. After this LET statement is executed A$ will contain 14 ELM STREET.

A string variable may be set equal to another string variable, as in the LET statement

    100 LET Q$ = P$

When the computer executes this statement, it takes the string in the P$ box and puts it in the Q$ box.

String variables may only be equated to other string variables or to strings. The following two LET statements are therefore illegal:

    100 LET A$ = P

    100 LET A$ = 46

The first LET statement is illegal because it sets a string variable equal to a numeric variable, and the second LET statement is illegal because it sets a string variable equal to a number.

Since you cannot do arithmetic with string variables, the LET statement in line 30 is illegal:

    10 LET A$ = "APPLES"

    20 LET B$ = "ORANGES"

    30 LET C$ = A$ * B$

We all learned in elementary school that you cannot multiply apples and oranges. Strings, however, may be added in a special way called concatenation, which we will study in Chapter 8.

String variables may also be assigned values using READ and DATA statements as follows:

```
10  READ A$
     .
     .
     .
100  DATA "14 ELM STREET"
```

Notice that the string 14 ELM STREET is enclosed in quotation marks when it occurs in a DATA statement, just as it was when we used it in the LET statement.

A string may contain any character you can type at your keyboard, except a quotation mark. The reason strings may not contain quotation marks is that the compiler cannot tell which quotation mark indicates the beginning, which indicates the end, and which are parts of the string. Some versions of BASIC even allow lowercase letters in a string. If your keyboard can type lowercase letters, try using them in a string to see whether your version of BASIC accepts them.

Since the number of characters a string variable may contain is limited, it may sometimes be necessary to abbreviate. For example, suppose that in some version of BASIC a string variable may contain a maximum of 18 characters. Suppose also that we want to assign the address 147 Thompson Street to a string variable. The string 147 THOMP-SON STREET is 19 characters long (remember that the blanks count as characters). If we try to assign this string to a string variable by using either a LET statement or a READ statement, we would have an error. In some BASICs the computer would print an error message and stop executing. In other versions of BASIC the computer might assign just the first 18 characters of the string and discard the rest. In either event we would not have what we want. Therefore any string that is longer than 18 characters must be abbreviated to contain 18 or fewer characters.

A program that uses a string variable is shown in Fig. 2.7. This program is based on the program of Fig. 2.6, modified to include reading and printing the employee's name. We have introduced a new variable, N\$, which represents the employee's name. In line 10 we read N\$ as well as R and H, and in the DATA statements we include the names as well as the rates of pay and hours worked. As usual, the order of the values in the DATA statement must agree with the order of the variables in the READ statement. In line 30 when we want to print the employee's name, we just include N\$ in the print list with R, H, and G.

Exercise

2.3 In this programming assignment you should develop your program by following our systematic procedure. Print the input data and the calculated answers. Your program should be able to process an

```
1 REM PAYROLL WITH EMPLOYEE NAMES
2 REM PROGRAMMER M. TROMBETTA
10 READ N$,R,H
20    LET G = R * H
30    PRINT N$,R,H,G
40 GO TO 10
50 DATA "TINKER,JOE",4,30
60 DATA "EVERS,JOHN",7,25
70 DATA "CHANCE,FRANK",5,40
80 END


RUN

FIG2#7       14:57    02/25/80

TINKER,JOE        4              30             120
EVERS,JOHN        7              25             175
CHANCE,FRANK      5              40             200

LINE    10:    END OF DATA

TIME 0.0 SECS.
```

Fig. 2.7. Using a string variable to print names.

arbitrary number of cases. Use REM statements to document your program.

For each salesperson we are given a name and sales. Write a program to calculate and print each salesperson's commission. Commission is calculated as 12% of sales. (*Hint:* 12% of a number is calculated by multiplying the number by .12.)

MORE COMPLICATED EXPRESSIONS

All of the expressions we have used so far have involved only two terms. Obviously, we sometimes must do more complicated arithmetic. This section explains the rules for writing complicated expressions.

Exponentiation

Besides adding, subtracting, multiplying, and dividing, which we discussed earlier, raising to a power is also possible in BASIC. This is called **exponentiation** and is indicated by the symbol $\wedge$. (Some versions of BASIC use $\uparrow$ and others use $**$. You should write the symbol used in your version of BASIC in the place provided on the inside front cover of this book.) If we wanted to raise A to the fourth power, in algebra we would write A^4, and in BASIC, A $\wedge$ 4.

Suppose that A equals 2, and B equals 3. What value will be assigned to C when the following LET statement is executed?

LET C = 4 * A + B

Some students assume that the computer will multiply 4 by A, which is 2, to get 8, and then add B, which is 3, to get 11, so that C will equal 11. Other students assume that the computer will add A and B to get 5, and then multiply by 4 to get 20, so that C will equal 20. In truth, both answers are "reasonable," but one is right and the other is wrong. To know which value C will have, we must understand the rules the computer uses when it evaluates expressions.

Rules of Precedence

When the computer evaluates an expression, it follows the **"rules of precedence."** This means that it scans the expression three times, from left to right and performs the arithmetic operations in the following order:

1. Exponentiation

2. Multiplication and division

3. Addition and subtraction

Let us see how these rules help us determine how the computer will evaluate the expression 4 * A + B. In step 1 the computer scans the expression looking for exponentiations to perform. This expression does not contain any exponentiations, so the computer goes to step 2. In step 2 the computer performs multiplications and divisions. It performs the multiplication, 4 * A and gets the answer 8. So by the start of step 3 the expression has been reduced to 8 + B. In step 3 the computer performs the addition and gets the answer 11. So we see that students who said C would equal 11 were correct, and those who said C would equal 20 were incorrect.

It is important to understand that, when the computer performs step 2, it does not do all the multiplications first and then all the divisions. It does multiplications and divisions as it encounters them, as it scans the expression from left to right. Suppose A equals 12, and B equals 2. What is the value of the expression A / 3 * B? Since there is no exponentiation, nothing happens when the computer performs step 1. During step 2, as the computer scans the expression from left to right, it first encounters the division. It divides 3 into A and gets 4. At this point the expression is 4 * B. The computer then multiplies 4 by B and gets 8 for the expression.

Similarly, when the computer performs step 3, it does additions and subtractions as it encounters them, as it scans the expression from left to right. So that if A equals 20, B equals 5, and C equals 3, the expression A − B + C equals 18.

It is particularly easy to make mistakes with expressions in which an arithmetic step follows division. For example, with A equal to 12 and B equal to 2, consider the expression A / B + 1. When it evaluates this expression, the computer will first divide A by B to get 6 and then add 6 and 1 to get 7. Many students would mistakenly add the B and 1 to get 3, and then divide A by 3 to get the wrong answer, 4.

Use of Parentheses

There is a difficulty. Suppose the logic of the problem required that in this last expression B and 1 be added before the division. Or in our earlier expression 4 * A + B suppose the logic of the problem required A and B to be added before the multiplication. How can we get the computer to do what we want instead of what it does automatically by following the rules of precedence? The answer is that we use parentheses. We really should add a zero step to our sequential rules of precedence:

0. Evaluate expressions inside parentheses.

Therefore if we wanted B and 1 to be added before the division, we would write the expression A / (B + 1). Similarly, if we wanted A and B to be added before the multiplication, we would write the expression 4 * (A + B). In this last expression note that the asterisk indicating multiplication must be present. In algebra, multiplication is often implied by simply writing two terms together, as $4(A + B)$. In BASIC this is totally wrong; if you want to indicate multiplication, you must use an asterisk.

The only rule to remember when using parentheses is that there must be the same number of right parentheses as left parentheses. You must also be careful to use the correct keys when you are typing. Many keyboards contain square brackets, [], as well as parentheses. Square brackets are illegal in BASIC; you must use parentheses.

You may use as many parentheses as you want. Unnecessary parentheses are simply ignored. So the following expressions are all legal and equivalent:

    A / (B + 1)

    (A) / (B + 1)

    (A / ((B) + 1))

These last two expressions are legal, but what the computer would think of you if you typed them, I'd rather not say.

A Savings Account Problem

Now that you know how to write complicated expressions, let's solve the following problem. If D dollars are deposited into a savings account that pays an interest rate R, the balance in the account after N years may be calculated by the equation

B = D * (1 + R) ^ N

Write a program that will read D, R, and N and calculate and print B.

The first step of our systematic procedure is to pick names for the variables. In this problem the names have already been assigned in the statement of the problem. I would, however, like to refine this step. Not only do I want to pick names for the variables, I also want to indicate which variables are input variables and which are output variables. The input variables are those variables whose values we know, and which are given to the computer in, for example, READ-DATA statements. In this problem the input variables are D, R, and N. The output variables are those variables whose values we do not know and which the computer is supposed to calculate. In this problem the output variable is B.

Two circumstances sometimes cause students to get confused about which are the input and which are the output variables. First, even though D, R, and N are input variables, we will print them. But remember we print D, R, and N to help us debug the program, and so we will know which B goes with which set of D, R, and N. It is important to remember that we know D, R, and N before we run the program. That is what makes them input variables.

That brings us to the second circumstance that sometimes causes students difficulty. Part of our systematic procedure is to calculate an answer by hand, so we will also know a value of B before we run the program. But remember we know only one value of B before we run the program, and we calculated that one value just to check our program. Once the program is written, we expect to use it to calculate many values of B.

From now on the variable names will be specified as follows:

Input variables
Amount deposited   D
Interest rate   R
Number of years   N

Output variable
Balance in account   B

The algorithm we will use is

1. Read values for D, R, and N.

2. Calculate B.

3. Print D, R, N, and B.

4. Repeat for all sets of D, R, and N.

Next we must calculate an answer by hand. Let's use values D = 1000, R = .05 (notice that R must be expressed as a decimal, not a percentage), and N = 20. Using a hand calculator, it is not too difficult to calculate that B equals 2653.30.

The flowchart for this problem is shown in Fig. 2.8. Notice how the structure of this flowchart is identical to the structure of the flowchart in Fig. 2.1. They both involve input, processing, output, and a loop to repeat.

Round-off Error

The program based on this flowchart is shown in Fig. 2.9. There seems, however, to be a problem, since the calculated answer of 2653.24 does not agree exactly with our hand-calculated answer of 2653.30. The pro-

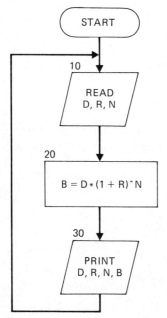

Fig. 2.8. Flowchart for savings account problem.

gram does not contain a logic error. The difference between the computer's answer and our hand-calculated answer is due to **round-off error.**

The term "round-off error" refers to small numeric errors that occur in computer-calculated answers because of the way computers store numbers. Numbers are stored in primary storage in binary form, but in everyday life we write numbers in decimal form. We do not have to be concerned with the complexities of the binary number system, except to note that, when numbers containing a fractional part like 1.05, are converted to binary form in primary storage, small errors sometimes occur. Often these errors have no detectable effect on the final answers, but sometimes, as in this case, they result in a small error. Notice that the error in this case is only six cents in more than two thousand dollars.

The size of the error depends on exactly how the computer stores numbers. If you execute the program in Fig. 2.9 on your computer, your answer may be slightly different from my answer, either closer or further from the correct answer. The main thing to remember about round-off error is that it sometimes may cause your computer to calculate an answer that is slightly different from an example in the text or from your hand-calculated answer.

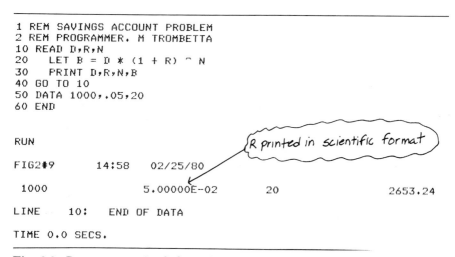

```
1 REM SAVINGS ACCOUNT PROBLEM
2 REM PROGRAMMER. M TROMBETTA
10 READ D,R,N
20    LET B = D * (1 + R) ^ N
30    PRINT D,R,N,B
40 GO TO 10
50 DATA 1000,.05,20
60 END


RUN                                    R printed in scientific format

FIG2#9       14:58    02/25/80

  1000                 5.00000E-02      20               2653.24

LINE    10:    END OF DATA

TIME 0.0 SECS.
```

Fig. 2.9. Program to print balance in a savings account.

Exercises

2.4 Identify the syntax errors, if any, in the following LET statements:

a) LET A = B PLUS C

b) LET 2 * P = Q

   c) LET M = 5 (N − S)

   d) LET W = R * ((S + T) * V − P / N

   e) LET A = B * ((1 + C) $^\wedge$ (E − F) + G) / (H + I)

2.5 Calculate the value assigned to A by the following LET statements if B = 3, C = 4, D = 2, and E = 1.

   a) LET A = B + C / D + E

   b) LET A = (B + C) / D + E

   c) LET A = (B + C) / (D + E)

   d) LET A = B + 3 * C / D $^\wedge$ 2 + E

   e) LET A = (B + 3 * C) / (D $^\wedge$ 2 + E)

2.6 Translate the following algebraic equations into LET statements.

   a) $a = \dfrac{b + c + d}{3}$

   b) $a = \dfrac{b + 2c + 3d}{6}$

   c) $t = \dfrac{d((1 + r)^n - 1)}{r}$

   d) $p = \dfrac{m \cdot r}{1 + (1 + r)^{-n}}$

MORE ABOUT THE PRINT STATEMENT

We have used PRINT statements in our programs to display answers, but we have not yet explained exactly how the PRINT statement works. The printer paper and CRT screen are divided into five zones. (On some systems there are only four zones.) The size of these zones varies slightly from one system to another, but on most systems they are 15 columns wide. The PRINT statements we have used so far print one value in each zone. Therefore a line of output can contain five values. If we specify more than five variables to be printed, the computer prints the values of five variables on a line and uses as many lines as necessary to print the values of all the variables. So if the PRINT statement were

   PRINT A, B, C, D, E, F, G, H

the values for A, B, C, D, and E would be printed on the first line, and the values for F, G, and H on the second. String variables are printed the same way. If we print a string variable that contains more than 15 characters, it will occupy more than one print zone, and the next variable will be printed at the start of the next zone. For example, if N$ contains 18 characters, the PRINT statement

PRINT N$, A

will cause the value of N$ to fill all of print zone 1 and the first three columns of print zone 2, and the value of A will be printed in print zone 3.

Use of Semicolons

It often happens that we want to print more than five values on a line. BASIC makes that very easy; just separate the variables by semicolons instead of commas. A legal PRINT statement would be

PRINT A; B; C; D; E; F; G; H

This PRINT statement would cause all eight values to be printed on one line.

When semicolons are used to separate the variables in a print list, the values are printed next to each other. Numbers are printed with a space in front and behind. The space in front of the number is used to show the sign of the number. If the number is positive, the space is left blank; if the number is negative, a minus sign is printed. The space behind the number is always left blank so that there will be at least one blank space between numbers. String variables are printed with no space in front or behind.

You might wonder how many values will be printed on a line when semicolons are used. Unfortunately, there is no simple answer because different values take different numbers of columns to print. For example, the number 1 requires only three columns to print (remember the space in front and behind), while the number 16976 requires seven columns.

Values Printed in Scientific Format

You noticed that in Fig. 2.9 the value of R looked strange. That is because it is printed in scientific format. If a variable has a very large value, say greater than ten million, or very small, say less than one hundredth, BASIC automatically prints the value in scientific format.[2]

The following examples illustrate how scientific format works. Suppose a variable equals 12,345,678. This value would be printed as 1.2345678E + 07. The E + 07 tells us that, to get the value represented by this number, we must shift the decimal point 7 places to the right. If you shift the decimal point 7 places to the right, you will get the original value, 12,345,678.

---

2. The version of BASIC used in Fig. 2.9 is unusual in that it prints values less than one tenth in scientific format.

Suppose a variable equals .00000001. This value would be printed as 1.0E − 08. In this case the minus sign in the E − 08 tells us that, to get the value represented by this number, we must shift the decimal point 8 places to the left. If you shift the decimal point 8 places to the left, you will get the original value .00000001. In Fig. 2.9 the value printed for R was 5.0E − 02. If you shift the decimal point 2 places to the left, you will get .05, which is the correct value of R.

In our problems values will not be printed in scientific format very often, but if they are you will not have any trouble reading them.

Hanging Punctuation

In the examples we have seen so far, whenever a PRINT statement was executed, it started printing on a new line. That is fine, since usually you want to keep the output for each case on its own line. If you put a comma or a semicolon after the last variable in a PRINT statement, however, the PRINT statement will not start on a new line the next time it is executed. Instead it will begin printing where the previous printing stopped. Under special circumstances that may be desirable, but most of the time it is not desirable because the output from different cases becomes mixed on the same line. A comma or a semicolon after the last variable is said to be hanging. Figure 2.10 shows the output produced by the program in Fig. 2.6 when the PRINT statement in line 30 contains a

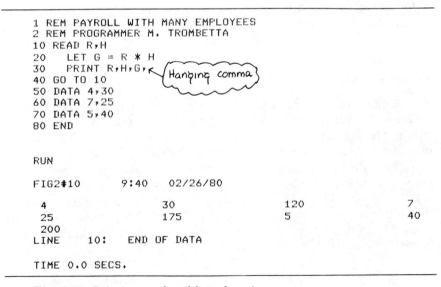

```
1 REM PAYROLL WITH MANY EMPLOYEES
2 REM PROGRAMMER M. TROMBETTA
10 READ R,H
20    LET G = R * H
30    PRINT R,H,G,       (Hanging comma)
40 GO TO 10
50 DATA 4,30
60 DATA 7,25
70 DATA 5,40
80 END


RUN

FIG2#10        9:40    02/26/80

4                  30            120          7
25                 175          5            40
200
LINE    10:   END OF DATA

TIME 0.0 SECS.
```

Fig. 2.10. Printing produced by a hanging comma.

hanging comma. (The version of BASIC used in Fig. 2.10 prints four values on a line.) Because that comma is legal, we did not get a syntax error message, but it sure made a mess of our output.

Exercises

In each of the following programming assignments you should develop your program by following our systematic procedure. You should print the input data and the calculated answers. Your programs should be able to process an arbitrary number of cases. Use REM statements to document your programs.

2.7 We are given each employee's name, rate of pay, and hours worked. Write a program to calculate and print each employee's gross pay, withholding, and net pay. Withholding is calculated as 20% of gross pay, and net pay is calculated as gross pay minus withholding. For each employee you should print the name, rate of pay, hours worked, gross pay, withholding, and net pay. To get all these variables to print on one line, semicolons must be used in the PRINT statement. (*Hint:* 20% of a number is calculated by multiplying the number by .20.)

2.8 For each student we are given his or her name and test scores on three tests. Write a program to calculate the student's average score by adding the three test scores and dividing by three. For each student you should print the name, three test scores, and average test score. If your BASIC has fewer than 5 print zones on a line, you will have to use semicolons in your PRINT statement to get all these values on one line.

2.9 Write a program to calculate the percentage of markup. If C is cost, S is selling price, and M is percentage of markup, then M is calculated by the formula

$$M = \frac{S - C}{C} \times 100$$

2.10 If D dollars are deposited into a savings account at the end of each year, and if interest rate R is paid on the accumulated balance, then after N years the total in the account, T, is

T = D * ((1 + R) ^ N − 1) / R

Write a program that will read D, R, and N, and calculate and print T. R must be expressed as a decimal, not a percentage. Since it may be difficult to calculate an answer to this problem by hand,

I will give you an answer. If D = 100, R = 0.05, and N = 20, T should be 3306.60. Because of round-off error, my computer-calculated answer was 3306.49.

MORE ON ERRORS

Now that you can write more sophisticated programs, you will make more sophisticated errors. It is important to know how to detect and correct these more sophisticated errors.

One kind of syntax error that frequently causes trouble occurs when you accidentally type the letter O instead of the number zero as part of a line number. Figure 2.11 shows what happens if, for example, when typing the program in Fig 2.6 you accidentally type line 30 incorrectly as

   3O PRINT R,H,G

where the character following the number 3 is the letter O, not the number zero. As Fig. 2.11 shows, this causes the perhaps unexpected error message

   LINE 3 SYNTAX ERROR IN STATEMENT

Your immediate response would probably be, "What nonsense; I don't even have a line 3!" If you follow the rule that whenever the computer tells you something you do not understand you should LIST your program, you will get the results shown in Fig. 2.11. Figure 2.11 shows that you do have a line 3 in your program, and it is printed in its proper numeric position. It should be clear by now that the computer took the line number to be 3, and the statement to be

   O PRINT R,H,G

Since this is not a legal BASIC statement, the computer printed a syntax error message.

Deleting a Line

To correct this error requires two steps. First, we must delete line 3 from our program. That is easy. On many systems, a line is deleted from a program by simply typing the line number followed immediately by a carriage return. On other systems, a line is deleted by typing the command DELETE followed by the line number of the line you want to delete. Write the method used in your BASIC on the inside front cover of this book. Second, we must type line 30 correctly. Figure 2.11 shows that, when these corrections are made, the program executes properly.

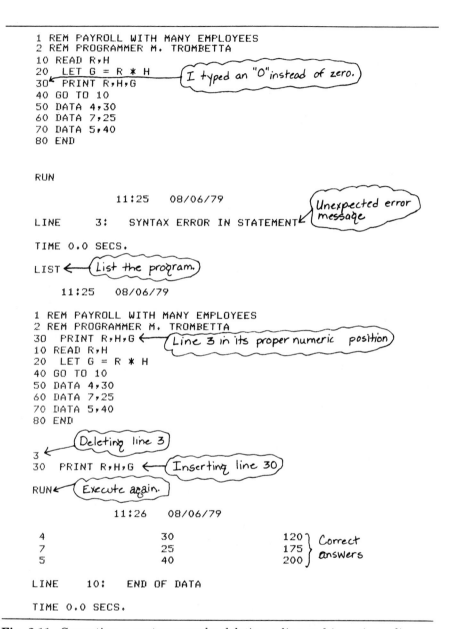

```
1 REM PAYROLL WITH MANY EMPLOYEES
2 REM PROGRAMMER M. TROMBETTA
10 READ R,H
20  LET G = R * H          I typed an "O" instead of zero.
30  PRINT R,H,G
40 GO TO 10
50 DATA 4,30
60 DATA 7,25
70 DATA 5,40
80 END


RUN

            11:25    08/06/79                Unexpected error
                                             message
LINE     3:    SYNTAX ERROR IN STATEMENT

TIME 0.0 SECS.

LIST          List the program.

     11:25    08/06/79


1 REM PAYROLL WITH MANY EMPLOYEES
2 REM PROGRAMMER M. TROMBETTA
30  PRINT R,H,G        Line 3 in its proper numeric   position
10 READ R,H
20  LET G = R * H
40 GO TO 10
50 DATA 4,30
60 DATA 7,25
70 DATA 5,40
80 END

             Deleting  line 3
3
30  PRINT R,H,G          Inserting  line 30

RUN       Execute again.

            11:26    08/06/79

4                  30              120   Correct
7                  25              175   answers
5                  40              200

LINE    10:    END OF DATA

TIME 0.0 SECS.
```

Fig. 2.11. Correcting a syntax error by deleting a line and inserting a line.

Inserting a Line

You sometimes may find that the source of a logic error in your program is a line that was left out of your program. Figure 2.12 shows the program in Fig. 2.6 with the PRINT statement omitted. (Although you might imagine that you would never leave out a line, be assured that with more complicated programs leaving out a line is a relatively easy error to make.) Notice that the program produces no output at all. When we examine the listing, we notice the missing PRINT statement. Logically the PRINT statement belongs between lines 20 and 30. We can insert a PRINT statement between lines 20 and 30 by typing

25 PRINT R,H,G

The computer will insert line 25 in its proper numeric position between lines 20 and 30. Figure 2.12 shows line 25 being added to the program. The program is then executed again, and this time we see the correct answers printed.

Now you understand why we number our statements by 10. This leaves us nine slots between every pair of statements in the program in which we can insert additional statements if we find they are required. We can insert new statements into our program any time we want simply by using a previously unused statement number. To execute the program after the new statements have been inserted we must type RUN again.

Endless Loops: The BREAK Key

Exercise 2.1(d) asked what output would be produced if line 40 in Fig. 2.2 were changed to GO TO 20. The answer is that the computer will keep printing the same three values of R, H, and G over and over, until something is done to stop it. By making that change in line 40 we created an endless loop. Since you might accidentally create an endless loop, you should know how to stop the computer from executing. This is done by hitting the BREAK key. On some keyboards the corresponding key is called the ATTN (for attention) key. Hitting the BREAK key stops the computer from executing.

Uninitialized Variables

Figure 2.13 shows a type of logic error that can be very difficult to correct. In line 20 I have accidentally typed a P instead of an R. Different BASICs respond to this error in different ways. In some BASICs, when the computer tries to execute line 20, it notices that we want to use the number in the P box but that we never put a number in the P box! The computer will stop executing our program and print an error message.

```
1 REM PAYROLL WITH MANY EMPLOYEES
2 REM PROGRAMMER M. TROMBETTA
10 READ R,H
20    LET G = R * H
30 GO TO 10
40 DATA 4,30
50 DATA 7,25
60 DATA 5,40
70 END


RUN

FIG2#12        9:42    02/26/80
        } No output produced
LINE    10:    END OF DATA

TIME 0.0 SECS.



25    PRINT R,H,G  ←[ Inserting line 25 ]

LIST ←( List the program. )

FIG2#12        9:42    02/26/80

1 REM PAYROLL WITH MANY EMPLOYEES
2 REM PROGRAMMER M. TROMBETTA
10 READ R,H
20    LET G = R * H
25    PRINT R,H,G  ←[ Line 25 was inserted
30 GO TO 10             in its proper place. ]
40 DATA 4,30
50 DATA 7,25
60 DATA 5,40
70 END


RUN ←( Execute again. )

FIG2#12        9:43    02/26/80

    4              30              120 }
    7              25              175 } Correct
    5              40              200 } answers

LINE    10:    END OF DATA

TIME 0.0 SECS.
```

Fig. 2.12. Inserting a statement in a program.

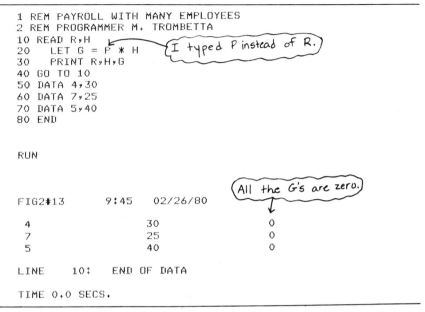

```
1 REM PAYROLL WITH MANY EMPLOYEES
2 REM PROGRAMMER M. TROMBETTA
10 READ R,H
20    LET G = P * H
30    PRINT R,H,G
40 GO TO 10
50 DATA 4,30
60 DATA 7,25
70 DATA 5,40
80 END


RUN


FIG2#13        9:45    02/26/80

   4                    30              0
   7                    25              0
   5                    40              0

LINE    10:    END OF DATA

TIME 0.0 SECS.
```

Fig. 2.13. Using an uninitialized variable.

In other BASICs, when the computer notices we are trying to use the number in the P box but that we never put a number in the P box, it assumes we wanted P to be zero! Of course we did not want P to be zero, we just made a mistake. But that does not occur to these BASICs; they just use a value of zero for P and go merrily along. The output produced in this case is shown in Fig. 2.13. This error is particularly difficult to correct because the output shows that R and H were assigned their proper values. This kind of error is called "using an **uninitialized variable**," because we use a variable before we assign it a value. If your BASIC does not warn you when you use an uninitialized variable, the only way to discover the error is by tracing the program.

Exercise

2.11 Write a program to determine how your BASIC responds to an uninitialized variable.

ADDITIONAL COMMANDS

When you sign-on, the computer presents you with a clean work area in which to develop your program. After you have finished working on one program and want to start another, you must clean the work area yourself. To clean the work area, use the command SCRATCH. (On some systems the proper command is CLEAR, and on others it is NEW.) Your instructor will tell you the command used in your BASIC, and you should write it on the inside front cover of this book. Be very careful when you use the SCRATCH command; it erases the current program. If your program has a simple error that could be corrected by retyping a single line, and you instead type SCRATCH, your whole program will be erased, and you will have to retype the whole thing. Use SCRATCH only when you are certain you are finished with a program.

Suppose you have an error in your program that you cannot correct in the time available. Or suppose you have program that you would like to use in the future. You can have the computer save a copy of your program in secondary storage by using the command SAVE. In some systems you must type SAVE filename, where "filename" is the name under which you want the program to be saved. File names are often your name or your initials. Your instructor will tell you the command used at your installation, and you should write it on the inside front cover of this book,

After the computer saves your program, it types the message READY. An example of saving a program is shown in Fig. 2.14. The file name used was EXAMPLE1. The copy of the program in secondary storage is not affected by the SCRATCH command. So you can save a program, scratch the work area, and work on a new program. The saved version of the program is still available to you.

A previously SAVED program can be retrieved by using the command OLD filename. (On some systems the command is LOAD filename.) Write the command used in your BASIC on the inside front cover of this book. The "filename" is the name you used when you saved the program

```
 1 REM PAYROLL WITH MANY EMPLOYEES
 2 REM PROGRAMMER M. TROMBETTA
10 READ R,H
20    LET G = R * H
30    PRINT R,H,G
40 GO TO 10
50 DATA 4,30
60 DATA 7,25
70 DATA 5,40
80 END


SAVE EXAMPLE1
READY  ←————(The SAVE operation is complete)
```

Fig. 2.14. Saving a program.

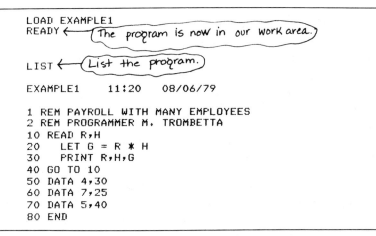

```
LOAD EXAMPLE1
READY ←    The program is now in our work area.

LIST ←    List the program.

EXAMPLE1    11:20    08/06/79

1 REM PAYROLL WITH MANY EMPLOYEES
2 REM PROGRAMMER M. TROMBETTA
10 READ R,H
20    LET G = R * H
30    PRINT R,H,G
40 GO TO 10
50 DATA 4,30
60 DATA 7,25
70 DATA 5,40
80 END
```

Fig. 2.15. Loading and listing a program.

or when you created it. After the computer retrieves your program, it types the message READY. An example of retrieving a program is shown in Fig. 2.15. When you type OLD (or LOAD), the program is retrieved from secondary storage and placed into the work area, but it is not listed or executed. When the computer responds with READY to your OLD (or LOAD) command, the situation is as though you had just typed the program. At that point you can correct the program, list it, or execute it. In Fig. 2.15 after retrieving the program EXAMPLE1, we listed it.

The space in secondary storage is limited, so when you are finished with a program, you should erase it from secondary storage to make room for other programs. This is done by using the command UNSAVE filename, or in some systems PURGE filename, or in still other systems KILL filename. Write the command used in your BASIC on the inside front cover of this book.

If you are using a personal computer with a cassette recorder as your secondary storage device, you can erase a program by simply recording over it.

Exercise

2.12 What command is used in your BASIC to

    a) Save a program on secondary storage
    b) Erase a program from secondary storage
    c) Retrieve a program from secondary storage
    d) Erase a program from the work area

SUMMARY

In this chapter you have learned

- How to use a loop in a program to process many cases
- How the computer evaluates complicated expressions by following the rules of precedence:

  0. Evaluate expressions inside parentheses.

  1. Exponentiation.

  2. Multiplication and division.

  3. Addition and subtraction.

- The rules for the following BASIC statements

  1. READ

  2. DATA

  3. GO TO

  4. REM

- Additional rules for the PRINT statement
- The rules governing string variables and how they are used in LET, READ, and PRINT statements
- How your system responds to uninitialized variables and how to delete statements from and insert statements into a program
- How to use the BREAK key to stop execution
- The commands to perform the following operations:

  1. Clearing the work area—SCRATCH (or CLEAR or NEW)

  2. Saving a program in secondary storage—SAVE

  3. Retrieving a program from secondary storage—OLD (or LOAD)

  4. Erasing a program from secondary storage—UNSAVE (or PURGE or KILL)

making decisions

OBJECTIVES

In this chapter you will learn

- How to draw a flowchart and write a program containing a decision
- The rules for the BASIC statements

  1. IF
  2. INPUT
  3. PRINT USING

- How to print strings
- How to use the TAB function with the PRINT statement

In addition you should learn the meanings of the following terms:

Compound condition   Condition

Conditional branching statement   Prompt

Relational symbol

In the problems we have considered so far we treated all cases identically. For example, in Exercise 2.3 every salesperson was paid the same 12% commission rate. In many problems, however, we would like to treat different cases differently. For instance, a commission rate might depend on sales; a company might pay a 20% commission rate if sales were greater than 500 dollars, and a 10% commission rate if sales were 500 dollars or less. Or a store might sell doughnuts for 20 cents each if a customer were to buy less than 12, but only 15 cents each if the customer were to buy 12 or more.

To solve these kinds of problems a program must execute different instructions depending on conditions. For example, if sales are greater than 500 dollars, the program must execute the statement in which commission is calculated using a 20% commission rate. But if sales are 500 dollars or less, the program must execute the statement in which commission is calculated using a 10% rate. In effect, the program must decide which statement to use in each case. To demonstrate how a program can make a decision we will develop a solution to the doughnut sales problem.

A SALES PROBLEM WITH A DECISION

Formally stated, the problem is to calculate and print bills for customers who purchase doughnuts. If fewer than 12 doughnuts are bought, they cost 20 cents each, but if 12 or more are bought, they cost only 15 cents each.

We begin by selecting names for the variables. Let's use the following:

> *Input variable*
>
> Number of doughnuts   D
> purchased
>
> *Output variable*
>
> Customer's bill   B

The next step is to develop an algorithm. For this problem we can use

1. Read D for a customer

2. Determine whether this customer bought 12 or more doughnuts

3. Calculate B using the appropriate cost

4. Print D and B

5. Repeat until all the customers have been processed

The only new step in the procedure is step 2, the decision step.

We must next calculate an answer by hand. If a customer buys 10 doughnuts, the bill will be 10 times 20 cents, or 2 dollars. The next step is to draw a flowchart, which is shown in Fig. 3.1. The new feature of this flowchart is the decision symbol, shown by a diamond.

Conditions

Inside the decision symbol we write a **condition.** In a condition a variable is compared with another variable or with a constant. The allowed comparisons and the symbols used to represent them are as follows:

Equal	$=$
Less than	$<$
Greater than	$>$
Less than or equal	$<=$
Greater than or equal	$>=$
Not equal	$<>$

To express the last three comparisons you must type two symbols

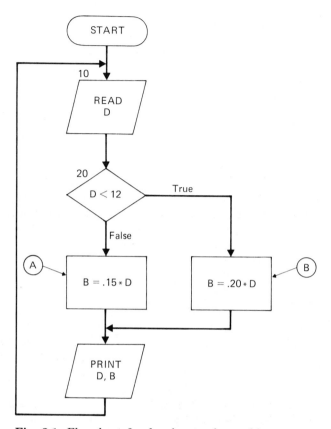

Fig. 3.1. Flowchart for doughnut sales problem.

next to each other. Because they indicate a relation like less than or greater than, they are called **relational symbols.**

A condition is read as a question. So the condition A < B is read, "Is A less than B?" If A is less than B, the condition is true; otherwise the condition is false. If we use an equal sign in a condition, as in the condition P = Q, it means "Is P equal to Q?" It does not mean "Put the number in the Q box into the P box," as it does when the equal sign is used in a LET statement. The condition P = Q is true only when P and Q are equal. The condition in Fig. 3.1 is read, "Is D less than 12?" If D is less than 12, the condition is true; otherwise the condition is false. (Question: if D is exactly 12, is the condition true or false?)

Let's now return to the flowchart in Fig. 3.1. Notice that there are two flowlines, or branches, leaving the decision symbol. One of the branches is labeled "true" and the other is labeled "false." If the condition is true, we leave the decision symbol along the true branch, and if the condition is false, we leave the decision symbol along the false branch. If D is less than 12, the condition is true. The true branch leads to process symbol Ⓑ, which shows B calculated using the equation B = 0.20 * D. In this equation the price of each doughnut is 20 cents, which is the correct price when D is less than 12. If D is 12 or greater, the condition is false. The false branch leads to process symbol Ⓐ, which shows B calculated using the equation B = 0.15 * D. In this equation the price of each doughnut is 15 cents, which is the correct price when D is 12 or greater.

So we see that the flowchart shows B calculated by the correct equation whether the customer buys less than 12 doughnuts or not. The rest of the flowchart involves steps with which you are already familiar. Notice that not all the symbols in the flowchart are numbered. Numbers are missing because we cannot complete the numbering of the flowchart until we write the program, which is the next step.

The IF Statement

We are now ready to write the program. The start of the program is shown in Fig. 3.2. Lines 1, 2, and 10 are similar to statements you have seen in earlier programs, but line 20 is new. The decision symbol in the flowchart is written in the program as an IF statement.

```
1 REM THE DOUGHNUT SALES PROBLEM
2 REM WRITTEN BY M. TROMBETTA
10 READ D
20    IF D < 12 THEN ?
```

Fig. 3.2. Start of the doughnut sales program.

As an illustration of how an IF statement works, consider the following statements:

50 IF A = 6 THEN 90

60 LET B = 10

.

.

.

90 LET B = 20

When the computer executes line 50, it evaluates the condition A = 6. If the number in the A box is 6, the condition is true, and the computer branches to the line number following the word THEN, in this case, line 90. On the other hand, if the number in the A box is not 6, the condition is false, and the computer executes the next statement, line 60. We say that, when the condition is false, the computer falls through the IF statement to the next line.

The general format of the IF statement is

IF condition THEN line number

The statement begins with the key word IF followed by a condition. The condition is written just as it is on a flowchart. If the condition is true, the computer branches to the "line number" that follows the word THEN. If the condition is false, the computer falls through to the next line.

Remember from Chapter 2 that a GO TO statement is called an unconditional branching statement. An IF statement is called a **conditional branching statement** because it does not branch all the time, only when the condition is true.

With this in mind, let's continue developing the program in Fig. 3.2. The false branch of the IF statement is written first. If the condition in line 20 is false, the rules of BASIC say that the next line executed will be line 30. The flowchart in Fig. 3.1 tells us that if the condition is false, we want to execute the statement in process symbol Ⓐ. Therefore this must be statement 30. Figure 3.3 shows the program with line 30 written. Notice that a question mark still follows the word THEN in line 20. This question mark indicates that we still do not know the line number to which we want to branch when the condition is true. We will have to figure that out later.

```
1 REM THE DOUGHNUT SALES PROBLEM
2 REM WRITTEN BY M. TROMBETTA
10 READ D
20    IF D < 12 THEN ?
30    LET B = .15 * D
```

Fig. 3.3. Doughnut sales program with line 30 added.

When we write the BASIC statement that corresponds to a particular flowchart symbol, we should number the symbol with the statement's line number to maintain the correspondence between the flowchart and the program. Figure 3.4 shows process symbol Ⓐ numbered 30.

We continue coding the false branch of the IF statement until the flowchart shows we have reached either the end of the false branch or the point where the true and false branches rejoin. In this example only

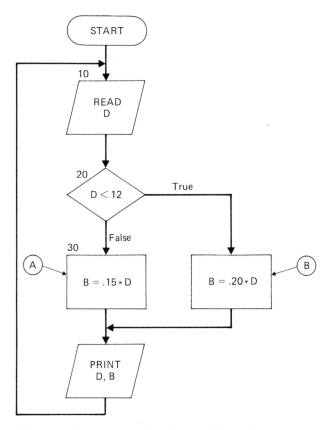

Fig. 3.4. Flowchart for doughnut sales problem, process symbol Ⓐ numbered.

one statement is in the false branch, which we have written as line 30, so we may now begin writing the true branch. The next available line number is 40, so we may assign line 40 to the first statement in the true branch. Figure 3.5 shows the statement in process symbol Ⓑ written as line 40. The PRINT statement may be written as line 50, the GO TO as line 60, the DATA as line 70, and the END as line 80.

The program as it now looks is shown in Fig. 3.5, and the flowchart with the new line numbers added is shown in Fig. 3.6. We must now replace the question mark on line 20 with the correct line number. Remember that the question mark stands for the line number we want to branch to when the condition is true. The flowchart in Fig. 3.6 shows that the true branch from the decision symbol leads to the process symbol that is numbered 40. Therefore the question mark must be replaced by

```
1 REM THE DOUGHNUT SALES PROBLEM
2 REM WRITTEN BY M. TROMBETTA
10 READ D
20    IF D < 12 THEN ?
30    LET B = .15 * D
40    LET B = .20 * D
50    PRINT D,B
60 GO TO 10
70 DATA 10,20
80 END
```

Fig. 3.5. Doughnut sales program, almost complete.

the number 40. Figure 3.7 shows the program with the question mark replaced by the number 40.

Whenever you write a program that contains IF statements, you should follow the procedure just illustrated. Always write the false

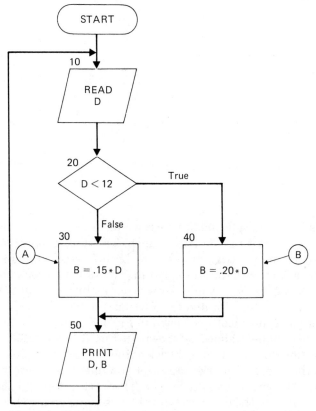

Fig. 3.6. Flowchart for doughnut sales problem, all symbols numbered.

```
1 REM THE DOUGHNUT SALES PROBLEM
2 REM WRITTEN BY M. TROMBETTA
10 READ D
20    IF D < 12 THEN 40
30    LET B = .15 * D
40    LET B = .20 * D
50    PRINT D,B
60 GO TO 10
70 DATA 10,20
80 END


RUN

FIG3#7        15:04    02/25/80

   10                   2. ← (Correct answer)
   20                   4. ← (Incorrect answer)

LINE    10:    END OF DATA

TIME 0.0 SECS.
```

Fig. 3.7. Execution of doughnut sales program, incorrect answer.

branch of the IF statement first. Use the flowchart to help you write the program, and use the program to number the flowchart.

Unfortunately the program developed here is not perfect. An execution of the program is shown in Fig. 3.7. The bill for the customer who bought 10 doughnuts is correct, but the bill for the second customer, who bought 20 doughnuts, should be 15 cents times 20, or 3 dollars. Instead the computer printed 4. Let's trace the program to determine where the error is.

Tracing the Program

In Fig. 3.8 we have set up a D box and a B box to help us trace the program. When we type RUN, the computer begins by executing the READ statement in line 10. It finds the DATA statement in line 70 and puts the first number, 10, into the D box, as we did also in Fig. 3.8(a). When line 20 is executed, the computer compares the 10 in the D box with 12. Since 10 is less than 12, the condition is true, and the computer branches to line 40. In line 40 the computer multiplies .20 by the 10 in the D box and puts the answer, 2, in the B box, as we did in Fig. 3.8(b). When the PRINT statement in line 50 is executed, the computer prints the 10 in the D box and the 2 in the B box. This is indeed our first line of output and agrees with our hand-calculated answer. So far, so good, but let's continue.

D   B
10   —

(a) After executing line 10

D   B
10   2

(b) After executing line 40

D   B
1̸0̸   2
20

(c) After executing line 10

D   B
1̸0̸   2̸
20   3

(d) After executing line 30

D   B
1̸0̸   2̸
20   3̸
     4

(e) After executing line 40

Fig. 3.8. Tracing the program in Fig. 3.7.

The GO TO statement in line 60 sends us back to line 10. This time when the READ statement is executed the 20 from the DATA statement is put in the D box, and the 10 that was there is erased as in Fig. 3.8(c). Now when line 20 is executed, the computer compares the 20 in the D box with 12 and determines that the condition is false. Since the condition is false, the computer does not branch to line 40 but instead falls through the IF statement to line 30. In line 30 the computer multiplies .15 by the 20 in the D box and puts the answer, 3, in the B box, as we did in Fig. 3.8(d). You will notice that 3 is in fact the correct bill for the second customer, but let's see what happens next.

After executing line 30 the computer executes line 40. But wait! We do not want to execute line 40. Line 40 calculates bills for customers who buy fewer than 12 doughnuts, and this customer bought 20. True, but remember that the computer does not understand anything about our problem. It always executes the statements in order unless a GO TO or an IF statement changes the order of execution. Let's follow the execution a little longer and then figure out how to fix the error.

When it executes line 40, the computer multiplies .20 by the 20 in the D box and puts the answer, 4, in the B box, erasing the correct answer, 3, as in Fig. 3.8(e). Next the PRINT statement in line 50 prints the 20 in the D box and the 4 in the B box. This is the second incorrect line of output.

The error occurs because, for customers who buy 12 or more doughnuts, the computer erases the correct bill calculated in line 30 and replaces it with the incorrect bill calculated in line 40. We must prevent the computer from executing line 40 for customers who buy 12 or more doughnuts. This is done by inserting a new statement between lines 30 and 40. Before you read on, try to figure out what that missing statement should be.

To make the computer skip over line 40 add the new statement

35 GO TO 50

Figure 3.9 shows a final, correct version of this program, and the output shows that the bill is calculated correctly for both customers.

The program was written initially without line 35 to show that forgetting that line is a very easy mistake to make. After going through this analysis, you should be alert and not leave out the GO TO in your

```
1 REM THE DOUGHNUT SALES PROBLEM
2 REM WRITTEN BY M. TROMBETTA
10 READ D
20    IF D < 12 THEN 40
30    LET B = .15 * D
35    GO TO 50    ← Statement added to correct error
40    LET B = .20 * D
50    PRINT D,B
60 GO TO 10
70 DATA 10,20
80 END

RUN

FIG3#9      15:05   02/25/80

   10           2.   ← Correct answers
   20           3.

LINE    10:   END OF DATA

TIME 0.0 SECS.
```

Fig. 3.9. Correct version of doughnut sales program.

programs. When you use an IF statement you almost always have to use a GO TO statement to skip over statements you do not want to execute.

The flowchart in Fig. 3.6 shows that, after we execute line 30, we want to execute line 50. Since we know that without a GO TO statement after line 30 the computer will execute line 40, we see that, if we had studied the flowchart carefully we would have been alerted to the need for a GO TO statement following line 30.

Notice that our program contained a logic error even though the first bill the program printed agreed with the bill we calculated by hand. Where does that leave the rule stating that, if the computer-calculated answers agree with the hand-calculated answers, the program is free of logic errors? Unfortunately, that rule is too simple. It must be replaced by the following rule:

> You must calculate answers by hand for all the branches in your program. Your program is free of logic errors only when the computer-calculated answers agree with all the hand-calculated answers.

In the doughnut problem we have two branches, D less than 12 and D not less than 12. We therefore need two hand calculations, one for each branch. Suitable values are D = 10 and D = 20. Since the output in Fig. 3.9 shows the computer-calculated bills agree with the hand-calculated bills for both of these cases, we can be sure the program is now free of logic errors.

Using String Variables in Conditions

String variables may also be used in conditions. You may compare a string variable to a string or to another string variable. So the condition A\$ = "YES" is perfectly legal. This condition is true if the variable A\$ contains the string YES. The condition N\$ < M\$ is a little more difficult to understand. What does it mean to say one string is less than another? Strings are compared according to the alphabet, so that ANDERSON is less than BAKER, and SMITH is greater than JONES. Notice that the number of characters in a string has no bearing on whether that string is greater or less than another string. Even though ANDERSON has more characters than BAKER, ANDERSON is less than BAKER because A comes before B in the alphabet.

If you compare strings that contain both letters and numbers, things get a little more complicated. On some computers numbers are "greater" than letters, while on other computers they are "less" than letters.

Other Sales Problems

Sometimes a price schedule is more complicated than the simple one we used for the doughnut problem. For example, suppose a parking lot charges as follows:

First 2 hours or less   5 dollars per hour

Additional hours   3 dollars per hour

The full solution to this problem is left for a homework exercise, but we will develop the LET statements to show how it is done. Let H stand for the number of hours parked and B stand for the customer's bill.

The bill for a customer who parks for 2 hours or less is straightforward; he is charged a flat 5 dollars per hour, so the LET statement is

LET B = 5 * H

The bill for a customer who parks for more than 2 hours is slightly more complicated. In such cases it is helpful to calculate a sample bill for the customer and to use the numeric calculations as an aid in developing the LET statements. Let's imagine a customer who parks for 6 hours, and calculate her bill. For the first 2 hours she is charged 5 dollars per hour, and for the next 4 hours she is charged 3 dollars per hour, so her bill is

$$B = 5 \times 2 + 3 \times 4 = 22$$

But we went too fast. We got 4 in this equation by subtracting 2 hours from the total time she was parked, which is 6 hours. Let's show that subtraction explicitly

$$B = 5 \times 2 + 3 \times (6 - 2) = 22$$

With this numeric equation as a guide, it is not too difficult to write the required LET statement

LET B = 5 * 2 + 3 * (H − 2)

Whenever you have difficulty writing a LET statement, do a calculation using numbers, and then use the resulting numeric equation to help you write the required LET statement. This does not involve any additional work, since you have to do a hand calculation anyway to check your program.

Exercises

3.1 Assume the following variables have the values indicated:

A = 6; B = 19; C = 19; X$ = "DONALD"; Y$ = "DUCK"

Which of the following conditions are true, and which are false?
a) A < C
b) B > C
c) C <= B
d) X$ < Y$
e) X$ <= Y$

In the following programming assignments you should develop your program by following our systematic procedure. You should print the input data as well as the calculated answers. Your programs should be able to process an arbitrary number of cases. Make sure you invent good test data.

3.2 A firm sells CRT terminals according to the following price schedule:

10 or less	1000 dollars each
More than 10	800 dollars each

Write a program to calculate and print customer's bills.

3.3 Solve the parking lot problem described in this section.

3.4 Write a program to determine whether, in your BASIC, the string 1 is greater than or less than the string A. The output of the program should be either LETTERS ARE GREATER THAN NUMBERS or NUMBERS ARE GREATER THAN LETTERS.

MORE COMPLICATED CONDITIONS

Sometimes problems involve more complicated conditions than we have met so far. For example, consider this problem. A company pays its salespeople according to the following schedule:

Sales under 100 dollars	10% commission rate
Sales 100 dollars or more and less than 500 dollars	20% commission rate
Sales 500 dollars or more	30% commission rate

Write a program that will calculate and print commissions.
We will use the following variable names:

Input variable

Sales   S

Output variable

Commission   C

The algorithm we can use for this problem is

1. Read S for a salesperson.

2. Determine this salesperson's commission rate category.

3. Calculate the commission.

4. Print the sales and commission.

5. Repeat until all the salespeople have been processed.

The algorithm is similar to the one used in the doughnut problem, but step 2 (determine the commission rate) is more difficult than the corresponding step in the doughnut problem. We could figure out how to carry out step 2 now, but it is easier to fill in the details later, when we draw the flowchart.

We must next calculate answers by hand. We need three test cases, corresponding to the three categories for commission rates. The three test cases and their answers are

Case number	Sales	Commission
1	50	5
2	200	40
3	1000	300

When you choose your test data for a hand calculation, you should follow the example used here and choose values that make your arithmetic easy. You do not have to check the program using values like 59.47, 246.37, and 976.36. These values would just make your hand calculation more difficult. If the program calculates commission correctly for sales of 50, 200, and 1000, we know that the program is correct and that it will calculate commission correctly for any sales we give it.

We must next draw the flowchart for this problem. The algorithm tells us that the first step is to read S for a salesperson and that is the first step shown in Fig. 3.10. The next step in the algorithm is to determine the commission rate category. We did not explain in detail exactly how that was to be done because it is easier to fill in the details while the flowchart is being drawn.

First we must determine whether this salesperson's sales are less than 100 dollars. This is determined using a decision, as shown in Fig. 3.10. If the condition is true, the commission rate is 10%. If the condition is false, we arrive at position (A). What do we do next? Many students are tempted to use a decision to determine whether S is greater than or equal to 100, as shown in Fig. 3.11, but that decision serves no

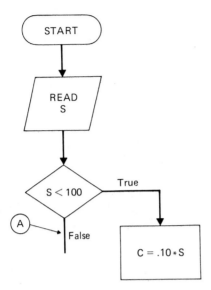

Fig. 3.10. Start of flowchart for commission problem.

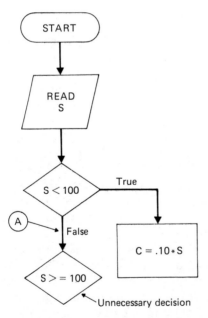

Fig. 3.11. Incorrect flowchart for commission problem.

purpose. If we get to position Ⓐ, we know that S is not less than 100 because we took the false branch from the first decision. But if S is not less than 100, it must be greater than or equal to 100, because these are two ways of saying the same thing. Therefore the answer to the second decision must be true. But using a decision that can have only one answer does not contribute to the solution of the problem.

To determine the correct way to continue the flowchart started in Fig. 3.10, we reason as follows. If we get to position Ⓐ, we know that

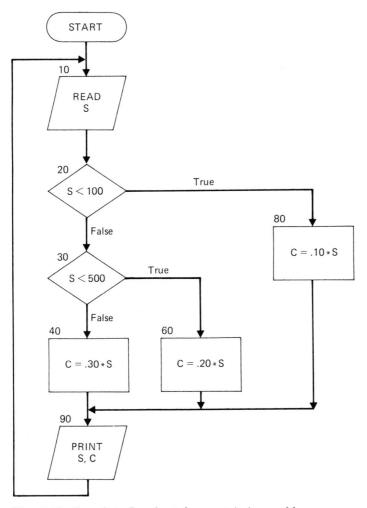

Fig. 3.12. Complete flowchart for commission problem.

S is not less than 100 dollars, but we do not know whether it is less than 500 dollars. This requires another decision, as shown in Fig. 3.12. If this second decision is true, we know that the correct commission rate is 20%. If the second decision is false, we know that S is 500 dollars or greater, so that the correct commission rate is 30%. All three commission calculations lead to the PRINT step. Finally we have a loop from the PRINT back to the READ step. (Although the flowchart symbols are numbered, you should understand that the numbering was done while the program was written in the next step.)

You have seen how drawing the flowchart actually helps develop the algorithm. So when you develop the algorithm as step 2 of our systematic procedure, it is not necessary to include every detail. The details can be filled in when the flowchart is drawn. When you develop the algorithm you only need to have a general idea of how to solve the problem.

The details of the algorithm are left to the flowchart step because the flowchart shows the logic of the algorithm so clearly. Most people find that thinking through the exact steps required is easier while drawing the flowchart. Of course, you cannot expect the drawing of your flowcharts to go as smoothly as it does when I show you a flowchart in this book. These are the finished products. When you draw your flowchart, you will have many mistakes and false starts. Do not be discouraged; that is why pencils have erasers.

The flowchart is helpful in two ways. First it helps to develop the algorithm. Then, after it is drawn, the flowchart helps to write the program. In our earlier problems we did not have to use the flowchart to help develop the algorithm because those problems were relatively simple. Whenever problems become complicated, especially when they involve more than one decision, a flowchart is particularly helpful.

After the flowchart is drawn, you should check it by tracing the test cases through it and making sure that the correct branches are taken and that the correct calculations are performed. You should not write the program until you are sure the flowchart is correct.

Figure 3.13 shows another incorrect flowchart for this problem. I have shown you this flowchart because it contains an error that students often make. You must never draw a flowchart symbol without having a flowline leaving it. Without an exit flowline from a symbol you have not specified what you want to do next. The only flowchart symbol that does not require an exit flowline is the termination symbol.

The next step is to write the BASIC program. Figure 3.14 shows the BASIC program based on the flowchart shown in Fig. 3.12. This program was written following the flowchart-to-program-to-flowchart procedure illustrated earlier. If you follow the rules, by always com-

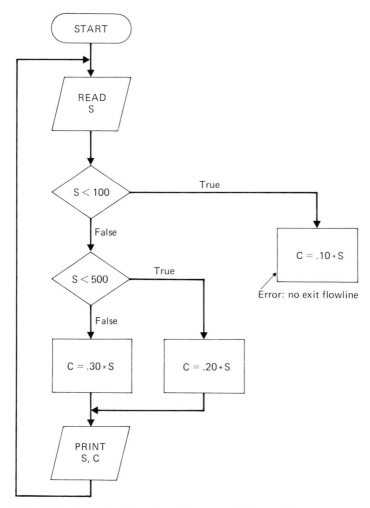

Fig. 3.13. Incorrect flowchart for commission problem.

pleting the false branch of an IF statement before starting the true branch and by using GO TO statements to skip statements you do not want to execute, you will not have any difficulty understanding how this BASIC program was written.

Decisions Involving More Than One Variable

There are other kinds of complicated decisions. Suppose we want to use a computer to help us pick horses to bet on. We will decide which horse

```
1 REM COMMISSION PROBLEM
2 REM PROGRAMMER. M. TROMBETTA
10 READ S
20    IF S < 100 THEN 80
30    IF S < 500 THEN 60
40    LET C = .30 * S
50    GO TO 90
60    LET C = .20 * S
70    GO TO 90
80    LET C = .10 * S
90    PRINT S,C
100 GO TO 10
110 DATA 50,200,1000
120 END


RUN

FIG3#14      9:46    02/26/80

50               5.
200              40.
1000             300

LINE    10:   END OF DATA

TIME 0.0 SECS.
```

Fig. 3.14. Program to calculate commissions.

to bet on by analyzing each horse's finishing position in its last race and its jockey's weight.

Let's use the following variables:

Input variables

Horse's name	H$
Horse's position in last race	P
Jockey's weight	W

Output variable

Amount to bet	B

For our first betting scheme let's say we will bet 10 dollars if a horse finished first in its last race and if its jockey weighs less than 115 pounds. If a horse does not meet both of these conditions, we will not bet. With our variables we can state the scheme as: if $P = 1$ and $W < 115$, then $B = 10$; otherwise $B = 0$.[1]

---

1. Please do not use this scheme, lose a lot of money, and send me a bill. This is a very simplified scheme; a realistic scheme would require analyzing lots of additional data, such as who the horse's grandmother was.

The algorithm is

1. Read H$, P, and W.
2. Determine B.
3. Print H$, P, W, and B.
4. Repeat for all horses.

     As usual, we will show how we determine B when we analyze the flowchart. The flowchart is shown in Fig. 3.15. Notice that, for B to be set equal to 10, both conditions must be true; if either one is false, we set B equal to 0.

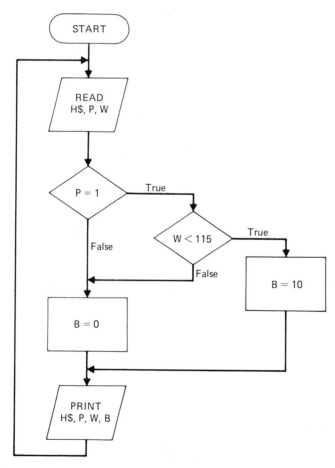

Fig. 3.15. Flowchart for first betting scheme.

You should be able to write a program based on this flowchart, so I will not write the program, but writing it is a homework assignment.

An Alternative Betting Scheme

Some people might prefer another betting scheme. Bet ten dollars if either a horse finished first in its last race or its jockey weighs less than 115 pounds. If the horse does not meet either of these conditions, we will not bet. With our variables, we can state the scheme as: if $P = 1$ or $W < 115$, then $B = 10$; otherwise $B = 0$. Notice that this betting scheme involves exactly the same conditions as the first scheme, but in this scheme we bet if either condition is true.

The algorithm for this scheme is exactly the same as the algorithm for the first scheme, since the difference in the two schemes is in how we determine B. The way B is determined is shown in the flowchart in Fig. 3.16. Notice that B is set equal to 10 if either condition is true; B is set equal to 0 only if both conditions are false.

Again, writing the program based on the flowchart if Fig. 3.16 is left to you as a homework exercise.

Compound Conditions

The solution of these two betting problems is simplified by the use of a **compound condition,** which some versions of BASIC allow. A compound condition is one or more simple conditions, like the ones we have studied so far, connected by the words AND or OR. Your instructor will tell you, and you should write, on the inside front cover of this book, whether your BASIC permits compound conditions.

For those versions of BASIC that permit compound conditions, the flowchart for the first betting scheme, which was originally shown in Fig. 3.15, could be drawn to include a compound condition as shown in Fig. 3.17. This flowchart is much simpler than the one in Fig. 3.15. That is the advantage of compound conditions—they allow complicated conditions to be written simply.

The decision step in Fig. 3.17 would be written as the IF statement

IF P = 1 AND W < 115 THEN 50

This IF statement involves two simple conditions: $P = 1$ and $W < 115$. When these two simple conditions are connected by the word AND, they form a compound condition. This compound condition is true only if both simple conditions are true. So in this IF statement we will branch to line 50 only if $P = 1$ and $W < 115$. Recalling the statement of the first

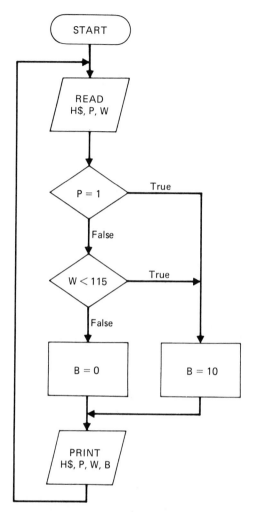

Fig. 3.16. Flowchart for second betting scheme.

betting scheme, we want B to be set equal to 10 exactly under those conditions.

Using a compound condition can also simplify the solution of the second betting problem. The flowchart, which was originally shown in Fig. 3.16, is modified to include a compound condition in Fig. 3.18. Again we see how the use of a compound condition simplifies the flowchart.

The decision step in Fig. 3.18 would be written as the IF statement

IF P = 1 OR W < 115 THEN 50

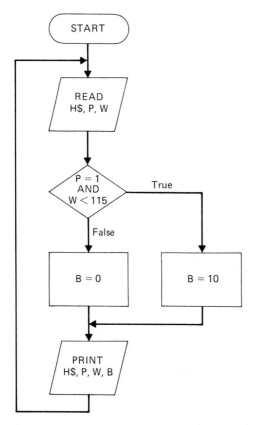

Fig. 3.17. Flowchart for first betting scheme using a compound condition.

In this IF statement the compound condition is formed by connecting the two simple conditions, P = 1 and W < 115 by the word OR. This compound condition is true if either simple condition is true. So in this IF statement we will branch to line 50 if P = 1 or W < 115. Recalling the statement of the second betting scheme, we want B to be set equal to 10 exactly under those conditions.

Exercises

In the following programming assignments you should develop your program by following our systematic procedure. You should print the input data as well as the calculated answers. Your programs should be able to process an abitrary number of cases. Make sure you invent good test data.

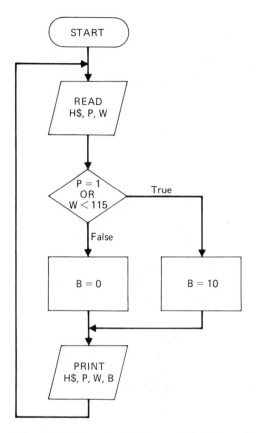

Fig. 3.18. Flowchart for second betting scheme using a compound condition.

3.5 A gas company measures the amount of gas its customers use in hundreds of cubic feet (ccf) and charges them according to the following schedule:

First 8 ccf   50 cents each
More than 8 ccf   30 cents each

Note that the 30-cent rate applies only to usage above 8 ccf. A customer who uses 10 ccf is charged 50 cents for the first 8 and 30 cents for the next 2 ccf. Write a program to calculate and print customers' bills.

3.6 An electric company measures the amount of electricity its customers use in kilowatt hours (kwh) and charges them according to the schedule:

First 12 kwh or less   2 dollars and 80 cents

Next 78 kwh   8 cents each kwh

Excess above 90 kwh   6 cents each kwh

Notice that the minimum bill is 2 dollars and 80 cents. Write a program to calculate and print customers' bills.

3.7 A firm pays its employees time and a half for overtime if they work more than 40 hours in a week. Write a program that will read hours worked and rate of pay for each employee and will calculate and print each employee's regular pay, overtime pay, and total pay. (This firm is located in paradise, where there are no taxes!) An employee's regular pay is the pay earned for the first 40 hours or less. Overtime pay is the pay earned for the hours worked beyond 40. Not every employee works more than 40 hours. For an employee who works 40 hours or less, overtime pay is zero. (Note that you calculate time and a half for overtime by multiplying the employee's usual rate by 1.5.)

3.8 Write a program to assign letter grades to students. The program should read each student's name and three test marks. It should calculate the average of the three test marks and then print the student's name, average, and letter grade. Letter grades are assigned as follows:

Average	Grade
>= 90	A
>= 80 but < 90	B
>= 70 but < 80	C
>= 60 but < 70	D
< 60	F

3.9 Write the program based on the flowchart in Fig. 3.15.

3.10 Write the program based on the flowchart in Fig. 3.16.

3.11 Write the program based on the flowchart in Fig. 3.17.

3.12 Write the program based on the flowchart in Fig. 3.18.

3.13 The following table involves two simple conditions, A and B, and two compound conditions, A AND B and A OR B. For each of the four cases indicate whether the compound conditions are true or false.

Case	A	B	A AND B	A OR B
1	True	True		
2	True	False		
3	False	True		
4	False	False		

3.14 It's the end of the year, and the ABC Company wants to use a computer to calculate bonuses for their salespeople. Salespeople who have been employed more than five years and have sales greater than 20,000 dollars get a bonus of 500 dollars; otherwise they get no bonuses. Write a program to calculate bonuses.

3.15 Resolve Exercise 3.14 to give a 500-dollar bonus to salespeople who have been employed more than five years or who have sales greater than 20,000 dollars. For each person, if neither condition is satisfied, no bonus is given.

MORE ON THE PRINT STATEMENT

Printing Strings

Besides printing values of variables, the PRINT statement can be used to print strings. For example, to print a heading simply convert the heading to a string by enclosing it in quotation marks and print it:

PRINT "MONTHLY SALES REPORT"

This PRINT statement causes MONTHLY SALES REPORT to be printed starting in the first print zone. To center the heading, have the computer skip print zones by adding commas:

PRINT,, "MONTHLY SALES REPORT"

The two commas tell the computer to skip the first two print zones and begin printing the heading in zone 3.

To print column headings you can print more than one string, as follows:

PRINT "RATE", "HOURS", "GROSS"

RATE will be printed in zone 1, HOURS in zone 2, and GROSS in zone 3. In fact you can mix strings and variables in the same PRINT statement:

PRINT "SALES ARE", S, "COMMISSION IS", C

If S = 200 and C = 40, this statement will print

SALES ARE   200   COMMISSION IS   40

As explained earlier, if semicolons are used instead of commas, the values will be printed more closely together. The statement

PRINT "SALES ARE"; S; "COMMISSION IS"; C

would print

SALES ARE 200 COMMISSION IS 40

If strings or string variables are printed with semicolons, they are printed right next to each other. For example, the statement

PRINT "RATE"; "HOURS"; "GROSS"

would print the line

RATEHOURSGROSS

which is probably not what you wanted.

When you print strings using semicolons, any blanks you want between the strings must be included in the strings. For example, if N$ is equal to SMITH, the PRINT statement

PRINT "NAME"; N$

would print the line

NAMESMITH

To get a blank between the E and the S, include the blank at the end of NAME as follows:

PRINT "NAME "; N$

This statement would print the line

NAME SMITH

which is a big improvement.

Figure 3.19 shows the simple gross pay program from Fig. 2.6 modified by the addition of two PRINT statements to print a report heading and column headings. Since we want to print the headings only once, the two new PRINT statements are inserted before the READ statement. If these two PRINT statements were inserted after the READ statement, they would be inside the loop and would be executed every time the READ statement was executed. Since that is not what we want, we must place the PRINT statements that print the headings before the READ statement.

PRINT with TAB

The output produced by the program in Fig. 3.19 is acceptable, but if we wanted to print more than five values on a line and therefore used

```
 1 REM PAYROLL WITH MANY EMPLOYEES
 2 REM PROGRAMMER M. TROMBETTA      } Statements that print
 5 PRINT,"PAYROLL REPORT"           } headings
 7 PRINT "RATE","HOURS","GROSS PAY"
10 READ R,H
20   LET G = R * H
30   PRINT R,H,G
40 GO TO 10
50 DATA 4,30
60 DATA 7,25
70 DATA 5,40
80 END


RUN

FIG3#19      15:03    02/25/80

                    PAYROLL REPORT
RATE                HOURS                GROSS PAY
  4                  30                  120
  7                  25                  175
  5                  40                  200

LINE    10:   END OF DATA

TIME 0.0 SECS.
```

Fig. 3.19. Printing headings.

semicolons instead of commas in the PRINT statement, we would run into some difficulties. Recall that, when semicolons are used, each variable is printed next to the previously printed variable. Since the number of columns occupied by a variable depends on the numeric value of that variable, the values for different cases would not be lined up under each other in neat columns. The solution to Exercise 2.7 was a good example of the irregular output produced by semicolons. When we want control over the spacing of our output, we can use the PRINT statement with the TAB function.

The TAB function is best explained using an example. Consider the statement

PRINT TAB(5); A; TAB(14); B; TAB(46); C

This statement tells the computer to space over to column 5 and print the value of A, then space to column 14 and print the value of B, and finally to space to column 46 and print the value of C. Notice that, when we use TAB, we use semicolons, not commas, to separate the items in the print list. A comma would cause the computer to space over to the start of the next print zone, and would destroy the spacing we were trying to achieve with the TAB.

TAB may also be used when printing headings. For example, the statement

PRINT TAB(6); "NAME"; TAB(21); "GROSS"

causes NAME to be printed starting in column 6 and GROSS to be printed starting in column 21.

Figure 3.20 shows a program that solves Exercise 2.7 and uses the TAB function to print headings and to produce output that is lined up in columns.

```
1 REM EXERCISE 2.7 WITH TAB
2 REM PROGRAMMER. M. TROMBETTA
10 PRINT TAB(24);"PAYROLL   REPORT"
20 PRINT TAB(8);"N$";TAB(24);"R";TAB(33);"H";TAB(40);"G";TAB(48);"W";TAB(56);"N"
30 READ N$,R,H
40    LET G = R * H
50    LET W = .20 * G
60    LET N = G - W
70    PRINT TAB(3);N$;TAB(22);R;TAB(31);H;TAB(38);G;TAB(46);W;TAB(54);N
80 GO TO 30
90 DATA "KIRK",4.50,20
100 DATA "SPOCK",15,20
110 DATA "BONES",8,40
120 END


RUN

FIG3#20    14:52    02/26/80

                   PAYROLL   REPORT
          N$         R         H        G        W        N
       KIRK         4.5       20       90       18       72
       SPOCK         15       20      300       60      240
       BONES          8       40      320       64      256

LINE   30:   END OF DATA

TIME   0.0   SECS
```

Fig. 3.20. Payroll program with TAB.

The TAB function gives much better-looking output than we would have using semicolons, but the TAB function has problems of its own. Notice that in the column headings only the variable names (N$, R, and so on) were printed, not the full names (NAME, RATE, and so on). This was done because the line that prints the column headings, line 20, is 80 characters long. If the full names had been used, the line would have been more than 100 characters long. Although the maximum line length allowed varies from one version of BASIC to another, many versions do not allow lines longer than 72 or 80 characters. Your instructor will tell you the maximum number of characters permitted in a line in your version of BASIC, and you should write this number on the inside front cover of this book.

You should understand that line 20 is so long not because the column headings are excessively long but because the TAB function is used six times in that line, and each use requires 7 or 8 characters. As you will see, when we use the PRINT USING statement, we can print the full column headings.

The PRINT USING Statement

The TAB function gives us a lot of control over how the output will look, but sometimes we want even more control. For example, in Fig. 3.20 the employee named Kirk earns four dollars and 50 cents per hour, but his rate of pay is printed as 4.5. Numerically 4.5 and 4.50 are equivalent, so the computer does not print the final zero. But since this number represents dollars and cents we would like it to be printed as 4.50. Also, although the TAB function produces pretty good columns, for really nice-looking output we would like the columns to be printed with the decimal points lined up.

The PRINT USING statement gives us complete control over exactly how our answers will be printed. Some versions of BASIC do not have a PRINT USING statement. If your version does not have a PRINT USING statement, you can skip this section. Furthermore, the BASICs that do have PRINT USING statements implement it differently. The two most widely used versions are described here, but your instructor may have to give you the details of exactly how your version works.

Suppose that R stands for rate of pay, H stands for hours, and G stands for gross pay. In some versions of BASIC, the PRINT USING statement might be written as

100 PRINT USING 101, R, H, G

This statement tells the computer that you want it to print the values of R, H, and G using the format specified in line 101. Line 101 is called an image statement. It is not necessary that the image statement be the next statement following the PRINT statement, but that is customary.

Line 101 might be written as

101: ##.## ## ###.##

Immediately after the line number the image statement has a colon (:). Then we use the number symbol, #, to define three numeric fields, corresponding to the three variables we specified in PRINT USING statement. Some BASICs use a different symbol to define number fields. You should write the symbol used in your BASIC on the inside front cover of this book.

Each # corresponds to one digit. These number fields may be placed anywhere in the image statement. The only requirement is that the number fields must be separated from each other by at least one blank. The value of R will be printed exactly in the position of the first number field, ##.##, the value of H in the position of the second number field, ##, and the value of G in the third number field, ###.##.

When you design a number field, you must consider the size of the number that will be printed in it and whether the number contains a decimal part. Since R and G represent dollars and cents, they contain a two-digit decimal part. Therefore a decimal point and two #'s were included to the right of the decimal point. Some employees in our company earn more than 10 dollars per hour, but none earns more than 99 dollars per hour. The pay rate field was therefore designed with two #'s to the left of the decimal point. Similarly, some employees in our company earn more than 100 dollars per week, but none earns more than 999 dollars per week. Therefore the gross pay field was designed with three #'s to the left of the decimal point. In our company employees do not work fractional parts of hours, so the hour field does not include a decimal point.

When the PRINT USING statement is executed, the numeric values of the variables replace the number symbols in the image line. What happens if there are more number symbols in the field than digits in the number to be printed? It depends on whether the extra number symbols are to the left or to the right of the decimal point. To the right of the decimal point the extra number symbols are replaced with zeros. Including two number symbols to the right of the decimal point forces the computer to print 4.50 instead of 4.5, which would be printed with an ordinary PRINT statement. To the left of the decimal point extra number symbols are replaced with spaces. This may sound complicated, but, to sum it up, the computer does what you would want it to do. Figure 3.21 shows a program with a PRINT USING statement that ought to clarify some of these rules.

The variable A was printed in the field ##.##. Since the value of A was 4.2, the extra # to the left of the decimal point was replaced by a space. The extra # to the right of the decimal point was replaced by a 0. The variable B was printed in the field ####. Since B was 1, the three extra #'s were replaced by spaces.

If a number is too large to fit in the number field we have designed for it, the computer prints a series of asterisks. This is also shown in Fig. 3.21. The variable C was printed in the field ##. Since C was 213, it could not fit in the field provided. The two #'s were therefore replaced by asterisks.

So we see that if a number field is too large for a number, the computer prints the number and just leaves spaces for the extra #'s. But

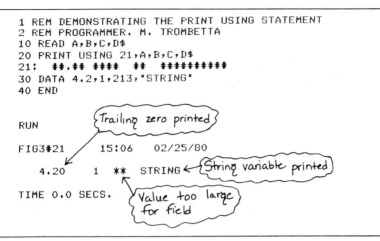

```
1 REM DEMONSTRATING THE PRINT USING STATEMENT
2 REM PROGRAMMER. M. TROMBETTA
10 READ A,B,C,D$
20 PRINT USING 21,A,B,C,D$
21: ##.## #### ## ##########
30 DATA 4.2,1,213,'STRING'
40 END

RUN                    (Trailing zero printed)

FIG3#21      15:06      02/25/80

   4.20      1   **   STRING ← (String variable printed)

TIME 0.0 SECS.      (Value too large for field)
```

Fig. 3.21. Demonstrating the PRINT USING statement.

if the number field is too small, the computer prints asterisks. It is therefore always better to make the field too large rather than run the risk that it might be too small. So, for example, if there is the slightest chance that some employees could work more than 99 hours, we should make the hours field ### instead of only ##.

String variables may be printed with a PRINT USING statement by simply defining a field for them, using number symbols in the image statement. Some BASICs use a different symbol to define string fields. You should write the symbol used in your BASIC on the inside front cover of this book. Fig. 3.21 shows an example of printing string variables.

Other characters besides number signs and periods may be included in an image statement. These other characters are printed exactly as they are written. For example, the image statement

101:    $##.##   ## HOURS $###.##

will print the dollar signs and the word HOURS, in addition to the numeric values of the three variables.

A PRINT USING statement may be used to print headings by simply not listing any variables. To print a heading, you can use the following statements

10 PRINT USING 11

11:      MONTHLY SALES REPORT

Notice that quotation marks are not used in the image statement. Figure 3.22 shows the program of Fig. 3.20 rewritten using the PRINT

```
1 REM EXERCISE 2.7 WITH PRINT USING STATEMENT
2 REM PROGRAMMER. M. TROMBETTA
10 PRINT USING 11
11:                     PAYROLL   REPORT
20 PRINT USING 21
21:    NAME          RATE    HOURS   GROSS    WITHHOLDING   NET PAY
30 READ N$,R,H
40    LET G = R * H
50    LET W = .20 * G
60    LET N = G - W
70    PRINT USING 71,N$,R,H,G,W,N
71: ############   ##.##    ##   ####.##    ####.##    ####.##
80 GO TO 30
90 DATA "KIRK",4.50,20
100 DATA "SPOCK",15,20
110 DATA "BONES",8,40
120 END


RUN

FIG3#22     20:08   11/26/80

                       PAYROLL   REPORT
        NAME         RATE    HOURS   GROSS   WITHHOLDING   NET PAY
        KIRK         4.50     20     90.00      18.00       72.00
        SPOCK       15.00     20    300.00      60.00      240.00
        BONES        8.00     40    320.00      64.00      256.00

LINE    30:   END OF DATA

TIME 0.0 SECS.
```

Fig. 3.22. Payroll program with PRINT USING statement.

USING statement. As you can see, the PRINT USING statement produces very attractive output.

We have described the version of the PRINT USING statement that uses an image line. In some versions of BASIC, a string variable is used instead of an image line to specify the format of the output line. In these versions of BASIC, the PRINT USING statement is written as

99 LET S$ = "$##.##   ## HOURS $###.##"

100 PRINT USING S$, R, H, G

This statement functions exactly like the statement shown earlier, which used the image line. Any string variable, not only S$, may be used. To print a heading, for example, we might use the statements

9 LET H$ = "   MONTHLY SALES REPORT"

10 PRINT USING H$

Just the simplest features of the PRINT USING statement have been described here. Many versions of BASIC include additional fancy features.

The way these fancier features are implemented varies so much from one version of BASIC to another, that your instructor will have to tell you about the special features of your version of BASIC.

Exercise

3.16 Resolve Exercise 3.7, this time printing a report heading and column headings. Use the PRINT USING statement or TAB function to make your output attractive.

THE INPUT STATEMENT

In the programs you have seen so far, variables have been assigned values by using either the LET or the READ statements. A third method of assigning values to variables, the INPUT statement, is often convenient. An example of the INPUT statement is

INPUT A,B

When this INPUT statement is executed, the computer prints a question mark at the terminal, stops executing the program, and waits for you to type the values you want to use for A and B. Suppose that when you see the question mark you type 9, 4 (followed by a carriage return, as usual). The computer puts the 9 in the A box and the 4 in the B box and then continues executing the program.

When you use an INPUT statement in a program, you are in effect saying to the computer, "I'll tell you the values I want to use for these variables later." Then, when the program is executed and the computer encounters the INPUT statement, the computer prints a question mark, which is in effect saying to you, "Now is the time to specify the values you want to use for these variables."

The general format of the INPUT statement is

INPUT variable, variable, variable

You can list as many variables as you want.

When the computer executes an INPUT statement and prints a question mark, you must enter one value for each variable in the INPUT list, and the values must be separated by commas. If you enter too many or too few values, the computer thinks you made a typing error, and it will ask you to retype the data. (In some versions of BASIC, if you type too few values, the computer uses what you typed and prints another question mark, so you can type additional data. In some versions of BASIC, if you type too many values, the computer uses what it needs and discards the rest.)

Entering String Variables

String variables can also be assigned values by using an INPUT statement, and, as an extra-nice feature, if the string does not contain a
comma, it does not have to be enclosed in quotation marks. For example,
suppose we were entering a person's name and age by using the INPUT
statement

INPUT N$,A

When the computer prints the question mark, we could type

MARY JONES, 24

MARY JONES would be put in the N$ box, and 24 would be put in the
A box. If we wanted to type the name as JONES, MARY, however, we
would have to use quotation marks:

"JONES, MARY", 24

If we did not use quotation marks in this case, the computer would
assume that both commas were separators and that we had typed three
values: JONES and MARY and 24. Since the INPUT statement contains
only two variables, the computer would print an error message.

Printing a Prompt

There is one small problem with the INPUT statement. When the question mark is printed, the user of the program (who might even be the
author) may not know what is supposed to be typed. In what order should
the data be typed: A followed by B or B followed by A? Of course the
user could LIST the program and examine the INPUT statement to see
which variables should be entered and their order, but it is much more
convenient to cause a message to be printed telling users what they are
supposed to do when they see the question mark. We call this message
a **prompt.**

An example of a program that uses an INPUT statement is shown
in Fig. 3.23. This program accepts miles traveled and gallons of gasoline
used and calculates and prints the gas mileage obtained. Notice especially that there are no DATA statements in this program. Because of
the prompt and the nicely labeled output, this program could be used
by someone who does not know anything about BASIC. The user would
not have to LIST the program; you would tell him or her to type RUN
and just follow directions.

Well, perhaps that is not all you must tell the user. Figure 3.23
shows that after entering three sets of data the user wanted to stop, but
the computer would not allow it. The problem is that the program is in

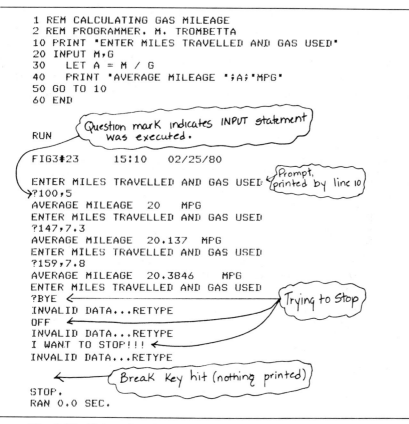

```
1 REM CALCULATING GAS MILEAGE
2 REM PROGRAMMER, M. TROMBETTA
10 PRINT "ENTER MILES TRAVELLED AND GAS USED"
20 INPUT M,G
30    LET A = M / G
40    PRINT "AVERAGE MILEAGE ";A;"MPG"
50 GO TO 10
60 END
```

Question mark indicates INPUT statement was executed.

```
RUN

FIG3#23      15:10    02/25/80

ENTER MILES TRAVELLED AND GAS USED
?100,5
AVERAGE MILEAGE   20    MPG
ENTER MILES TRAVELLED AND GAS USED
?147,7.3
AVERAGE MILEAGE   20.137  MPG
ENTER MILES TRAVELLED AND GAS USED
?159,7.8
AVERAGE MILEAGE   20.3846    MPG
ENTER MILES TRAVELLED AND GAS USED
?BYE
INVALID DATA...RETYPE
OFF
INVALID DATA...RETYPE
I WANT TO STOP!!!
INVALID DATA...RETYPE

STOP.
RAN 0.0 SEC.
```

Prompt, printed by line 10

Trying to Stop

Break Key hit (nothing printed)

Fig. 3.23. Using the INPUT statement.

an INPUT loop. When the computer executes the INPUT statement and prints the question mark, it is waiting for the user to enter two numbers, and that is all it will accept. If you type anything else, BYE, OFF, or I WANT TO STOP, for example, the computer thinks you have made a typing error, and it asks you to retype the data. The way to get out of the INPUT loop is to hit the BREAK key.

The INPUT statement is particularly useful when you do not know the values you want to use as data until the program is running. This situation often arises when computers are used to play games. Figure 3.24 shows a program that plays a game. One player enters a number between 1 and 100 without letting a second player see it, and then the second player tries to guess the number. The computer tells the second player whether the guesses are too high or too low and when the guess is correct.

The program in Fig. 3.24 illustrates the use of an empty PRINT statement, in lines 40 through 80. An empty PRINT statement causes the computer to print a blank line, which amounts to skipping a line. The appearance of a report can often be improved by skipping a line or two between headings. In the program in Fig. 3.24 the lines are skipped to permit the first player to rip off the part of the output showing the

```
1 REM GUESS THE NUMBER GAME
2 REM PROGRAMMER. M. TROMBETTA
10 PRINT "ENTER A NUMBER BETWEEN 1 AND 100"
20 PRINT "DON'T LET YOUR OPPONENT SEE THE NUMBER"
30 INPUT N
40 PRINT
50 PRINT
60 PRINT      Blank PRINT statements to skip lines
70 PRINT
80 PRINT
90 PRINT "GUESS THE NUMBER YOUR OPPONENT ENTERED"
100 PRINT "THE NUMBER IS BETWEEN 1 AND 100"
110 INPUT G
120    IF G = N THEN 180
130    IF G > N THEN 160
140    PRINT "YOU GUESSED TOO LOW"
150    GO TO 110
160    PRINT "YOU GUESSED TOO HIGH"
170 GO TO 110
180 PRINT "YOU HIT IT ON THE HEAD!"
190 END


RUN

FIG3#24      15:13    02/25/80

ENTER A NUMBER BETWEEN 1 AND 100
DON'T LET YOUR OPPONENT SEE THE NUMBER
?63

          Lines skipped by blank PRINT statements

GUESS THE NUMBER YOUR OPPONENT ENTERED
THE NUMBER IS BETWEEN 1 AND 100
?45
YOU GUESSED TOO LOW
?97
YOU GUESSED TOO HIGH
?63
YOU HIT IT ON THE HEAD!

TIME 0.0 SECS.
```

Fig. 3.24. A program that plays "Guess the number."

number entered. Study this program so that you understand how it works.

Exercises

3.17 Remove line number 150 from the program shown in Fig. 3.24. What output will this modified program produce if the hidden number is 43 and the guess is 36?

3.18 Modify the game playing program in Fig. 3.24 so that, in addition to printing YOU GUESSED TOO HIGH and YOU GUESSED TOO LOW, it will also print YOU ARE GETTING CLOSE whenever the guess is within five of the hidden number.

SORTING*

Sorting, or putting things in order, is a very important computer task. In fact sorting is so important that whole books have been written about it. In Chapter 6 we will learn how to sort any number of numbers, but in this chapter we will consider the problems of sorting two and three numbers.

Sorting Two Numbers

Let's first consider sorting two numbers. We want to write a program that will accept two numbers and print them in numeric order. To simplify the program we assume the numbers are not equal. Since these numbers do not represent anything like rate of pay or sales, we can use the variable names A and B. Since the values of these two variables will be entered into the computer as well as printed out, they are both the input and the output variables in this problem.

The algorithm we can use is

1. Input two numbers.
2. Sort the two numbers.
3. Print the two numbers.
4. Repeat until all the sets of numbers have been sorted.

Step 2 was deliberately left vague, since it will be easier to figure out exactly how to sort the numbers when we draw the flowchart.

Calculating the answer by hand is simple. There are only two ways you can mix up two numbers: small followed by large or large followed

---

* This section may be omitted without loss of continuity.

by small. In both cases the program should print the numbers in the order of small followed by large. So our test data and the expected answers are

Case	Data	Answers
1	1, 2	1, 2
2	2, 1	1, 2

A flowchart for this problem is shown in Fig. 3.25 and a program in Fig. 3.26. Notice that, although the program contains a statement to print a prompt in line 10, that step is not shown on the flowchart. That step is left out because the flowchart shows the logical structure of the program. We know that every INPUT statement is preceded by a PRINT statement, but we do not show that step because it is not an important part of the logic of the program. If we clutter the flowchart with non-essential steps, it will be harder to see the underlying logical structure. The printing of the prompt was not included in the algorithm for the same reason. When we are developing an algorithm, we want to concentrate on the essentials and not be distracted by details.

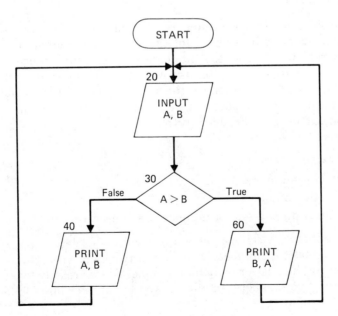

Fig. 3.25. Flowchart to sort two numbers.

```
1 REM SORT TWO NUMBERS
2 REM PROGRAMMER. M. TROMBETTA
10 PRINT "ENTER THE TWO NUMBERS TO BE SORTED"
20 INPUT A,B
30    IF A > B THEN 60
40    PRINT A,B
50    GO TO 10
60    PRINT B,A
70 GO TO 10
80 END


RUN

FIG3#26      15:14    02/25/80

ENTER THE TWO NUMBERS TO BE SORTED
?1,2
 1                    2
ENTER THE TWO NUMBERS TO BE SORTED
?2,1
 1                    2
ENTER THE TWO NUMBERS TO BE SORTED
?

STOP.
RAN 0.0 SEC.
```

Fig. 3.26. Program that sorts two numbers.

Sorting Three Numbers

You must agree that sorting two numbers is a rather simple problem (sorting one number is even simpler), but sorting three numbers is not so easy. We can call the three variables A, B, and C and use the algorithm we used to sort two numbers by simply changing the word "two" to "three." As before, we assume that no two numbers are equal.

If you think about it, you will see that there are six ways to mix up three numbers. They are

Case	Data
1	1, 2, 3
2	1, 3, 2
3	2, 1, 3
4	2, 3, 1
5	3, 1, 2
6	3, 2, 1

In all six cases the program should print 1,2,3. Of course we do not have to use only the numbers 1, 2, and 3 in our test data, but restricting

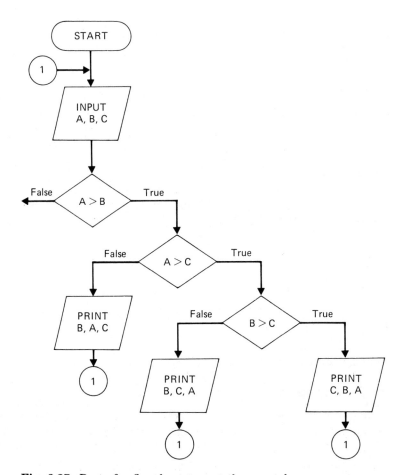

Fig. 3.27. Part of a flowchart to sort three numbers.

ourselves to these three numbers makes it easy to ensure that we have tested the program with every possible combination of small, middle, and large.

Part of a flowchart for this problem is shown in Fig. 3.27. Let's see how this flowchart was developed. The first thing you might notice on this flowchart is the new symbols:

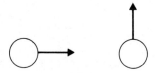

The symbol on the left is called an input connector, and the symbol on the right is called an output connector. After every print step we want to return to the input step to enter the next case. If we drew all those flowlines, the flowchart would be confusing. So instead of drawing the flowlines, we use connectors. Since there may be several sets of connectors in one flowchart, we distinguish among them by putting an identification inside the connector. In Fig. 3.27 we used the number 1 as the identification. An output connector in a flowchart just means to go to the input connector with the same identification.

After the input step is the condition, A > B. If this condition is true, we know that A is greater than B, but we do not know anything about the relative size of C. To determine the relative size of C, we will use the condition A > C. If this condition is false, we know that C is greater than A, and since we already knew that A was greater than B from the previous condition, the three variables must be in the order B,A,C. Therefore the variables are printed in this order.

Now let's follow the true branch of the A > C condition. If this condition is true, we know that A is greater than C, and since we already knew from the previous condition that A was greater than B, we can conclude that A is greater than both B and C. At this point we do not know anything about the relative size of B and C. So the third condition is B > C. If this condition is true, we know that B is greater than C, and since A was already greater than both B and C, the variables must be in the order C,B,A, and they are printed in this order. Similarly, if the condition is false, the variables must be in the order B,C,A. When you fill in the other half of the flowchart, follow the same reasoning. This, along with writing the BASIC program based on the flowchart, can be a homework exercise.

You might be interested to know that using this method to sort 10 numbers would require a program with 3,628,799 IF statements! Since computers are routinely used to sort thousands (and even hundreds of thousands) of numbers, it is clear that a smarter sorting scheme is needed. We will learn one such smarter scheme in Chapter 6.

Exercises

3.19 Complete the sorting flowchart started in Fig. 3.27. After the flowchart is complete, write the program based on it.

3.20 Figure 3.28 shows part of a flowchart to sort three numbers. You may use any statements you like to replace the question marks, but you may not use any decisions or print steps. That is, the

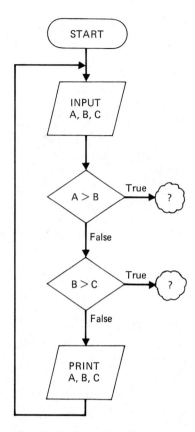

Fig. 3.28. Part of a flowchart to sort three numbers.

flowchart will contain just the two decisions and the one print step already shown. Complete the flowchart, and write the program.

SUMMARY

In this chapter you have learned

- How to draw a flowchart and write a program containing a decision
- The two functions of a flowchart—to help develop the algorithm and to help write the program
- That you must make up test data to test all the branches in your program

- How to use a numeric calculation to guide your development of a complicated LET statement
- The rules for the following BASIC statements:

  1. IF
  2. PRINT USING
  3. INPUT

- How to print strings and headings, and how to use the TAB function with the PRINT statement
- The following flowchart symbols:

1. The decision symbol—the diamond

2. The connector symbol—the circle

loops

OBJECTIVES

In this chapter you will learn

- How to control the number of times a loop is executed
- How to continue processing after all the data have been read
- The rules for the BASIC statements

  1. GOSUB
  2. RETURN
  3. STOP
  4. ON-GO TO

- How to use PRINT statements whose only function is to help debug the program
- How to use subroutines

  In addition you should learn the meanings of the following terms:

Accumulator	Control break
Counter	Subroutine
Trailer data	

In all the problems we have solved so far, when we ran out of data, the computer simply stopped executing the program. In many cases, however, additional processing must be done after all the data have been read. For example, suppose we were calculating and printing gross pay for employees. After the gross pay had been calculated and printed for the last employee, we might want to print the total gross pay. To solve this kind of problem requires some new techniques, which you will learn in this chapter.

A PAYROLL PROBLEM WITH TOTALS

Let's change slightly a problem we solved in Chapter 2. Given the rate of pay and hours worked for each of three employees, write a program to calculate and print the gross pay. In addition, calculate and print the total gross pay. The rate of pay and hours worked for the three employees are given along with the calculated gross pay and total gross pay.

Employee number	Rate of pay	Hours worked	Gross pay
1	4.00	30	120.00
2	7.00	25	175.00
3	5.00	40	200.00
			495.00

The only new thing about this problem is the calculation and printing of the total gross pay, 495 dollars.

The variable names we will use are

Input variables

Rate of pay	R
Hours worked	H

Output variables

Gross pay	G
Total gross pay	G1

We could have used T to stand for the total gross pay, but using G1 emphasizes that G1 stands for the total of all the Gs.

Before we develop the algorithm for this problem, let's think about exactly what is required. To print the total gross pay we must execute the READ statement exactly three times. If we stop the read-loop before the READ statement is executed three times, some employees will not be processed. On the other hand, if the READ statement is executed four times, it will run out of data, causing the computer to print the message LINE 10 END OF DATA and stop executing.

Using Trailer Data

We will control the number of times the READ statement is executed by adding a DATA statement for an imaginary employee after the DATA statements for the real employees. We will invent data for this imaginary employee that is so peculiar that, when we read it, we will have no difficulty identifying it as the data for the imaginary employee and not data for a real employee. What do we mean by peculiar data? We mean data that could not possibly be data for a real employee. For instance, the rate of pay for a real employee could never be zero, so zero is a fine choice for the imaginary employee's rate of pay. Every time we execute the READ statement we have to check to determine whether on this execution we encountered the data for the imaginary employee. Since the data for the imaginary employee is placed after the data for the real employees, we say we are using **trailer data** to control the read-loop.

Using an Accumulator

When we encounter the trailer data, we know that all the real employees have been processed, so all that remains is to calculate and print the total gross pay. But here we run into a problem. At this point we would like to say to the computer, "Remember all those Gs you calculated for me? Please add them up to get the total gross pay." If we could say that to the computer, you know it would answer us, "No, I don't remember all those Gs I calculated. The G box can only hold one number, and the only G that I remember is the last one I calculated, in this case 200." You cannot carry out this fanciful conversation with the computer, but it does illustrate an important point. Every time a new G is calculated, the old G is erased. We cannot wait until the end of processing to add up all the Gs, because by that time they are no longer in the computer. We must add each G to the total when we calculate it. Adding the Gs to the total one at a time requires an **accumulator**. In this program G1 will be the accumulator. Exactly how an accumulator is used will be shown when we develop the flowchart and the program.

Developing the Program

We are now in a position to develop the algorithm for this problem:

1. Set G1 equal to zero.
2. Read R and H for an employee.
3. If this is the imaginary employee, go to step 8.
4. Calculate G.
5. Accumulate G into G1.
6. Print R, H, and G.
7. Repeat steps 2–6 for all employees.
8. Print G1.

Why step 1 is necessary and how step 5 is done in BASIC will be explained when we see the BASIC program.

We must next calculate answers by hand. Hand-calculated gross pay and total gross pay were presented in the statement of the problem.

To be sure the total gross pay is calculated properly we must use more than one employee. Checking with two employees would probably uncover any logic errors, but we use three as an extra check. If the program calculates total gross pay properly for three employees, we can feel confident that it will work for any number of employees.

The flowchart based on this algorithm is shown in Fig. 4.1. You can see that step 3 of the algorithm is carried out by checking whether the R that was just read is equal to zero. The BASIC program, which follows directly from the flowchart, is shown in Fig. 4.2. Notice especially the DATA statement for the imaginary employee in line 130. The only function of this DATA statement is to set R equal to zero. However, since the READ statement contains two variables, we must include two numbers in the DATA statement. It does not matter what value is used for the second number since it is never used, so we will use zero.

To make sure we understand exactly how this program works let's trace it. We set up boxes for all the variables as shown in Fig. 4.3. When the computer executes line 10, it puts 0 in the G1 box as shown in Fig. 4.3(a). When it executes line 20, it puts 4 in the R box and 30 in the H box, as in 4.3(b). When it executes line 30, it finds that the condition is false, so it falls through to line 40. When line 40 is executed, 120 is put in the G box, as in 4.3(c). So far this has been old hat, but line 50 introduces something new. Remember how a LET statement works. First the computer does the arithmetic specified in the expression on the right of the equal sign. In this case it takes the 0 from the G1 box and adds to it the 120 from the G box, getting 120 as the answer. After the computer reduces the expression on the right to a number, that number is put into the box of the variable on the left. In this case the 120 is put into the G1 box, as shown in Fig. 4.3(d).

Recall that I said G1 was an accumulator. What makes G1 an accumulator is the way it is used in a LET statement. An accumulator is always used in a LET statement as follows:

LET accumulator = accumulator + something else

The critical fact is that the accumulator variable appears on both sides of the equal sign. Each time it is executed it accumulates the value of the "something else" variable. In our example, G1 accumulates the values of G.

You can now see why line 10 is required. If we had not put 0 in the G1 box initially, we might have run into trouble. The first time the computer executes line 50 it has to use the number in the G1 box. If we had not assigned a value to G1, we would have been using an unintialized variable. As you remember from the discussion in Chapter 2, many systems will stop execution if you try to use an uninitialized variable. Even if your system is one of those that sets uninitialized

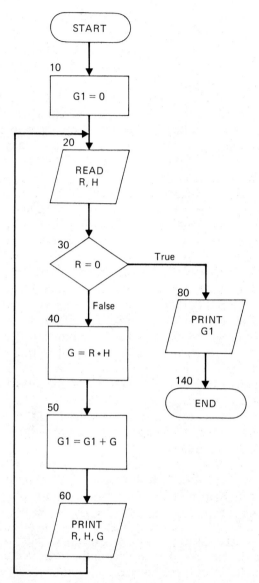

Fig. 4.1. Flowchart for payroll with total pay.

```
1 REM PAYROLL REPORT WITH TOTAL PAY
2 REM PROGRAMMER M. TROMBETTA
10 LET G1 = 0    ← (G1 initialized)
20 READ R,H
25   REM CHECK IF WE JUST READ DATA FOR IMAGINARY EMPLOYEE
30   IF R = 0 THEN 80
40   LET G = R * H
50   LET G1 = G1 + G ← (G1 used as an accumulator)
60   PRINT R,H,G
70 GO TO 20
80 PRINT,"TOTAL GROSS PAY",G1
90 DATA 4,30
100 DATA 7,25
110 DATA 5,40
120 REM DATA FOR IMAGINARY EMPLOYEE FOLLOWS
130 DATA 0,0
140 END


RUN

FIG4#2       15:15    02/25/80

4                30               120
7                25               175
5                40               200
                 TOTAL GROSS PAY  495

TIME 0.0 SECS.
```

Fig. 4.2. Program to print a payroll report with total gross pay.

variables to 0, it is good practice to set your accumulators to 0 yourself in a LET statement.

Let's return to tracing the program. We will skip the next few steps (although you should make sure you can trace them) and see what happens when line 50 is executed the second time. At that time the variables have the values shown in Fig. 4.3(e). Can you figure out what the vaue of G1 will be after line 50 is executed? The computer evaluates the expression by adding the number in the G1 box, 120, to the number in the G box, 175, and puts the total, 295, in the G1 box. Skip ahead to the third time line 50 is executed. Do you know what the value of G1 will be now? You should have figured out that G1 will be equal to 495.

After line 50 is executed for the third time, line 60 prints the answers for the third employee, and line 70 returns us to line 20. This time when the READ statement is executed, the data for the imaginary employee is read, causing R and H to be set equal to zero. When line 30 is executed, the condition is true, and the program branches to line

R	H	G	G1
–	–	–	0

(a) After executing line 10

R	H	G	G1
4	30	–	0

(b) After executing line 20

R	H	G	G1
4	30	120	0

(c) After executing line 40

R	H	G	G1
4	30	120	0̸
			120

(d) After executing line 50

R	H	G	G1
4̸	3̸0̸	1̸2̸0̸	0̸
7	25	175	120

(e) After executing line 40

Fig. 4.3. Tracing the program in Fig. 4.2.

80, which prints the value of G1, 495. The comma in line 80 causes the value of G1 to be printed in print zone 3, under the values of G. (Of course, if we wanted really fancy output we could print headings and use the PRINT USING statement.) Now that we have traced the program we understand exactly how it works.

Exercises

4.1 Which of the following could be used as the trailer DATA statement for the program in Fig. 4.2?

   a) DATA 0,40
   b) DATA 0, −1
   c) DATA 5, 0
   d) DATA −1, −1

4.2 What output will be produced if the following changes are made to the program in Fig. 4.2. Trace the program to determine what the output will be. Before making each new change, assume the program is restored back to its original form.

a) The GO TO statement in line 70 is changed to

70 GO TO 10

b) The IF statement in line 30 is moved to line 65.

4.3 For each depositor we are given a name and a balance. Write a program to read and print each depositor's name and balance and the total balance.

4.4 Resolve Exercise 2.7 to include calculating and printing total gross pay, total withholding, and total net pay. Use the PRINT USING statement or the TAB function to produce an attractive report.

CALCULATING THE AVERAGE TEST SCORE

Trailer data are used in many applications to control the number of times a read-loop is executed. As another example consider the following problem. Given the following students' names and test scores, read and print each student's name and test score, and calculate and print the average test score.

Student number	Student name	Test score
1	Melita	90
2	Benito	80
3	Angela	86
4	Mickey	74

To check the program we calculate the average test score by hand as (90 + 80 + 86 + 74) divided by 4 equals 82.5

To have the computer calculate the average test score we will accumulate the individual test scores to get the total and then divide the total by the number of students. In the statement of the problem we are given data for four students. Whenever you write a program, you should try to make it as general as possible. Instead of writing a program that can handle only four students, let's develop a program that can handle any number of students.

Using a Counter

To calculate the average test score we must divide by the number of students. Since the program is supposed to handle any number of students, to get the proper number by which to divide we will count each student as he or she is processed. To count the students we will need a new variable to act as a **counter**. As you will see, a counter is used very much like an accumulator.

We will use trailer data to control the number of times the read-loop is executed. Since in this problem we are reading names and test marks, we may invent peculiar data for either of these variables. For example, since no student will ever get a test mark of -10 (we hope!) we can use -10 as the test mark in the trailer data. It is clearer, however, to use a peculiar name in the data statement. For example, I will use END as the name in the trailer data

The variable names we will use are

Input variables

Student name	N$
Test score	T

Internal variable

Counter	C

Output variables

Test score accumulator	T1
Average test score	A

Notice we have a new kind of varible, an internal variable. The counter, C, is neither read in nor printed out. It is used only in the program. We call this kind of variable an internal variable. You might wonder how I realized I needed an internal variable. The answer is that at first I didn't. Most often you will not realize you need an internal variable until you start to draw the flowchart. At that time simply come back and add the names of the internal variables to the list of variable names.

We can use the following algorithm for this problem:

1. Set T1 and C to zero.

2. Read N$ and T for a student.

3. If this is the imaginary student, go to step 8.

4. Count the student who was just read.

5. Accumulate the test score for this student.

6. Print N$ and T.

7. Repeat steps 2–6 for all students.

8. Calculate and print A.

The flowchart based on this algorithm is shown in Fig. 4.4. One new feature in this flowchart is shown in box 10. Remember, the flow-

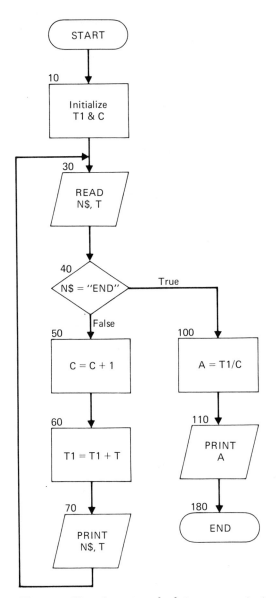

Fig. 4.4. Flowchart to calculate average test score.

chart is drawn to help us develop the algorithm and to write the program. It is not necessary to show every step in the flowchart. Recall that we do not show the step that prints the prompt when we use an INPUT statement. So in the flowchart shown in Fig. 4.4, in box 10 we simply say "Initialize T1 and C." This reminds us that both T1 and C must initially be set equal to zero. When we write the program, box 10 will translate into two LET statements.

The program based on this flowchart is shown in Fig. 4.5. The trailer data is in line 170, and in line 40 we determine whether we have read it by checking IF N$ = "END". You must be careful when you compare strings. Remember that spaces are significant in strings. Because of the space in " END" the following version of line 40 would not work:

    40 IF N$ = " END" THEN 100

```
1 REM CALCULATE AVERAGE TEST SCORE
2 REM PROGRAMMER M. TROMBETTA
10 LET T1 = 0
20 LET C = 0   ← ( C Initialized )
30 READ N$,T
40    IF N$ = "END" THEN 100
50    LET C = C + 1   ← ( C used as a counter )
60    LET T1 = T1 + T
70    PRINT N$,T
80 GO TO 30
90 REM CALCULATION OF AVERAGE TEST SCORE
100 LET A = T1/C
110 PRINT "AVERAGE TEST SCORE IS",A
120 DATA "MELITA",90
130 DATA "BENITO",80
140 DATA "ANGELA",86
150 DATA "MICKEY",74
160 REM NEXT DATA IS FOR IMAGINARY STUDENT
170 DATA "END",0
180 END


RUN

FIG4#5      12:01    09/14/79

MELITA            90
BENITO            80
ANGELA            86
MICKEY            74
AVERAGE TEST SCORE IS              82.5

TIME 0.0 SECS.
```

Fig. 4.5. Program to calculate average test score.

When the computer reads the trailer data, N$ will contain END. But "END" and " END" are not equal, and therefore the computer will never branch to line 100.

Testing IF N$ = "END" would not work if we ever had a student named END. Do you think it would be better if we used THAT'S ALL FOLKS as the name in the trailer data? If you do, what, if any, other changes would also have to be made to the program? The answer is given at the end of this chapter.

The counter variable C is used in line 50. The similarity to the way the accumulator variable T1 is used in line 60 is clear. Let's trace the execution of line 50 for several cycles to see how the counter works. C is assigned the initial value of zero in line 20. The first time line 50 is executed, the computer adds the zero in the C box to 1 and puts the answer, 1, back in the C box. The second time line 50 is executed, the computer adds the number in the C box, which is now 1, to 1 and puts the answer, 2, back in the C box. Each time line 50 is executed the number in the C box is increased by one. When we finally read the trailer data and branch to line 100, C will be 4.

The accumulator T1 works just like the accumulator G1 worked in our previous program. When we get to line 100, we calculate the average by dividing the total of all the test scores by the number of students.

Exercises

4.5 Suppose the program in Fig. 4.5 were run with 30 students. How many times would line 10 be executed? How many times would line 30 be executed?

4.6 Resolve the problem on pages 74–80 to include calculating and printing average sales, average commission, and average commission rate.

4.7 The program in Fig. 4.5 calculates the average test score. In statistical studies it is useful to calculate the standard deviation of the test scores as well as the average score. The standard deviation of the test scores is calculated using the equation.

$$S = (T2 / C - A \char`\^ 2) \char`\^ .5$$

In this equation A stands for the average test score, C stands for the number of students, and T2 stands for the sum of the squares of the test scores. Modify the program in Fig. 4.5 to calculate and print the standard deviation as well as the average text score.

FINDING THE HIGHEST SALES*

As a final example of the use of trailer data to control a read-loop consider the following problem. Given a series of salesperson's names and sales, find and print the highest sales.

We will use the following variable names:

Input variables

Salesperson name   N$

Sales   S

Output variables

Highest sales   H

Let's use the following test data:

Salesperson's name	Sales
Hart, M.	300
Lee, G. R.	700
Rand, S.	200

If our program functions properly, it should print 700 as the highest sales. We will use an imaginary salesperson named END to control the read-loop.

The algorithm for this problem involves a trick, which is easier to explain when the program is traced. For now I will just state the algorithm and explain it later.

1. Set H to zero.

2. Read N$ and S

3. If this is the imaginary salesperson, go to step 6.

4. If this S is higher than H, set H equal to S. Otherwise do nothing.

5. Repeat steps 2–4 for all salespeople.

6. Print H.

The flowchart for this problem is shown in Fig. 4.6, and the program based on this flowchart is shown in Fig. 4.7. Let's trace the program to see how it works. We start by setting up boxes for the H, N$, and S variables, as shown in Fig. 4.8. When the computer executes line 10, it puts a zero in the H box as shown in Fig. 4.8(a). When line 20 is executed, HART, M. is put in the N$ box, and 300 is put in the S box,

---

* This section may be omitted without loss of continuity.

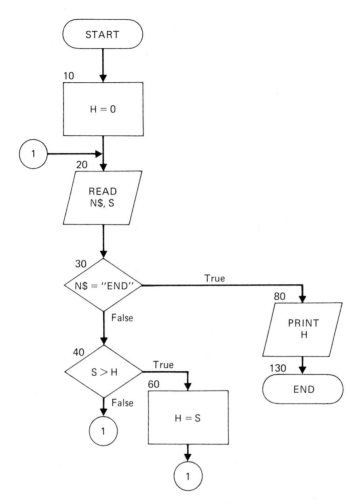

Fig. 4.6. Flowchart to find highest sales.

as shown in Fig. 4.8(b). N\$ is not equal to "END", so we fall through line 30 to line 40. Since S is greater than H, line 40 sends us to line 60. In line 60 the number in the S box, 300, is put in the H box, as shown in Fig. 4.8(c). We then return to the READ statement in line 20, which causes LEE, G.R. to be put in the N\$ box and 700 to be put in the S box, as in Fig. 4.8(d). We drop through line 30 again and in line 40 find again that S is greater than H, so we branch to line 60. Once more the number in the S box is put in the H box, as shown in Fig. 4.8(e).

The third time the READ statement is executed RAND, S. is put in the N\$ box, and 200 is put in the S box, as shown in Fig. 4.8(f). This

```
1 REM FINDING HIGHEST SALES
2 REM PROGRAMMER M. TROMBETTA
10 LET H = 0
20 READ N$,S
30    IF N$ = "END" THEN 80
40    IF S > H THEN 60
50       GO TO 20
60    LET H = S
70 GO TO 20
80 PRINT ,"HIGHEST SALES",H
90 DATA "HART, M.",300
100 DATA "LEE, G. R.",700
110 DATA "RAND, S.",200
120 DATA "END",0
130 END


RUN

FIG4#7        11:36    07/14/80

               HIGHEST SALES      700

TIME 0.0 SECS.
```

Fig. 4.7. Program to find highest sales.

time, when we get to line 40, we find that S is not greater than H, so we do not branch to line 60 but rather fall through to line 50, which then sends us to line 20. Notice that this time, since S was not greater than H, we did not change the number in the H box. That is the basic idea behind this algorithm: when we have an S that is greater than H, we save that value of S in the H box; when we have an S that is not greater than H, we ignore that value of S.

When we execute the READ statement the fourth time, we encounter the imaginary salesperson, so line 30 sends us to line 80 where we print the value of H.

For this scheme to work H must be given an initial value less than the highest sales. The easiest way to do that is to give H an initial value of zero, since sales can never be less than zero. If we wanted to find the lowest sales, we might let L stand for lowest sales. We would then have to give L an initial value greater than the lowest sales. To do that we would have to know how high sales could be. If sales were always less than 1000 dollars, for example, we could give L an initial value of 1000.

Exercises

4.8 What output would be produced by the program in Fig. 4.7 if the following changes are made:

H   N$ S
0   —   —
(a) After executing line 10

H   N$ S
0   HART, M.   300
(b) After executing line 20

H   N$ S
0̶   HART, M.   300
300
(c) After executing line 60

H   N$ S
0̶   H̶A̶R̶T̶, M.   3̶0̶0̶
300   LEE, G.R.   700
(d) After executing line 20

H   N$ S
0̶   H̶A̶R̶T̶, M.   3̶0̶0̶
3̶0̶0̶   LEE, G.R.   700
700
(e) After executing line 60

H   N$ S
0̶   H̶A̶R̶T̶, M.   3̶0̶0̶
3̶0̶0̶   L̶E̶E̶, G̶.R̶.   7̶0̶0̶
700   RAND, S.   200
(f) After executing line 20

Fig. 4.8. Tracing the program in Fig. 4.7.

a) Line 10 is changed to

10 LET H = 1000

b) Line 70 is changed to

70 GO TO 10

4.9 Modify the program in Fig. 4.7 to find and print the name of the salesperson with the highest sales, along with the numeric value of the highest sales.

4.10 For each contestant we are given a name and a time to run the marathon. Write a program to find and print the lowest time.

HOW TO BECOME A MILLIONAIRE

We do not control a loop only by using values read from a trailer DATA statement; sometimes a calculated value can be used to determine when to exit from a loop. To illustrate this kind of control let's solve the following problem. A bank pays R interest rate. Suppose that, starting a year from now, you deposit D dollars into this bank every year for N years. At the end of that time the total amount of money you will have, T, can be calculated by the equation

$$T = D * ((1 + R)\ ^{\wedge}\ N - 1) / R$$

This equation was used in Exercise 2.10. For some particular values of R and D we want to find the N necessary for T to be a million dollars. It should be clear from the statement of the problem that R and D are the input variables, and N and T are the output variables.

If we used logarithms, we could develop an equation to calculate N, but let's see how we can have the computer search for the required N.

The basic idea of the algorithm is to use larger and larger values of N until we find the N that causes T to become greater than or equal to one million. The algorithm is

1. Input R and D.

2. Set N equal to 1.

3. Calculate T by using successively larger values of N until T becomes greater than or equal to one million.

4. Print N and T.

5. Repeat until all sets of R and D have been processed.

Our next step would normally be to calculate an answer by hand, but we will postpone that step and draw the flowchart first because the flowchart will make the algorithm easier to understand. A flowchart is shown in Fig. 4.9. Notice the Calc T in box 30. The whole equation to calculate T does not fit in this little box, so Calc T reminds us to calculate T at this point. Of course, the complete equation must be used when the program is written.

The flowchart clearly shows the loop consisting of boxes 30, 40, and 50. We calculate T in box 30. We test T in box 40. If T is not greater than or equal to one million, we increase N by 1 in box 50 and repeat the loop. Sooner or later we will get up to an N that causes T to become greater than or equal to one million, and then we can print N and T.

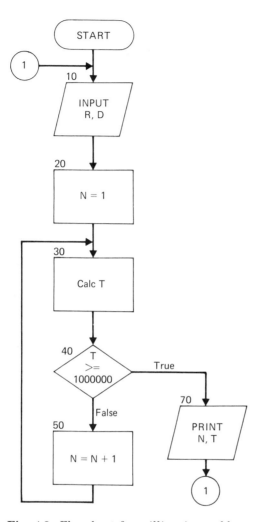

Fig. 4.9. Flowchart for millionaire problem.

We have to check whether T is greater than or equal to one million, rather than whether it is equal to one million, because it is likely that T will jump from below one million to above it and never be exactly equal to one million.

Using a PRINT Statement for Debugging

It would be very difficult to calculate an answer to this problem by hand. Fortunately we do not have to. We can reason that the critical step is the calculation of T. If we can be sure that T is calculated properly, and if, when we exit from the loop and print N and T, we see that T is in fact greater than or equal to one million, we can have confidence in our program.

We can be sure that T is calculated properly by checking the computer's calculation against a hand calculation. Let's pick R = .08 (8% interest), and D = 500, and calculate T for N = 1, 2, and 3. That is not very hard, particularly if we use a calculator. The answers are

N	T
1	500.00
2	1040.00
3	1623.20

But this does not do us any good, since the computer does not print the T it calculated when N was 1, 2, or 3. It only prints N and T when T becomes greater than or equal to one million.

This kind of problem occurs from time to time. The solution is to add a PRINT statement, which is just used for debugging. Figure 4.10 shows a BASIC program based on the flowchart in Fig. 4.9, with a PRINT statement added in line 35. When we RUN the program, we see the debugging output produced by this PRINT statement. After the first three lines of output we hit the BREAK key to stop execution. We now compare the computer-calculated T against the hand-calculated T for N equal 1, 2, and 3. We see they agree to within a penny, so we know that T is being calculated properly and that N is being incremented properly. (The values do not agree exactly because of round-off error.)

We conclude that the program is correct, and we have no further need for line 35. So we delete line 35, and type RUN again. This time the program runs until T becomes greater than or equal to one million. We see that it takes 67 years for T to become 1,078,311 dollars. That's not such a long time; is it?

Exercises

4.11 Sara Smith won 100,000 dollars in a lottery. She put the money in a savings account that pays 8% interest. At the end of each year she withdraws 15,000 dollars from the account and spends it on a big bash. Write a program to determine how many years she can do this before her account balance is down to zero.

To be sure you understand the problem, let's look at what happens during the first two years. During the first year the full 100,000 dollars is on deposit, so the interest earned is 0.08 ×

```
1 REM MILLIONAIRE PROBLEM
2 REM PROGRAMMED BY M. TROMBETTA
9 PRINT "ENTER INTEREST RATE AND ANNUAL DEPOSIT"
10 INPUT R,D
20    LET N = 1
30    LET T = D * ((1 + R) ^ N - 1) / R
35      PRINT N,T  ←
40      IF T >= 1000000 THEN 70
50      LET N = N + 1
60    GO TO 30
70    PRINT N,T
80 GO TO 9
90 END

RUN

FIG4#10      15:50    09/19/79

ENTER INTEREST RATE AND ANNUAL DEPOSIT
?.08,500
  1                 500.
  2                 1039.99
  3                 1623.19
```

PRINT statement used only for debugging (annotation)

Debugging output (annotation)

Break Key hit to stop execution

```
STOP.
RAN 0.0 SEC.

35  ←
```

Line 35 deleted (annotation)

```
RUN

FIG4#10      15:50    09/19/79

ENTER INTEREST RATE AND ANNUAL DEPOSIT
?.08,500
  67                1078311
ENTER INTEREST RATE AND ANNUAL DEPOSIT
?

STOP.
RAN 0.0 SEC.
```

Answers (annotation)

Fig. 4.10. Program for millionaire problem.

100,000 = 8000. On December 31, therefore, the balance is 100,000 + 8000 = 108,000. However, Sara now withdraws 15,000, so her balance goes down to 108,000 − 15,000 = 93,000. During the second year interest is earned on 93,000, and is only 0.08 × 93,000 = 7440. When at the end of the second year Sara withdraws her usual 15,000, her balance is reduced to 93,000 + 7440 − 15,000 = 85,440. This process continues until her balance becomes less than or equal to zero.

A SALES PROBLEM WITH SUBTOTALS

Let's write a program to solve the following problem. A store has a number of departments. Each department is identified by a department number. Every time a department makes a sale a DATA statement containing the department number and the amount of the sale is created. The management of the store would like to have a BASIC program that prints every sale and the total of all the sales. So far, this problem is exactly like ones we solved earlier, but one more condition is added to the problem to make it different. In addition to the total of all the sales, the program should also print the subtotal of sales for each department.

To make sure you understand the problem, let's assume we have the data:

Department number	Amount of sale
46	500
46	200
49	150
57	200
57	600
57	50

What is particularly significant about the data is that the number of sales for each department is variable. Notice that department 46 has two sales, department 49 has only one sale, and department 57 has three sales.

With these data, the program should produce the following output:

Department number	Amount of sale
46	500
46	200
Total sales for department 46	700
49	150
Total sales for department 49	150
57	200
57	600
57	50
Total sales for department 57	850
Grand total sales	1700

We would have no trouble accumulating the sales for each department. The problem comes in determining when to print the subtotal for a department. How do we know when we have read all the sales for department 46 and are therefore ready to print the subtotal for that department? The scheme we will use is this: when the department number changes, we know we have started reading the data for a new department. We must therefore have finished reading the data for the previous department, and we should print the subtotal for that department. For this scheme to work all the sales for a department must obviously be together, as they are in the previously listed data.

When the department number changes, we say we have encountered a **control break**. When we encounter a control break, we know we should print the total for the previous department.

Since we want to print the grand total of all the sales, we know we must use trailer data. We will use a DATA statement with a department number equal to 9999 as the trailer data.

The variables we will use are

Input variables

Department number	D
Sales	S

Internal variables

Previous department number	D1

Output variables

Total sales for a department	S1
Total sales for all departments	S2

The algorithm we will use is

1. Read D and S.

2. If D = 9999, go to step 6.

3. If D is different from the previous D, calculate and print the subtotal for the previous department.

4. Print D and S.

5. Repeat steps 1–4 for all the data.

6. Print the subtotal for the last department.

7. Print the grand total.

As usual we will explain the algorithm completely when we draw the flowchart, but now we will look at steps 3 and 6 in a little more detail. In step 3, how are we going to know whether D is different from the previous D? The way to do that is to save the previous D in the variable D1. So step 3 really involves comparing D and D1.

In step 6, which we execute after reading the trailer data, why do we print the subtotal for the last department? When we read the trailer data, aren't we ready to print the grand total? No, we are not. When we read the trailer data, we have read all the data for the last department, but we have not yet printed the subtotal for that department. That is why we must first print the subtotal for the last department and then print the grand total.

Flowchart: Subroutines

The flowchart is shown in Fig. 4.11. This flowchart introduces a new flowchart symbol:

A rectangle with two vertical lines drawn as shown is the flowchart symbol for a **subroutine**. A subroutine is simply a group of BASIC statements that performs some function or calculation. These statements are not included in the main body of the program, where they are needed. Rather they are inserted somewhere else in the program, usually near the end, and called, or executed, when they are needed.

You might wonder why anyone would use a subroutine instead of simply putting the statements in the main body of the program. There are several reasons. In this problem notice that we must calculate a subtotal at two places in the program. Instead of repeating the BASIC statements that calculate the subtotal, it is easier to group the statements as a subroutine and execute them from the main body of the program whenever they are needed.

A second reason for using subroutines is they make the algorithm, the flowchart, and the BASIC program easier to understand. Recall that when we developed the algorithm, in step 3, we simply said, "Calculate and print the subtotal." Similarly, in the flowchart, and, as you will see, in the program, when we come to the point where we must calculate and print the subtotal, we simply say, "Execute the instructions that calculate and print the subtotal." At this point we do not have to be concerned with the details of exactly how the subtotal calculation and printing will be done. This permits us to concentrate on the main logic of the problem. Once we have the main logic clear, we can then go back and program the subroutine. Because up to now our programs have been

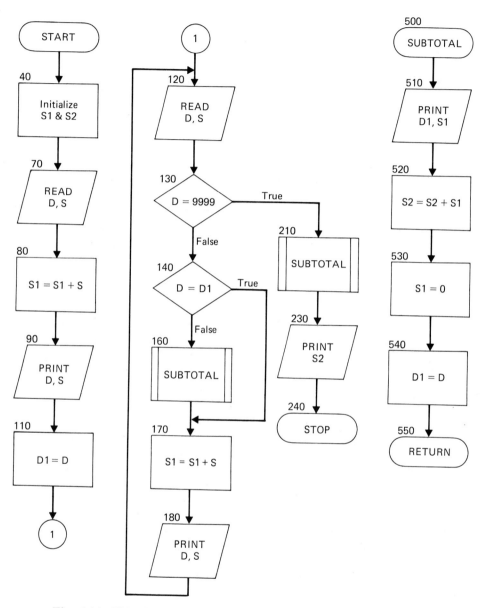

Fig. 4.11. Flowchart for a report with subtotals.

relatively simple, we have not had occasion to use subroutines. But in more complicated problems you will find subroutines very useful.

Let's now examine the flowchart in detail. The variable D1 is supposed to contain the previous department number. When we start, however, there is no previous department number. Therefore the first reading must be handled in a special way. We read the first D and S; we accumulate this S into S1; we print this D and S; and we set D1 equal to D. Now D1 is equal to the previous department number, so we can enter the main loop.

Inside the main loop we read D and S and test to see whether the trailer data were just read. If the trailer data were just read, we execute the subtotal subroutine to print the subtotal for the last department and then print the grand total. If the trailer data were not read, we check if the department number has changed. If it has, we again execute the subtotal subroutine to print the subtotal for the previous department. Whether the department number has changed or not, we next process the current data, and then go back to the READ statement to continue the loop. Now that we understand the flowchart for the main program, let's examine the flowchart for the subtotal subroutine.

The first thing we notice about the flowchart for the subtotal subroutine is that the terminal symbols do not contain the words START and END. It is customary to start the flowchart of a subroutine with a terminal symbol that contains the name of the subroutine, in this case SUBTOTAL. It is also customary to end the flowchart of a subroutine with a terminal symbol that contains the word RETURN. We do that because, when we reach the end of a subroutine, we want to return to the main body of the program. Hence the word RETURN.

In the subtotal subroutine we print the subtotal for the previous department. (Using, notice, D1 not D. D1 contains the department number of the previous department; D contains the department number of the current department.) We then accumulate the department subtotal into the grand total, reset the department subtotal back to zero, and set the previous department number equal to the current department number. Notice that the subtotal subroutine involves several steps besides merely printing the subtotal.

There is one small point that deserves discussion. In the list of the variables used in this problem D1 was listed as an internal variable, but the flowchart shows it being printed. Isn't that a contradiction? No, because the primary use of D1 is as an internal variable, to indicate when the department number has changed. In any event, and this is the important point, remember that we list the variables in the problem to help us write the program. Therefore D1 could correctly be listed as either an internal variable or an output variable, depending on what you think its primary use is.

BASIC Program: GOSUB, RETURN, and STOP Statements

The program for the subtotals problem is shown in Fig. 4.12. The only things new about the program are the statements that involve the subroutine: the GOSUB statement in lines 160 and 210, the RETURN statement in line 550, and the STOP statement in line 240.

The GOSUB statement is similar to the GO TO statement. When the computer executes the statement GOSUB 500, it branches to statement 500 just as it would if it executed the statement GO TO 500. When it executes a GOSUB statement, however, the computer not only branches to the specified line number, it also remembers the line number of the statement following the GOSUB. In the program in Fig. 4.12, when the computer executes the GOSUB statement in line 160, it remembers the line number of the next statement, line 170. When the computer executes the RETURN statement in line 550 it "returns," or branches, to line 170.

Notice that the RETURN statement always returns to the correct line number. If the subroutine is executed from the GOSUB statement in line 160, the RETURN statement causes a branch to line 170. If, on the other hand, the subroutine is executed from the GOSUB statement in line 210, the RETURN statement causes a branch to line 220. Speaking loosely we can say that the RETURN statement tells the computer, "Go back where you came from!" The computer remembers where it came from and goes back.

There is nothing special about line number 500, which was used as the first line in the subroutine. You can use any line number you want for the start of a subroutine, but it should be much greater than the highest line number in the main program. By giving a subroutine line numbers much higher than those in the main program, we physically separate it from the main program. Since a subroutine is logically self-contained, it is a good idea to make it physically self-contained too.

Another reason for making a subroutine physically separate from the main program is that a physically separate subroutine helps avoid the error of "falling into" a subroutine. "Falling into" a subroutine means executing the instructions in a subroutine without using a GOSUB statement. You might, for example, branch into a subroutine as a result of a GO TO or IF statement. Or, as the computer executes statements sequentially, it might arrive at the subroutine statements. Falling into a subroutine is an error because, when the RETURN statement is executed, the computer will not know where to return to. Remember that

```
10 REM A REPORT WITH SUBTOTALS
20 REM PROGRAMMER. M. TROMBETTA
30 REM INITIALIZE ACCUMULATORS
40 LET S1 = 0
50 LET S2 = 0
55 PRINT USING 56
56:                          DEPARTMENT    SALES
60 REM READ AND PROCESS FIRST DATA STATEMENT
70 READ D,S
80 LET S1 = S1 + S
90 PRINT USING 91,D,S
91:                              ###        #####
100 REM INITIALIZE PREVIOUS DEPARTMENT NUMBER
110 LET D1 = D
115 REM PROCESS REMAINING DATA
120 READ D,S
130    IF D = 9999 THEN 200
140    IF D = D1 THEN 170
150    REM DEPARTMENT NUMBER CHANGED EXECUTE SUBTOTAL SUBROUTINE
160    GOSUB 500
170    LET S1 = S1 + S
180    PRINT USING 91,D,S
190 GO TO 120
200 REM ALL DATA READ. PRINT TOTAL FOR LAST DEPARTMENT
210 GOSUB 500
220 REM PRINT GRAND TOTAL
230 PRINT USING 231,S2
231: GRAND TOTAL SALES                    #####
240 STOP
500 REM SUBTOTAL SUBROUTINE
510 PRINT USING 511,D1,S1
511: TOTAL SALES FOR DEPARTMENT ###       #####
520 LET S2 = S2 + S1
530 LET S1 = 0
540 LET D1 = D
550 RETURN
600 DATA 46,500
610 DATA 46,200
620 DATA 49,150
630 DATA 57,200
640 DATA 57,600
650 DATA 57,50
660 REM TRAILER DATA FOLLOWS
670 DATA 9999,0
999 END

RUN

FIG4#12      20:03   11/26/80

                              DEPARTMENT    SALES
                                  46         500
                                  46         200
TOTAL SALES FOR DEPARTMENT        46         700
                                  49         150
TOTAL SALES FOR DEPARTMENT        49         150
                                  57         200
                                  57         600
                                  57          50
TOTAL SALES FOR DEPARTMENT        57         850
GRAND TOTAL SALES                           1700

TIME 0.0 SECS.
```

Fig. 4.12. A program that prints subtotals.

it is the GOSUB statement that remembers the line number to which the RETURN statement branches. You should execute a subroutine only as a result of a GOSUB statement.

In the program in Fig. 4.12 the STOP statement in line 240 prevents us from falling into the subroutine. The STOP statement simply stops the execution of the program. In some versions of BASIC you can continue execution by typing the command CONT. In most versions of BASIC, however, the only way to execute the program again is by using the command RUN.

Exercise

4.12 The coach of a hockey team wants to use a computer to keep track of the performance of her players. After each game a DATA statement is written with each player's name and the number of goals she made during that game. (If a player did not score any goals during a particular game, no DATA statement is made for her for that game.) Write a program that will read and print these data and will also calculate and print subtotals for each player as well as a grand total for all players.

THE ON-GO TO STATEMENT

BASIC provides another conditional branching instruction that is sometimes handy, the ON-GO TO statement. The ON-GO TO statement is used as follows:

ON X GO TO 300, 150, 200

X is the name of a variable in the program and should be equal to an integer. The numbers 300, 150, and 200 are line numbers in the program. (In some versions of BASIC the same statement is written GO TO 300, 150, 200 ON X. Your instructor will tell you the format used in your BASIC, and you should write it on the inside front cover of this book.)

If X is 1, the computer branches to line number 300 because 300 is the first line number listed. If X is 2, the computer branches to the second line number listed, 150. Finally, if X is 3, the computer branches to the third line number listed, 200.

Following the word ON you may have a variable or an expression, and following the words GO TO you may have as many line numbers as you like. You should make sure that the variable or expression following the word ON does not have a value less than one or greater than the number of line numbers listed. In this example if X were less than 1 or greater than 3, the computer would not be able to figure out which line number we wanted to branch to. If that happened, most BASICs would stop executing and print an error message. Some BASICs, however, would fall through the ON-GO TO statement and execute the next statement.

As an example of when an ON-GO TO statement could be used, consider the following problem. A fast-food chain has assigned a code number to each possible order, as follows:

Code number	Order	Price
1	Hamburger	$0.60
2	Fries	0.40
3	Shake	0.50
4	Hamburger and fries	1.00
5	Hamburger, fries, and shake	1.50

Write a program that will accept as input the code number of a customer's order, and calculate and print the customer's bill. The variables to use are

Input variable	
Code number of the order	C

Output variable	
Customer's bill	B

The algorithm is

1. Input C.

2. Calculate and print B.

3. Repeat for all customers.

The flowchart is shown in Fig. 4.13. This problem could be solved using five IF statements, but it is much easier to use an ON-GO TO statement. Unfortunately the flowchart symbol for the ON-GO TO statement has not been standardized. A diamond is used here to remind us that the ON-GO TO is a conditional branching instruction. The many branches leaving the diamond show immediately that the diamond does not represent an IF statement. To make the flowchart as clear as possible each branch is labeled with the value of the ON variable that causes the computer to take that branch.

The program is shown in Fig. 4.14. The program follows directly from the flowchart, and you should not have any trouble understanding it. Particularly after our discussion, the way the ON-GO TO statement

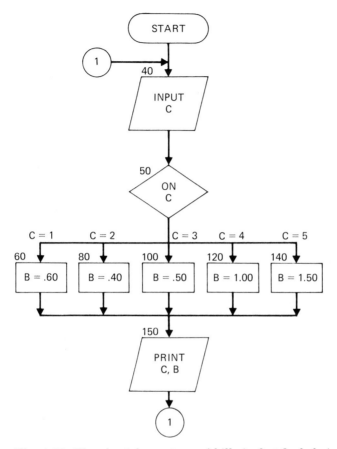

Fig. 4.13. Flowchart for customers' bills in fast-food chain.

works should be clear. Notice how all five codes are used to check the program.

Exercises

4.13 Consider the following ON-GO TO statement

ON P GO TO 50, 70, 60, 40, 90

What line number will the computer branch to if P has the following values:

a) 4
b) 2
c) 50

```
10 REM CUSTOMER BILLS IN A FAST-FOOD CHAIN
20 REM PROGRAMMER. M. TROMBETTA
30 PRINT "ENTER CODE NUMBER OF CUSTOMER'S BILL"
40 INPUT C
50    ON C GO TO 60,80,100,120,140
60    B = .60
70    GO TO 150
80    B = .40
90    GO TO 150
100   LET B = .50
110   GO TO 150
120   LET B = 1.00
130   GO TO 150
140   LET B = 1.50
150   PRINT USING 151,C,B
151:      #          #.##
160 GO TO 30
170 END


RUN

FIG4#14      20:10    11/26/80

ENTER CODE NUMBER OF CUSTOMER'S BILL
?4
        4          1.00
ENTER CODE NUMBER OF CUSTOMER'S BILL
?1
        1           .60
ENTER CODE NUMBER OF CUSTOMER'S BILL
?3
        3           .50
ENTER CODE NUMBER OF CUSTOMER'S BILL
?5
        5          1.50
ENTER CODE NUMBER OF CUSTOMER'S BILL
?2
        2           .40
ENTER CODE NUMBER OF CUSTOMER'S BILL
?

STOP.
RAN 0.0 SEC.
```

Fig. 4.14. A program to calculate bills in a fast-food chain.

4.14 A company has classified their salespeople into three categories. Those in category 1 get a 5% commission, those in category 2 get a 10% commission; and those in category 3 get a 15% commission. Write a program that will read sales and category numbers for each salesperson and will calculate and print commissions.

SUMMARY

In this chapter you have learned

- How to use trailer data to control the number of times a read-loop is executed
- How to use accumulators and counters
- How to use a calculated value to control the exit from a loop
- How to insert PRINT statements in your program to help debugging
- How to program a subroutine
- The rules for the following BASIC statements:

   1. GOSUB
   2. RETURN
   3. STOP
   4. ON-GO TO

- The following flowchart symbols:

   1. The subroutine symbol—a rectangle with two vertical lines

   2. The ON-GO TO symbol—a diamond with multiple branches

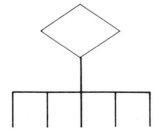

- The answer to question in this chapter: the IF statement in line 40 would be changed to

   40 IF N$ = "THAT'S ALL FOLKS" THEN 100

counter-controlled loops

OBJECTIVES

In this chapter you will learn

- How a counter can be used to control the number of times a loop is executed
- How FOR and NEXT statements are used to create a counter-controlled loop
- How to use hanging commas in print lists
- How to use the BASIC functions

  1. INT

  2. RND

- The rules for the BASIC statement RANDOMIZE

  In addition you should learn the meaning of the following terms:

  Argument   Counter-controlled loops
  Function   Independent loops
  Nested loops

In the problems we discussed in Chapter 4 we exited from the loop when a variable was assigned a particular value, through the execution of either a READ statement or a LET statement. In many instances, however, we want to execute a loop a certain number of times. Such loops are called **counter-controlled loops.**

A SIMPLE COUNTER-CONTROLLED LOOP

The program shown in Fig. 5.1 contains a counter-controlled loop. Before you read further, determine what output will be produced by this program. You should be able to trace the program and figure out that it will print the numbers 1–10.

Let's see whether we can understand why the loop in Fig. 5.1 is called a counter-controlled loop. The variable C is the counter. In line 10 C is assigned an initial value of one. We call this the initialization step. In line 20 C is printed. In line 30 C is increased by 1. We call this the incrementation step. In line 40 C is tested. If C is greater than 10,

```
1 REM A COUNTER-CONTROLLED LOOP
2 REM PROGRAMMED BY M. TROMBETTA
10 LET C = 1
20 PRINT C
30   LET C = C + 1
40   IF C > 10 THEN 60
50 GO TO 20
60 END
```

Fig. 5.1. A program with a counter-controlled loop.

we exit from the loop by branching to line 60. If C is not greater than 10, we fall through to line 50, which sends us back to the top of the loop.

Every counter-controlled loop must contain these steps: (1) the counter must be initialized; (2) the counter must be incremented; and (3) the counter must be tested. These three steps don't have to be in the order shown in Fig. 5.1. You might find it interesting to determine the output that would be produced if the program in Fig. 5.1 were modified by putting the incrementation step after the testing step or the PRINT statement after the incrementation step.

The FOR and NEXT Statements

Counter-controlled loops are so important that BASIC provides the FOR and NEXT statements to make writing them easy. The program in Fig. 5.2 uses the FOR and NEXT statements to create a counter-controlled loop. It produces exactly the same output as the program in Fig. 5.1. The FOR and NEXT statements are always used together. They define a counter-controlled loop with the FOR statement indicating the start of the loop and the NEXT statement indicating the end of the loop. The FOR statement in line 10 essentially says to the computer, "Execute all the statements between here and the NEXT statement, first with C equal to 1, then with C equal to 2, and so on with C finally equal to 10."

We can gain a deeper understanding of how the FOR and NEXT statements work by tracing the program in Fig. 5.2. The first time the computer executes the FOR statement in line 10, it sets C equal to 1. It then executes the PRINT statement in line 20 and prints 1. When it executes the NEXT statement in line 30, the computer first sets C equal to the next value, which is 2, and then checks to see whether C is greater than 10, which is the upper limit specified in the FOR statement. If C is less than 10, as it is in this case, the computer branches back to the line following the FOR statement, which in this example is line 20, and the loop is executed again, this time with C equal to 2.

```
 1 REM COUNTER-CONTROLLED LOOP
 2 REM WITH FOR AND NEXT STATEMENTS
 3 REM WRITTEN BY M. TROMBETTA
10 FOR C = 1 TO 10
20    PRINT C
30 NEXT C
40 END


RUN

FIG5#2        15:19    09/14/79

 1
 2
 3
 4
 5
 6
 7
 8
 9
10

TIME 0.0 SECS.
```

Fig. 5.2. Using the FOR and NEXT statements
to create a counter-controlled loop.

This procedure is repeated until the loop is executed with C equal to 10. When C is 10 and the computer executes the NEXT statement in line 30, it sets C equal to the next value, which is 11. Now C has become greater than 10, the upper limit in the FOR statement. Instead of branching back to the top of the loop, the computer exits from the loop by falling through to the statement following the NEXT statement.

It is important to realize that the FOR and NEXT statements do all the work for you. They initialize the counter; they increment the counter; and they test the counter. I showed you the program in Fig. 5.1 so that you would understand what is involved in a counter-controlled loop. But when you use the FOR and NEXT statements, you do not have to write the initialization, incrementation, or testing steps.

Notice in Fig. 5.2 that I indented the PRINT statement. BASIC doesn't require this indentation, but to make it easier to see the beginning and end of the loop, the statements between the FOR and NEXT statements will be indented two spaces. You should follow the same convention.

To simplify the program in Fig. 5.2 I did nothing inside the loop except print the value of the counter. Understand, however, that the FOR and NEXT statements can be as far apart as you like, and you can do anything you want inside the loop.

I will illustrate the use of the FOR and NEXT statements by using them to solve a problem.

Printing an Interest Table

Suppose we make a deposit into a bank account. Each year the balance in the account earns interest, and that interest is added to the balance, so that the balance gradually increases. Write a program that will calculate and print the interest earned and the balance in the account for each of the next five years.

The clue that we should use a counter-controlled loop in this problem is that we want to repeat the calculation for each of the next five years. That tells us to set up a loop that is executed five times.

The variables we will use are

Input variables

Interest rate	R
Deposit	D

Output variables

Balance	B
Interest earned	I
Year counter	Y

The algorithm is

1. Input D and R.

2. Set B equal to D.

3. Repeat step 4 five times.

4. Calculate and print interest earned and new balance.

You may not immediately see the reason for step 2. B stands for the balance in the account, and step 2 simply says that, when we start, the balance in the account is equal to the deposit.

I will calculate answers by hand only for the first two years. If the computer-calculated answers for the first two years agree with our hand-calculated answers, we may assume that the program is correct. Let's assume we deposit 1000 dollars at a 7% interest rate. The results for the first two years are shown as follows:

Year	Interest earned	Balance at end of year
1	$70.00	$1070.00
2	74.90	1144.90

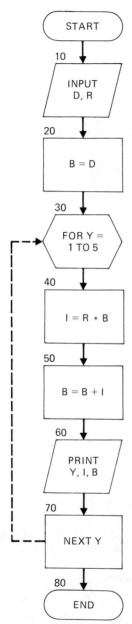

Fig. 5.3. Flowchart to print an interest table.

It is important to understand how I calculated these numbers because the program will follow essentially the same steps. For the first year the balance is equal to the original deposit of 1000 dollars. The interest earned during the first year is 7% of 1000 dollars, which is 70 dollars. At the end of the first year this 70 dollars is added to the balance of 1000 dollars so that the balance at the end of the first year is 1070 dollars. During the second year 7% interest is earned on the balance of 1070 dollars. This interest is 74 dollars and 90 cents. At the end of the second year this interest is added to the balance of 1070 dollars so that the balance at the end of the second year is 1144 dollars and 90 cents. The program will follow this procedure for the full five years.

The flowchart for this problem is shown in Fig. 5.3. Unfortunately, the flowchart symbols for the FOR and NEXT statements have not been standardized, and different authors use different symbols. I use a hexagon for the FOR statement and a rectangle for the NEXT statement. Furthermore, to show the loop clearly, I draw the flowline from the NEXT symbol back to the FOR symbol. I draw this flowline dotted, because, if it were solid you might get the mistaken idea that the flowline represented a GO TO statement.

This flowchart translates directly into the BASIC program shown in Fig. 5.4. I used a PRINT USING statement to make the output more attractive. We see that the computer-calculated answers agree with our hand-calculated answers, so we conclude that the program is correct.

Exercise

5.1 Modify the "Guess the Number" program in Fig. 3.24 to use a FOR-NEXT loop to count the number of guesses that have been made. If the player guesses the number, print a message like YOU WIN IN 5 GUESSES. If the player doesn't guess the number in 10 tries, print a message like YOU LOSE; THE NUMBER WAS 37.

The FOR and NEXT Statements in Detail

The format of the FOR statement is

FOR variable = starting value TO final value

The "variable" named in the FOR statement is called the counter variable because it is used as a counter to control the number of times the FOR-NEXT loop is executed. In the program in Fig. 5.2 the counter variable is C; the starting value is 1; and the final value is 10. The starting and final values are not, however, restricted to numbers; they can be variables and even expressions.

```
1 REM PRINT AN INTEREST TABLE
2 REM PROGRAMMER M. TROMBETTA
9 PRINT "ENTER DEPOSIT AND INTEREST RATE"
10 INPUT D,R
20 LET B = D
21 PRINT USING 22
22:    YEAR        INTEREST        BALANCE
25 REM LOOP FOR 5 YEARS
30 FOR Y = 1 TO 5
40    LET I = R * B
50    LET B = B + I
60    PRINT USING 61,Y,I,B
61:    ##        #####.##      ######.##
70 NEXT Y
80 END


RUN

FIG5#4      15:21   09/14/79

ENTER DEPOSIT AND INTEREST RATE
?1000,.07
      YEAR        INTEREST        BALANCE
        1          70.00         1070.00
        2          74.90         1144.90
        3          80.14         1225.04
        4          85.75         1310.80
        5          91.76         1402.55

TIME 0.0 SECS.
```

Fig. 5.4. A program that prints a five-year interest table.

The program in Fig. 5.5 is a generalized version of the program in Fig. 5.2. By using S for the starting value and F for the final value, we can have this program print the numbers between any two numbers we like.

Notice that the NEXT statement in Fig. 5.5 is the same as it was in Fig. 5.2: NEXT C. The format of the NEXT statement is simply

NEXT variable

Where the "variable" must be the same as the "variable" in the FOR statement. That is very important. As we shall see later, there may be more than one FOR-NEXT loop in a program. The computer pairs a NEXT statement with the FOR statement that has the same "variable."

The STEP Clause

In the examples you have seen so far, when we executed the NEXT statement, we have calculated the next value of the counter variable by

```
1 REM USING VARIABLES FOR STARTING AND FINAL
2 REM VALUES IN FOR STATEMENT
3 REM PROGRAMMER M. TROMBETTA
9 PRINT "ENTER STARTING AND FINAL VALUE"
10 INPUT S,F
20 FOR C = S TO F
30    PRINT C
40 NEXT C
50 END


RUN

FIG5#5        15:22    09/14/79

ENTER STARTING AND FINAL VALUE
?6,13
   6
   7
   8
   9
  10
  11
  12
  13

TIME 0.0 SECS.
```

Fig. 5.5. A FOR-NEXT loop with variable starting and final values.

adding one to the old value. We may not, however, always want to go up in steps of one. The STEP clause of the FOR statement permits us to use any step size we like. The full format of the FOR statement is

FOR variable = starting value TO final value STEP step size

Like the starting value and the final value the step size may be a number, a variable, or an expression. We did not have to use the STEP clause in our earlier problems because we were using a step size of one. If you omit the STEP clause, the computer will automatically use a step size of one.

Suppose we wanted to print only the odd numbers from 1 through 10. Fig. 5.6 shows the program in Fig. 5.2 modified to print only odd numbers. The only change that was made to the program in Fig. 5.2 was the addition of the STEP clause to the FOR statement. This FOR statement can be interpreted as instructing the computer to give C the values 1–10, going up in steps of 2.

Let's trace the program. The first time line 10 is executed C is set to 1. Line 20 prints the 1. In the NEXT statement in line 30 the next value of C is calculated by adding the step size to the current value of C. In this case the step size is 2, so the next value of C is calculated to be 3. Since the new value of C is not greater than the final value of 10

```
1 REM USE OF STEP CLAUSE
2 REM PROGRAMMER M. TROMBETTA
10 FOR C = 1 TO 10 STEP 2
20    PRINT C
30 NEXT C
40 END


RUN

FIG5#6        15:22    09/14/79

  1
  3
  5
  7
  9

TIME 0.0 SECS.
```

Fig. 5.6. Using the STEP clause to print only odd numbers.

specified in the FOR statement, the computer branches back to the top of the loop and repeats the loop with C equal to 3.

This process is repeated with C equal to 3, 5, 7, and 9. When C is 9 and the NEXT statement is executed, the next value of C is calculated to be 11. Since 11 is greater than the final value of 10, the computer does not branch back to the top of the loop but falls through to the statement following the NEXT statement.

At this point what is the value of C? In some versions of BASIC C is 11. Other versions of BASIC set C back to the previous value, in this case 9. You may want to experiment to determine what your BASIC does.

What happens if the final value is less than the starting value? Suppose, for example, the FOR statement were written as follows.

FOR C = 10 TO 1

In some BASICs the loop would not be executed at all. In other BASICs the loop is executed once. You might like to experiment to determine what your BASIC does.

Noninteger and Negative Step Size

The step size does not have to be an integer, and it does not even have to be positive. For example, the FOR statement

FOR N = 0 TO 1 STEP 0.25

causes N to have the values 0, 0.25, 0.50, 0.75, and 1. Nothing new is involved here; we still get the next N by adding the step size to the old N.

To show the use of a negative step size consider the FOR statement

FOR C = 10 TO 1 STEP −1

If this statement replaced the FOR statement in Fig. 5.2, the program would print the numbers 10, 9, 8, 7, 6, 5, 4, 3, 2, and 1. We still add the step size to the old C to get the next C, but when we add −1 to 10, we get 9, and when we add −1 to 9, we get 8, and so on until we add −1 to 2 and get 1.

When a negative step size is used, we exit from the loop when the calculated value of the counter becomes *less* than the final value specified in the FOR statement. So in the above example, the loop is executed when C is equal to 1. But then in the NEXT statement C is calculated to be 0. Since 0 is less than the final value of 1, we exit from the loop by falling through to the statement following the NEXT statement. So, for a negative step size to work properly, the final value must be less than the starting value.

A Payroll Problem with Totals

All of the problems we solved in Chapter 4 using a trailer DATA statement could also be solved using a FOR-NEXT loop. When using a FOR-NEXT loop you must know in advance how many cases are to be processed. This number is used as the upper limit in the FOR statement to cause the FOR-NEXT loop to be executed just the right number of times.

These ideas can be made much clearer if we actually solve a problem. Let's resolve the problem on page 108, in which we are given a rate of pay and hours worked for each employee, and we calculate and print each employee's gross pay and the total gross pay. We will use the following variable names:

Input variables

Rate of pay	R
Hours worked	H
Number of employees	N

Internal variable

Employee counter	E

External variables

Gross pay	G
Total gross pay	G1

I have used the same variable names we used in the earlier problem and have introduced two new variables: N for the number of employees and E for the employee counter. N will be used as the final value in the FOR statement, and E will be used as the counter variable.

The algorithm we will use is

1. Initialize G1.

2. Read N.

3. Repeat steps 4–6 N times.

4.   Read R and H.

5.   Calculate and accumulate G.

6.   Print R, H, and G.

7. Print G1.

The flowchart for this problem is shown in Fig. 5.7, and the program is in Figure 5.8. The first thing you might wonder about in this program is why line 30 wasn't written simply as

30 FOR E = 1 TO 3

Writing the FOR statement this way would simplify the program, but then the program could only be used with 3 employees. By writing the program as we did, the program can be used with any number of employees by just changing the DATA statements. The rest of the program would not have to be changed at all.

Notice that the READ N step is outside the FOR-NEXT loop. The READ N step is outside the FOR-NEXT loop because we want to execute it once. Furthermore we must assign a value to N before we execute line 30; otherwise we would be using an uninitialized variable.

It is important to understand the difference between N and E. N is the number of employees we want to process. It is set once during each run of the program. E is the number of employees we have processed. E starts out as one and increases by one each time an employee is processed. When E becomes equal to N, the number of employees we have processed is equal to the number of employees we want to process, and the loop is finished.

Since the problems we solved in Chapter 4 can be solved using either a trailer DATA statement or a counter-controlled loop, you might wonder which method is preferable. Unfortunately there is no one best way. In some problems the number of cases to be processed is known, or easily determined, and using a counter-controlled loop is the most convenient way to solve the problem. In other problems determining the

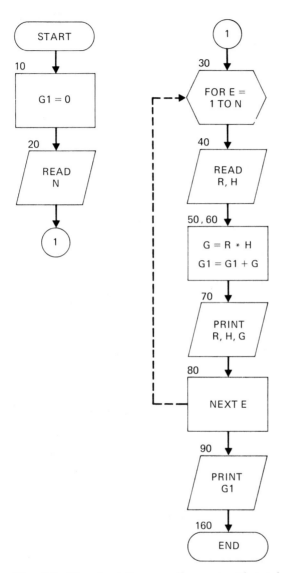

Fig. 5.7. Flowchart for payroll report with total pay.

```
1 REM PAYROLL WITH TOTAL PAY
2 REM USE OF FOR-NEXT LOOP
3 REM PROGRAMMER M. TROMBETTA
10 LET G1 = 0
20 READ N
30 FOR E = 1 TO N
40    READ R,H
50    LET G = R * H
60    LET G1 = G1 + G
70    PRINT R,H,G
80 NEXT E
85 REM PRINT TOTAL GROSS PAY
90 PRINT ,"TOTAL GROSS PAY",G1
100 REM THE NUMBER OF EMPLOYEES FOLLOWS
110 DATA 3
120 REM RATE AND HOURS FOR EACH EMPLOYEE FOLLOW
130 DATA 4,30
140 DATA 7,25
150 DATA 5,40
160 END


RUN

FIG5#8      15:29    02/25/80

4              30            120
7              25            175
5              40            200
            TOTAL GROSS PAY   495

TIME 0.0 SECS.
```

Fig. 5.8. Payroll report with total gross pay–solution using FOR-NEXT loop.

number of cases is troublesome, and using trailer data is most convenient. Each problem must be analyzed individually.

Finding the Highest Sales*

To illustrate an important point we will use a FOR-NEXT loop to solve the problem on page 120 and find the highest sales.

The variable names we will use are

Input variables

Salesperson's name	N$
Sales	S
Number of salespeople	N

---
* This section may be omitted without loss of continuity.

Internal variable

Salespeople   C
counter

Output variable

Highest sales   H

As before, I have used the same variable names we used in Chapter 4, and have introduced two new variables, N and C. The flowchart for this problem is shown in Fig. 5.9, and the program in Fig. 5.10.

You should not have any trouble understanding either the flowchart or the program, but you should be aware of one important point. If the condition in line 50 is false, we want to ignore the current S, and read N$ and S for the next salesperson. But notice that line 60 is not GO TO 40, which would take us to the READ statement. Nor is it GO TO 30, which would take us to the FOR statement. Rather it is GO TO 80, which takes us to the NEXT statement.

We must branch to the NEXT statement because, when we use a FOR-NEXT loop, the FOR and NEXT statements are controlling the loop for us. The NEXT statement increments and tests the counter and then branches back to the top of the loop if the counter is less than or equal to the final value. If we branched to the FOR statement or to the READ statement, the value of the counter, C, would be incorrect. When you use a FOR-NEXT loop, you must execute the NEXT statement each time you go through the loop.

You must follow two other rules to make sure that a FOR-NEXT loop works properly.

1. You must never branch into a FOR-NEXT loop; the loop should always be started by executing the FOR statement.

2. Once inside the loop, you must not change the value of the counter variable, the starting variable, the final variable, or the step variable.

You do not have to make a special effort to follow these two rules since, when you logically develop a program, it is not likely that you would violate them.

A Depreciation Problem*

We will use a FOR-NEXT loop to solve a new problem, one we did not solve in Chapter 4. Machinery used in businesses wears out, and the monetary value of this wearing out is called depreciation. Calculating

---

* This section may be omitted without loss of continuity.

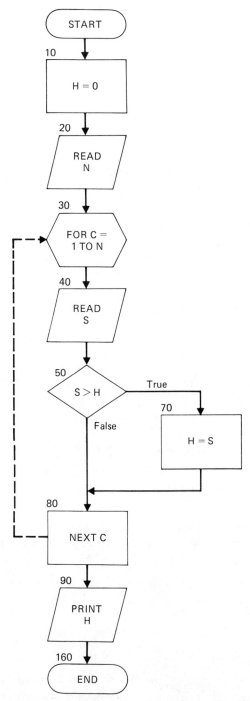

Fig. 5.9. Flowchart to find highest sales.

```
1 REM FINDING HIGHEST SALES USING FOR-NEXT LOOP
2 REM PROGRAMMER. M. TROMBETTA
10 LET H = 0
20 READ N
30 FOR C = 1 TO N
40    READ N$,S
50    IF S > H THEN 70
60    GO TO 80
70    LET H = S
80 NEXT C
90 PRINT "HIGHEST SALES",H
100 REM THE NUMBER OF SALESPEOPLE FOLLOWS
110 DATA 3
120 REM NAME AND SALES FOR EACH SALESPERSON FOLLOWS
130 DATA "HART,M.",300
140 DATA "LEE, G.R.",700
150 DATA "RAND, S.",200
160 END


RUN

FIG5#10       15:27    02/25/80

HIGHEST SALES       700

TIME 0.0 SECS.
```

Fig. 5.10. Program to find the highest sales solution using a
FOR-NEXT loop.

depreciation is important because the Internal Revenue Service (IRS)
allows businesses to deduct depreciation on their income tax returns.

To calculate the depreciation of a machine we have to know its
useful life. The useful life of different machines may be obtained from
tables published by the IRS. Let's use the following variable names:

Input variables

Useful life   L

Cost   C

Internal variable

Year counter   Y

Output variables

Depreciation   D

Book value   B

Depreciation can be calculated in a number of ways. The simplest
way is the straight-line method. In the straight-line method the depreciation each year is calculated by the equation $D = C / L$.

The value of the machine at the end of its useful life, called the salvage value, should be included in the calculation, but to simplify our problem we will assume that the salvage value is 0.

When we calculate the depreciation of a machine, we also calculate the machine's book value. The book value is simply the value of the machine on the business's books. At the end of each year the book value is calculated as the book value at the end of the previous year minus the depreciation during the year. At the start the book value is equal to the cost.

Now that we understand some of the basic concepts of depreciation we can solve the following problem. Write a program that will accept as input the cost and useful life of a machine and will print a depreciation report. For each year during the useful life the report should contain the year number, the depreciation during that year, and the book value at the end of that year. Depreciation should be calculated using the straight-line method.

The algorithm for this problem is

1. Input C and L.

2. Set B equal to C.

3. Repeat Steps 4 and 5 L times.

4.   Calculate D and B.

5.   Print Y, D, and B.

In this algorithm the only step that might not be clear is step 2. In step 2 we are just saying that, when we first buy the machinery, the book value is equal to the cost. That makes sense, since the machinery is brand new and has not yet begun to depreciate.

As we did in the interest table problem, we will calculate answers by hand only for the first two years. If the computer-calculated answers for the first two years agree with our hand-calculated answers, we may assume the program is correct. Let's assume that C is 10,000 dollars, and L is 5 years. The depreciation, which is calculated by dividing C by L, is 2000 dollars. The answers for the first two years are given as follows:

Year	Depreciation	Book value
1	2000	8000
2	2000	6000

The book value at the end of the first year is calculated by subtracting the depreciation of 2000 dollars from the original cost of 10,000 dollars, to give 8000 dollars. The book value at the end of the second year is calculated by subtracting the depreciation of 2000 dollars from the book value at the end of the first year, to give 6000 dollars. The program will follow this procedure for each year during the useful life.

The flowchart for this program is shown in Fig. 5.11, and the program based on this flowchart in Fig. 5.12. The only part of the program that might not be immediately clear is line 50. If you remember how a LET statement works, you should have no difficulty understanding line 50. The computer will subtract the number in the D box from the number in the B box and put the answer in the B box. This is equivalent to saying that the book value at the end of a year is equal to the book value at the end of the previous year minus the depreciation during that year.

If you look at the output, you will notice that the depreciation is 2000 dollars every year. Recall that our hand calculation also showed that the depreciation was 2000 dollars every year. We should have expected that the depreciation would be constant, since it is calculated by dividing the cost by the useful life (see line 40), and both cost and useful life are constant. I have written the program so that the depreciation is calculated every time we go through the FOR-NEXT loop. In the example in Fig. 5.12 the computer calculated depreciation five times, even though depreciation never changed. It wastes computer time to have the computer do unnecessary calculations, and the program could be improved by moving the calculation of depreciation outside of the FOR-NEXT loop, to line 29 for example. You should get into the habit of examining your programs to see whether they can be improved.

Exercises

5.2. Consider the following program.

```
10 FOR C = 13 TO 27 STEP 4
20    PRINT C
30 NEXT C
40 END
```

a) What output is produced?
b) What output is produced if line 10 is changed to

```
10 FOR C = 5 TO 6 STEP .1
```

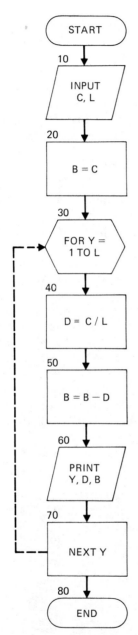

Fig. 5.11. Flowchart to print depreciation report, straight-line method.

```
1 REM DEPRECIATION REPORT USING STRAIGHT-LINE METHOD
2 REM PROGRAMMER. M. TROMBETTA
9 PRINT "ENTER COST AND USEFUL LIFE"
10 INPUT C,L
19 REM AT START BOOK VALUE EQUALS COST
20 LET B = C
25 PRINT USING 26
26:   YEAR    DEPRECIATION    BOOK VALUE
30 FOR Y = 1 TO L
40    LET D = C / L
50    LET B = B - D
60    PRINT USING 61,Y,D,B
61:   ##         #####.##        #####.##
70 NEXT Y
80 END


RUN

FIG5#12     15:24    09/14/79

ENTER COST AND USEFUL LIFE
?10000,5
   YEAR    DEPRECIATION    BOOK VALUE
    1        2000.00         8000.00
    2        2000.00         6000.00
    3        2000.00         4000.00
    4        2000.00         2000.00
    5        2000.00            0.00

TIME 0.0 SECS.
```

Fig. 5.12. A program that prints a depreciation report, straight-line method.

c) What output is produced if line 10 is changed to

10 FOR C = 20 TO 10 STEP -2

5.3. In some versions of BASIC, when the FOR-NEXT loop in Exercise 5.2(a) is complete and line 40 is executed, the value of C is 25, while in other versions of BASIC the value of C is 29. Write a program to determine the value of C in your version of BASIC. The program should print either C = 25 or C = 29.

5.4. Consider the following program.

10 READ J, K, L

20 FOR I = J TO K STEP L

30   PRINT I

40

```
50 DATA    2, 9, 4
60 END
```

a) What statement belongs in line 40?
b) What output is produced by this program?
c) What output is produced if line 20 is changed to

```
20 FOR I = L TO K STEP J
```

5.5. How would the output of the program shown in Fig. 5.8 be changed if we added the following trailer DATA statement

```
155 DATA 0,0
```

5.6. Resolve Exercise 2.7 using a FOR-NEXT loop to calculate and print total gross pay, total withholding, and total net pay. Use the PRINT USING statement or the TAB function to produce an attractive report.

5.7. Resolve the average test score problem on page 115 using a FOR-NEXT loop instead of a trailer DATA statement.

5.8. Write a program to print a depreciation report.

a) Calculate depreciation using the declining-balance method. In the declining-balance method the depreciation is calculated using the equation $D = 2 * B / L$, where the variables have the meanings we used in the depreciation problem we solved in this section. (Note that, when depreciation is calculated using the declining-balance method, the final book value is not zero.)

b) Calculate depreciation using the sum-of-the-years-digits method. To use this method you must first calculate the sum of the numbers from 1 to L (i.e., $S = 1 + 2 + 3 + \ldots + L$). Then the depreciation in the first year is $L * C / S$; in the second year it is $(L - 1) * C / S$, and so on. In general, in year Y the depreciation is $(L + 1 - Y) * C / S$.

5.9. If a bank makes a mortgage of M dollars for N years at R interest rate, the annual payment is $P = M * R / (1 - (1 + R)^{\wedge}(-N))$ (We assume that the payments are made annually instead of monthly to make the problem a little easier.) Part of the payment P is used to pay the interest on the loan that is still owed to the bank, and the rest is used to reduce the loan, so that after N years the person, not the bank, owns the house. If at the start of any year the amount of the loan still owed the bank is called L, then the interest that year is $R * L$. The difference, $P - R * L$, is used to reduce the loan. At the start of the first year, naturally, $L = M$.

Write a program that will accept as input R, M, and N, will calculate and print P, and then for each year will print the number of the year, interest for that year, the amount used to reduce the loan, and the loan outstanding at the end of the year. (At the end of N years, the loan outstanding should be zero, or very close to zero.) The program should also keep track of the sum of all the interest payments and should print the total interest paid.

As an example, if M = 10,000 dollars, R = 0.08, and N = 20 years, P should be 1018.52, and the first few lines of output should be as follows (because of round-off errors you may not get exactly the same answers).

Year	Interest	Amount used to reduce loan	Loan outstanding at end of year
1	$800.00	$218.52	$9781.48
2	782.52	236.00	9545.48

NESTED FOR-NEXT LOOPS

A program may have more than one FOR-NEXT loop. The simplest example is shown in Fig. 5.13(a). Here the A loop and the B loop are completely independent. When the program is executed, the A loop is executed, and then the B loop is executed. FOR-NEXT loops used this way are called **independent loops.**

Figure 5.13(b) shows two FOR-NEXT loops, with the B loop inside the A loop. FOR-NEXT loops used this way are called **nested loops.** I

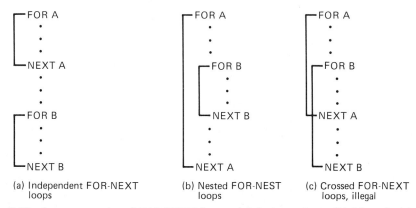

(a) Independent FOR-NEXT loops

(b) Nested FOR-NEST loops

(c) Crossed FOR-NEXT loops, illegal

Fig. 5.13. Arrangements of FOR-NEXT loops. (a) Independent. (b) Nested. (c) Crossed and illegal.

have shown two FOR-NEXT loops, but you may nest as many as you like as long as the inner loops are completely inside the outer loops. Before I show you an example of a program with nested FOR-NEXT loops, I would like to call your attention to the FOR-NEXT loops shown in Fig. 5.13(c). These loops are said to be crossed and are illegal. If you want to use more than one FOR-NEXT loop in a program, they must be independent, as shown in Fig. 5.13(a), or nested with the inner loops completely inside the outer loops, as shown in Fig. 5.13(b).

When FOR-NEXT loops are nested, the inner loop is completely executed each time we pass through the outer loop. Let's trace the program in Fig. 5.14 to make these ideas clearer. When the computer executes line 10, it puts 1 in the A box, as in Fig. 5.15(a). When it executes line 20, it puts 1 in the B box, as in Fig. 5.15(b). When it executes line 30, it puts 1 in the C box, as in Figure 5.15(c), and line 40 prints that 1. When the computer executes the NEXT B statement in line 50, it puts 2 in the B box, as in Fig. 5.15(d), and branches back to line 30. Notice that the number in the A box has not changed. When the computer executes line 30, it puts 2 in the C box, as in Fig. 5.15(e), and line 40 prints that 2. Now when the computer executes the NEXT B statement in line 50, it finds that B has become 3, which is larger than the final value of 2 specified in line 20. So instead of branching back to line 30, the computer exits from the B loop by falling through line 50, and it executes line 60.

```
1 REM NESTED FOR-NEXT LOOPS
2 REM PROGRAMMER M. TROMBETTA
10 FOR A = 1 TO 3
20    FOR B = 1 TO 2
30       LET C = A * B
40          PRINT C
50    NEXT B
60 NEXT A
70 END


RUN

FIG5#14      15:26    09/14/79

   1
   2
   2
   4
   3
   6

TIME 0.0 SECS.
```

Fig. 5.14. Illustration of nested FOR-NEXT loops.

A	B	C
1	–	–

(a) After executing line 10

A	B	C
1	1	–

(b) After executing line 20

A	B	C
1	1	1

(c) After executing line 30

A	B	C
1	~~1~~	1
	2	

(d) After executing line 50

A	B	C
1	~~1~~	~~1~~
	2	2

(e) After executing line 30

A	B	C
~~1~~	~~1~~	~~1~~
2	2	2

(f) After executing line 60

A	B	C
~~1~~	~~1~~	~~1~~
2	~~2~~	2
	1	

(g) After executing line 20

Fig. 5.15. Tracing the program in Fig. 5.14.

When the computer executes the NEXT A statement in line 60, the computer puts 2 in the A box, as in Fig. 5.15(f), and branches back to line 20. When it executes line 20, it puts 1 in the B box, as in Fig. 5.15(g), and starts the B loop again. We will stop here, but you should continue tracing the program to make sure you understand how the rest of the output was generated.

Printing a Balance Table

I will illustrate nested FOR-NEXT loops by writing a program that will print the balance in an account after 5, 10, 15, and 20 years, when the interest rate is 8%, 10%, and 12%.

We will use the following variable names:

Input variables

Deposit   D

Internal variable

Interest rate   R

Year counter   Y

Output variable

Balance   B

In the interest table problem on page 145 we calculated the balance in the account by adding the interest earned to the previous balance. Since in this problem we are not interested in the interest earned, we can calculate the balance in the account using the compound interest formula

$$B = D * (1 + R) \char`\^ Y$$

The algorithm for this problem is

1. Input D.

2. Repeat step 3 for Y equals 5, 10, 15, and 20.

3. Repeat step 4 for R equals 8%, 10%, and 12%.

4. Calculate and print balance.

The flowchart based on this algorithm is shown in Fig. 5.16, and the program based on that flowchart in Fig. 5.17. Just a few of the statements in this program require discussion. In line 50 R is expressed as a decimal, not a percentage. In line 40 we print the value of Y so that each row in the table will be labeled with its year number. Line

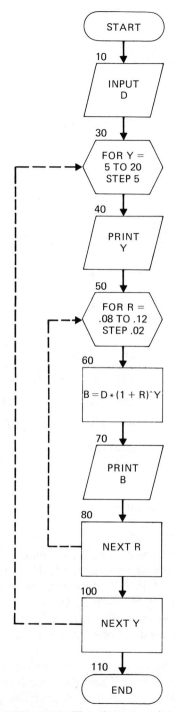

Fig. 5.16. Flowchart to print balance table.

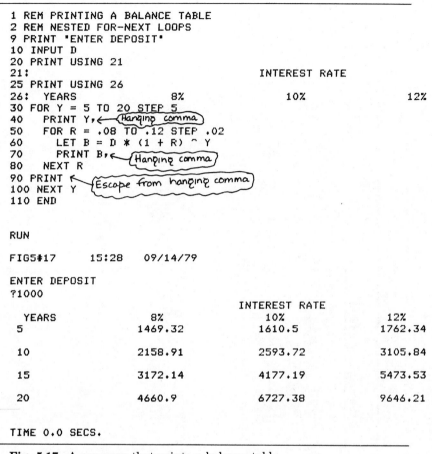

```
1 REM PRINTING A BALANCE TABLE
2 REM NESTED FOR-NEXT LOOPS
9 PRINT "ENTER DEPOSIT"
10 INPUT D
20 PRINT USING 21
21:                          INTEREST RATE
25 PRINT USING 26
26:   YEARS           8%           10%              12%
30 FOR Y = 5 TO 20 STEP 5
40    PRINT Y,        ← Hanging comma
50    FOR R = .08 TO .12 STEP .02
60       LET B = D * (1 + R) ^ Y
70       PRINT B,     ← Hanging comma
80    NEXT R
90 PRINT  ←  Escape from hanging comma
100 NEXT Y
110 END


RUN

FIG5#17     15:28    09/14/79

ENTER DEPOSIT
?1000
                             INTEREST RATE
   YEARS          8%           10%              12%
   5            1469.32       1610.5           1762.34

   10           2158.91       2593.72          3105.84

   15           3172.14       4177.19          5473.53

   20           4660.9        6727.38          9646.21


TIME 0.0 SECS.
```

Fig. 5.17. A program that prints a balance table.

40 and line 70, in which we print B, both use hanging commas. You may recall the discussion of hanging commas in Chapter 2. If a print list ends with a hanging comma, the next PRINT statement executed does not start a new line, but instead starts printing in the next print zone. By using hanging commas in lines 40 and 70 we cause Y and the three Bs that belong to that Y to be printed on one line, and in that way we generate a nice table.

After Y and three Bs have been printed on one line, we want to escape from the hanging comma so that the next Y and its three Bs will be printed on a new line. The PRINT statement in line 90 provides the escape from the hanging comma. Since no print list is associated with the PRINT statement in line 90, nothing is printed when it is executed.

Since line 90 does not contain a hanging comma, however the next PRINT statement executed, which will be line 40, will start a new line. That is exactly what we want.

Exercises

5.10. What output is produced by the program

```
10 FOR A = 1 TO 2
20    FOR B = 3 TO 1 STEP -1
30       LET C = A * B
40       PRINT C
50    NEXT B
60    NEXT A
```

5.11. A delivery service charges its customers based on the weight of the package and the distance it must be shipped. It has divided the area it serves into zones. Let's use the following variables:

Input variables

Weight of package	W
Zone to which package is delivered	Z

Output variable

Charge for delivery	C

The company calculates the charge using the equation

$$C = .75 + .03 * W * Z$$

Write a program that will print a table of charges for W equals 2, 4, 6, 8, and 10, and Z equals 1, 2, and 3. The W loop should be the outer loop, and the Z loop should be the inner loop.

FUNCTIONS

To simplify programming, BASIC provides an easy way to perform a number of common programming tasks. That easy way is through the use of **functions.** Most BASIC functions perform trigonometric or algebraic calculations that are not of interest to us, but two of them, the INT and the RND functions, are generally useful and are discussed here.[1]

The INT Function

The INT function is used as follows:

    LET Y = INT (X)

X is called the **argument** of the INT function, and as you can see, it is enclosed in parentheses. The argument of the INT function must be a constant, a variable, or an expression. The INT function assigns to Y the greatest integer less than or equal to X. That sounds complicated, but if X is positive, as it will be in all of our problems, the INT function assigns to Y the integer part of X. We say the INT function returns the integer part of its argument. So if X = 4.5, Y = 4, and if X = 6.99999, Y = 6. (If X = −3.7, Y = −4, which is the greatest integer less than or equal to −3.7.)

We can think of a function as a subroutine, but it is one supplied by BASIC and not one written by us. When the name of a function appears in an expression, the computer branches to the function subroutine, performs the required calculations, and returns to our program.

When would you want to calculate the integer part of a variable? It turns out that there are many such occasions, especially when in a problem only an integer makes sense as an answer. For example, suppose a farmer can only sell eggs by the dozen. Let the number of eggs the chickens lay be E, and the number of dozens sold be D. Given E, how can we calculate D?

You might suppose that D could be calculated using the LET statement

    LET D = E / 12

But a moment's thought will show you that is not correct. Suppose E is 50. This statement would make D equal 4.166667. But we said the farmer can only sell eggs by the dozen. We want a LET statement that would make D equal to 4. The following LET statement works:

    LET D = INT (E / 12)

To understand how this statement works, remember that the computer does the arithmetic inside the parentheses first. Therefore the computer

---

1. Functions that manipulate strings are discussed in Chapter 8.

will first divide E by 12 and get 4.166667, just as we did. The number 4.166667 is the argument of the INT function. The INT function will strip off the fractional part of this number and assign 4 to D.

After the farmer makes as many dozens as possible, how many eggs are left over? Let R be the number of eggs left over. In D dozen there are 12 * D eggs. Since we started with E eggs, the number left over is calculated by the LET statement

LET R = E − 12 * D

With E = 50 and D = 4, this LET statement makes R = 2, which is the correct answer.

The Change Program

Another example of the use of the INT function is the following problem. A vending machine sells items that cost less than one dollar and accepts one dollar as payment. Write a program to calculate the number of half dollars, quarters, dimes, nickels, and pennies required to make change.

Let's use the following variables:

Input variables	
Purchase price	P
Internal variable	
Change	C
Output variables	
Number of half dollars	N1
Number of quarters	N2
Number of dimes	N3
Number of nickels	N4
Number of pennies	N5

The algorithm we will use is (1) calculate the change and (2) calculate the number of half dollars, quarters, dimes, nickels, and pennies, in that order.

The logic of this program is not so complicated that we need a flowchart, so we will go directly to the program in Fig. 5.18. In this problem round-off error can be troublesome, so to eliminate round-off error we write the program in cents, not dollars, and the purchase price is entered as 43, not .43. Similarly, in line 50 the change is calculated in cents, as 100 − P, not in dollars.

```
10 REM CHANGE PROGRAM
20 REM PROGRAMMER. M TROMBETTA
30 PRINT "ENTER PURCHASE PRICE IN CENTS"
40 INPUT P
50    LET C = 100 - P
60    LET N1 = INT (C / 50)
70    LET C = C - 50 * N1
80    LET N2 = INT (C / 25)
90    LET C = C - 25 * N2
100   LET N3 = INT (C / 10)
110   LET C = C - 10 * N3
120   LET N4 = INT (C / 5)
130   LET C = C - 5 * N4
140   LET N5 = C
150   PRINT USING 160,N1,N2,N3,N4,N5
160:  HALF DOLLARS #  QUARTERS #  DIMES #  NICKELS #  PENNIES #
170 GO TO 30
180 END


RUN

FIG5#18      10:50    02/26/80

ENTER PURCHASE PRICE IN CENTS
?43
   HALF DOLLARS 1   QUARTERS 0   DIMES 0   NICKELS 1   PENNIES 2
ENTER PURCHASE PRICE IN CENTS
?

STOP.
RAN 0.0 SEC.
```

Fig. 5.18. A program that calculates change.

Let's trace the program to understand how it works. With P equal to 43, when line 50 is executed, C will be 57. How many half dollars do we need to make 57 cents' change? The answer is calculated in line 60. When line 60 is executed, 57 is divided by 50, giving an answer of 1.14. The INT function strips off the fractional part of this number and assigns the value 1 to N1, indicating 1 half dollar. The amount of change that now remains to be returned is calculated in line 70. The logic of line 70 is identical to the logic we used to calculate the number of eggs remaining after the farmer made up the dozens. In line 70 50 * N1 is the amount of change accounted for by N1 half dollars, and therefore C − 50 * N1 is the amount of change that now remains to be returned.

We repeat the same calculation for quarters in lines 80 and 90, for dimes in lines 100 and 110, and for nickels in lines 120 and 130. Any change that remains to be returned after the nickels are accounted for must be made up of pennies, so we can calculate the number of pennies directly in line 140 without using the INT function.

The RND Function

The RND function[2] is used as follows:

    LET A = RND

Notice that the RND function does not have an argument. The RND function returns a random number between 0 and 0.999999. What is a random number? The random numbers returned by the RND function have two characteristics. The first characteristic is that their values are unpredictable. Everytime we use the RND function we get a different, unpredictable number. If the preceding LET statement were executed three times, A might be assigned the values 0.46921, 0.91752, and 0.36147. Another time A might be assigned three completely different values. The second characteristic of the random numbers returned by the RND function is that all the numbers between 0 and 0.999999 are equally likely to be returned.

Why would anyone want to calculate a random number? People do so because many events in the world are influenced at least partially by random factors. For example, the amount of rainfall in Kansas in July varies randomly. The number of telephone calls made in New York City on a weekday morning varies randomly. When computers are used to study such events, it is useful to have an RND function.

We will not study such involved problems, but let's look at an easy problem that uses the RND function. Remember the "Guess the Number" program in Fig. 3.24? In that program one player entered an integer between 1 and 100, and a second player had to guess the integer. Using the RND function we can have the computer randomly select an integer that a player must guess.

But here we run into a problem. We want the computer to select an integer between 1 and 100, but the RND function returns a number between 0 and 0.999999. Fortunately there is an easy way to get the integers in the range we want. First multiply the RND function by 100:

    LET N = 100 * RND

Since RND returns a value between 0 and 0.999999, N will be between 0 and 99.9999. Next use the INT function

    LET N = INT (100 * RND)

---

2. Unfortunately different versions of BASIC have implemented the RND function differently. Your instructor will tell you how the RND function is used in your BASIC, and you should write this information on the inside front cover of this book.

Now N has integer values between 0 and 99. To get N to have the range 1 to 100, we just add 1, so the statement we finally use for N is

LET N = 1 + INT (100 * RND)

With this statement N will have random integer values between 1 and 100.

We can generalize this result. If we want a variable, say M, to have random integer values in the range A–B, the statement to use is

LET M = A + INT ((B − A + 1) * RND)

Figure 5.19 shows the program from Fig. 3.24 modified to have the computer randomly select the integer between 1 and 100, which must be guessed. The first thing we notice is line 10:

10 RANDOMIZE

```
1 REM GUESS-THE-NUMBER GAME USING THE RND FUNCTION
2 REM PROGRAMMER. M. TROMBETTA
10 RANDOMIZE
20 LET N = 1 + INT (100 * RND)
90 PRINT "GUESS THE NUMBER THE COMPUTER PICKED"
100 PRINT "THE NUMBER IS BETWEEN 1 AND 100"
110 INPUT G
120    IF G = N THEN 180
130    IF G > N THEN 160
140    PRINT "YOU GUESSED TOO LOW"
150    GO TO 110
160    PRINT "YOU GUESSED TOO HIGH"
170 GO TO 110
180 PRINT "YOU HIT IT ON THE HEAD!"
190 END



RUN

FIG5#19      15:38    02/25/80

GUESS THE NUMBER THE COMPUTER PICKED
THE NUMBER IS BETWEEN 1 AND 100
?50
YOU GUESSED TOO LOW
?75
YOU GUESSED TOO LOW
?87
YOU GUESSED TOO HIGH
?82
YOU HIT IT ON THE HEAD!

TIME 0.0 SECS.
```

Fig. 5.19. A program that plays "Guess the number" using the RND function.

This statement requires some explanation. I said that the RND function returns a series of unpredictable random numbers. That is not exactly true. When a program is being debugged, it is convenient to have the RND function return the same series of "random" numbers. Having the same series of random numbers makes it easier to trace and debug the program. Once the program has been debugged, then we would like the RND function to return a series of unpredictable random numbers. The RANDOMIZE statement causes the RND function to return a series of unpredictable random numbers. Normally you would not use a RANDOMIZE statement while a program was being debugged. After the program was working perfectly, you would then insert a RANDOMIZE statement near the beginning of the program.

We now return to the program in Fig. 5.19. In line 20 the computer randomly selects the integer between 1 and 100, which is to be guessed, using the LET statement we derived earlier. The rest of the program is identical to the program in Fig. 3.19.

Exercises

5.12 Write a program which converts inches to feet and inches. For example, if the input data is 27 inches, the program should print 27 INCHES IS 2 FEET AND 3 INCHES.

5.13 A vineyard measures the amount of wine in its storage tanks in gallons, but it must ship the wine in barrels. There are 42 gallons in a barrel. Write a program that will accept as input the number of gallons and will calculate and print the numbers of barrels that can be shipped. Also calculate and print the number of gallons remaining after as many barrels as possible have been filled.

5.14 A sewing store sells material by the yard. Write a program that will accept as input the number of feet required and will calculate and print the number of yards that must be purchased. (*Hint*: This problem is not as simple as it might at first appear. If six feet of material are required, then two yards must be purchased, but if seven feet are required, then 3 yards must be purchased.)

5.15 Write a program to help your kid brother improve his addition. The program should randomly select two integers between 1 and 10. Assume the integers are 6 and 2. The program should print the message WHAT IS THE SUM OF 6 AND 2? The program should accept your kid brother's answer as input, check whether his answer is correct, and print an appropriate message, either THAT'S RIGHT or SORRY THE CORRECT ANSWER IS 8.

If you want to make the program more elaborate, you can use a FOR-NEXT loop to propose 10 problems and keep track of how many problems are answered correctly. After all ten problems have been answered, you can print the number that was answered correctly.

SUMMARY

In this chapter you have learned

- How to use a counter to control the number of times a loop is executed
- The rules for the FOR and NEXT statements, including noninteger and negative step sizes
- How to use nested FOR-NEXT loops
- How to use a hanging comma when printing a table
- The flowchart symbol for the FOR-NEXT loop: a hexagon and a rectangle connected by a dotted line

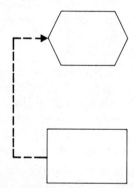

- How to use the functions
  INT
  RND
- How to use the RANDOMIZE statement

arrays

OBJECTIVES

In this Chapter you will learn

- What an array is
- The rules for the BASIC statement DIM
- How to process one- and two-dimensional arrays

In addition you should learn the meaning of the following terms:

Arrays, one and two dimensional	Flag
	Subscript
Master data	
Transaction data	

You know that the storage location set up by the compiler to hold the value of a variable can store only one value at a time. By being clever we have been able to solve some problems, such as calculating total gross pay, that at first glance seem to require having all the values of a variable stored in the computer.

Nevertheless, some problems really do require us to have all the values of a variable stored in the computer. For example, consider this problem: given a set of numbers, calculate their average. Then print each number and the difference between it and the average. Calculating the average of a set of numbers would present no difficulty, since we solved that problem in Chapter 4. But to print the differences requires that the original numbers be available. Using only the BASIC you know now you could not solve this problem, but it is easy to solve if we use an array.

WHAT IS AN ARRAY?

Before we can solve a problem using arrays, I must explain what they are and how they work. An **array** is a collection of storage locations that have the same variable name. If you want to use an array in your program, you must tell the compiler that you want a particular variable to be an array, rather than an ordinary variable, and you must indicate the number of storage locations you want associated with that variable. You do that by using a DIM statement like the one following:

DIM A(7), F$(15)

This DIM statement tells the compiler that you want A and F$ to be arrays, not ordinary variables, and that the compiler should set up 7 storage locations for the A array and 15 storage locations for the F$ array.[1] From their names you can tell that A is an ordinary or numeric array, which will contain numeric values, and that F$ is a string array, which will contain strings. DIM is short for "dimension," and the DIM statement gets its name because we use it to specify the size, or the number of storage locations, that should be reserved for each array. As many variables as you like may be listed in a DIM statement, and you can have as many DIM statements as you like in a program.

It is customary to put the DIM statement near the beginning of the program, and some versions of BASIC require that the DIM statement be placed before the first instruction that uses any array variable. In many versions of BASIC only a letter may be used as the name of an array, while in other versions of BASIC any legal variable name may be used as the name of an array. Your instructor will tell you the rules for your version of BASIC, and you should write them on the inside front cover of this book.

In response to the DIM statement

DIM B(5), P(12)

the compiler will set up 5 storage locations for the B array and 12 for the P array, as shown in Fig. 6.1(a). Since we want to be able to reference the individual members of an array, they are numbered, as shown in Fig. 6.1(a). If, for example, we want to print the value of the third member of the B array, we would write

PRINT B(3)

We say that B(3) is a subscripted variable and that 3 is the **subscript.** The subscript is always enclosed in parentheses. Notice that B(3) and B3 are entirely different. B(3) refers to the third member of the B array, while B3 is an ordinary variable.

If we declare a variable to be an array by listing it in a DIM statement, then whenever we use that variable in the program, we must specify the subscript. For example, writing

---

1. In most BASICs it is not necessary to list in a DIM statement any array that has 10 or fewer storage locations. Your programs are much clearer, however, if you list all arrays in a DIM statement, even those with fewer than 10 storage locations. That is what we will do in all the programs in this book.

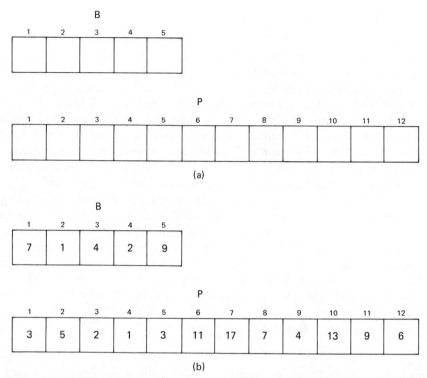

Fig. 6.1. (a) Storage locations for the B and P arrays. (b) B and P arrays with numeric values assigned to the members.

PRINT B

is wrong.[2] The computer might say to us, "I don't know what you want done. You told me to set up five storage locations for B; which one do you want printed?"

Using Arrays

As long as we specify a subscript, we may use an array variable anywhere that we could use an ordinary variable. Suppose the numeric values shown in Fig. 6.1(b) were assigned to the members of the B and P arrays.

---

2. Some BASICs have MAT statements that permit the use of an array name without a subscript. MAT statements are used in mathematical and scientific problems and will not be discussed in this book.

(For now do not worry about how the values were assigned; you will see that later.) The following statement is legal:

LET A = B(4) + P(7)

Before reading further, can you determine the value of A? The LET statement will be evaluated by adding the value of the fourth member of the B array, which is 2, to the value of the seventh member of the P array, which is 17, and the sum, 19, is assigned to A. Notice that the subscripts tell us which members of the arrays are to be added. We do *not* simply add the subscripts and say that A is equal to 11.

A subscripted variable may also be used on the left side of the equal sign in a LET statement. Before you read further, determine the value assigned to P(9) by the statement

LET P(9) = P(2) + P(8)

The answer is given at the end of the chapter.

In these examples I have used numbers as subscripts, but variables, and even expressions may also be used as subscripts. Consider the following LET statements:

100 LET J = 1

110 LET K = 2

120 LET W = B(J) + B(K)

130 LET X = B(K) * B(J + K)

140 LET Y = B(K - J) - B(K)

When the computer executes statement 100, it puts a 1 in the J box, and when it executes statement 110, it puts a 2 in the K box. When the computer gets to statement 120, it requires the value of B(J). At that point it looks in the J box and finds the 1 that was just put there. The computer therefore evaluates B(J) as though we had written B(1). Similarly, the computer requires B(K), so it looks in the K box, finds the 2 that was just put there, and evaluates B(K) as though we had written B(2). At this point statement 120 looks as though we had written it as

120 LET W = B(1) + B(2)

By using the values of the B array in Fig. 6.1(b), we see that W will be assigned the value of 8. The only thing that is different about statement 130 is that one of the subscripts is an expression. The computer evaluates B(J + K) as B(1 + 2) or B(3). After the subscripts are evaluated, statement 130 looks as though we had written it as

130 LET X = B(2) * B(3)

By using the values of the B array in Fig. 6.1(b), we see that X will be assigned the value 4. You should be able to determine the value assigned to Y when statement 140 is executed. The answer is given at the end of the chapter.

Assigning Values to an Array

Now that we know how to use arrays in LET statements, we come back to the question of how values are assigned to the members of an array.

Suppose we wanted to use READ and DATA statements to assign the values shown in Figure 6.1(b) to the B array. We could use the following statements:

10 DIM B(5)

20 READ B(1), B(2), B(3), B(4), B(5)

.

.

.

100 DATA 7, 1, 4, 2, 9

This would work, but if B were larger, if it had 100 or 500 members, this scheme would be inconvenient, to say the least.

The following statements provide a more convenient way to assign values to the members of the B array:

10 DIM B(5)

20 FOR J = 1 TO 5

30   READ B(J)

40 NEXT J

.

.

.

100 DATA 7, 1, 4, 2, 9

The idea here is to put the READ statement inside a FOR-NEXT loop, and to use the counter variable of the FOR-NEXT loop as the subscript in the READ statement. Let's make sure we understand how these statements work by tracing them. When statement 20 is executed the first time, J is assigned the value 1. To execute line 30 the computer requires the value of J. Since the current value of J is 1, the computer interprets line 30 as though we had written

30 READ B(1)

Therefore the first value from the DATA list, 7, is put into the B(1) box.

When line 40 is executed, J is assigned the value 2, and the computer branches back to line 30. Since the current value of J is 2, this time when line 30 is executed, the computer interprets it as though we had written

30 READ B(2)

Therefore the second value from the DATA list, 1, is put into the B(2) box.

The loop is repeated with J equal to 3, 4, and 5, and the last three values from the DATA list are put into the B(3), B(4), and B(5) boxes. By the time the loop is finished and we fall through the NEXT statement in line 40, all the members of the B array have been assigned the values shown in Fig. 6.1(b).

Notice that if the B array had 500 members, we would just change the final value of the FOR statement from 5 to 500 and add more DATA statements. The executed section of the program, lines 20 to 40, would be no longer and no more complicated.

This is the fundamental idea behind the use of arrays. We write one or more statements that use subscripted variables like the READ statement in the previous example. We then put these statements inside a FOR-NEXT loop and have the computer execute the statements as many times as we like. The size and complexity of our program does not depend on how many times the statements are executed or on how many members the array contains. By using an array this way we will be able to write a program to sort any number of numbers. You remember that the sorting method we used in Chapter 3 became impossibly complicated when we tried to sort more than four numbers.

Errors

When working with arrays there are some new kinds of errors you might make. For example, students frequently write the previous example as follows:

10 DIM B(5)

20 READ B(J)

.

.

100 DATA 7, 1, 4, 2, 9

They leave out the FOR and NEXT statements. You can avoid this kind of error if you remember that you want the READ statement to be executed five times. The READ statement shown in this program will be executed only once. You must almost always put statements that use subscripted variables inside a FOR-NEXT loop.

Another kind of error you might make is shown in the following example:

10 DIM R(5)

20 LET K = 20

30 LET R(K) = 10

When the computer executes statement 30, it tries to put 10 into R(20). Since the DIM statement specifies that the R array contains only five members, there is no R(20). The computer will therefore print the message SUBSCRIPT OUT OF BOUNDS and will stop executing. You will get the same message if the subscript is accidentally made negative. The message indicates either that your DIM statement is wrong or that the subscript was assigned an incorrect value. You must trace your program to determine the source of the error.

Exercises

6.1 The array V is defined to have seven members with the values shown here:

1	2	3	4	5	6	7
4	9	7	1	6	8	9

Suppose J = 3, K = 4, and L = 6. What value is assigned to A when each of the following LET statements is executed?

a) LET A = V(J) − V(K)
b) LET A = V(L) * V(K−J)
c) LET A = V(K) − V(J−K)

6.2 Trace the following program to determine its output.

```
10 DIM X (16)
20 FOR J = 1 TO 16
30   LET X (J) = J
40 NEXT J
50 FOR J = 2 TO 4
60   IF X(J) = 0 THEN 100
70   FOR K = 2 * J TO 16 STEP J
80     LET X(K) = 0
90   NEXT K
100 NEXT J
110 FOR J = 1 TO 16
120   IF X(J) = 0 THEN 140
130   PRINT X(J);
140 NEXT J
150 END
```

Can you recognize the output?

PRINTING THE DIFFERENCE FROM THE AVERAGE

Now that we know the characteristics of arrays we can use them to solve some problems. The first is a problem mentioned earlier: given students' names and test scores, calculate and print the average test score; also calculate and print each score and the difference between that score and the average.

A simpler version of this problem, without printing the differences, was solved in Chapter 4 on page 115. When we solved this problem, we used trailer data to indicate the end of the data. This time we will use the method developed in Chapter 5, in which the number of students is given as part of the data. We will use the number of students as the final value in a FOR statement.

The variable names we will use are

Input variables

Student name array	N$
Test score array	T
Number of students	S

Internal variables

Subscript	C
Test score accumulator	T1

Output variables

Average test score	A
Difference, test score minus	
average	D

Notice that we use two arrays in this problem. N$ is the array of student names, and T is the array of test scores. We can use the following algorithm for this problem:

1. Set T1 to zero.
2. Read S.
3. Repeat step 4 S times.
4. Read N$ and T.
5. Repeat step 6 S times.
6. Accumulate the test scores.
7. Calculate and print A.
8. Repeat step 9 S times.
9. Print N$, T, and D.

We can use the same data we used in Chapter 4. There the average test score was 82.5, so we can expect the following output from our program:

Average test score is 82.5.

Name	Score	Difference
Melita	90	7.5
Benito	80	−2.5
Angela	86	3.5
Mickey	74	−8.5

The flowchart based on this algorithm is shown in Fig. 6.2. The first thing we notice is that this flowchart contains three FOR-NEXT loops. Since the loops are independent, we can use the same counter

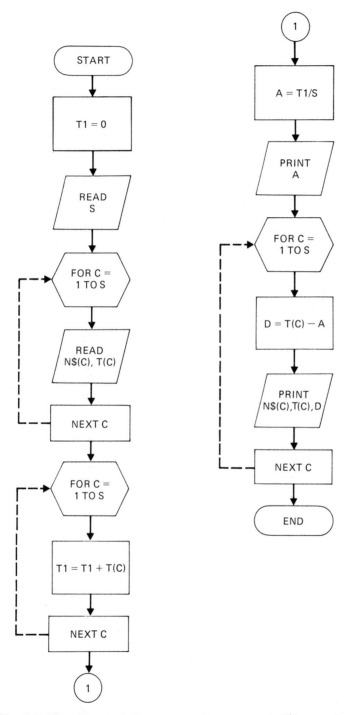

Fig. 6.2. Flowchart to print average test score and difference from average.

variable, C, in all three FOR-NEXT loops. Notice also how C is used as the subscript for the statements inside the FOR-NEXT loops.

If you think about this flowchart, you will realize that we do not need a separate FOR-NEXT loop to accumulate the test scores. After we read T(C), it is available to us to do anything we want with it, including accumulate it into T1. So we can move the accumulation step inside the FOR-NEXT loop, which does the reading, and eliminate the second FOR-NEXT loop. The revised flowchart is shown in Fig. 6.3. You should make it a practice to examine your flowcharts critically, because often you will find ways of improving them.

The program based on Fig. 6.3 is shown in Fig. 6.4. Notice that in the DIM statement, N$ and T are each allocated 40 storage locations. I choose 40 storage locations because I believe that the program will never be used to process more than 40 students, but I include a REM statement to warn users of this restriction, and I told them how the program could be modified to process more students. I could have made both arrays larger, but if I did, my program would take up more space in the computer's primary storage. Since there is a limited amount of space in primary storage, we do not make arrays bigger than they have to be.

If, when we execute the program, the number of students is less than 40 some of the members of N$ and T will not be assigned values. Since we will never use those members, the fact that they have not been assigned values will not cause any problems. The rest of the program follows directly from the flowchart and should not be difficult to understand. Notice that the computer's answers agree with our hand-calculated answers.

Exercises

6.3 Suppose in the program shown in Fig. 6.4, line 120 were changed to

FOR K = 1 TO S

What other changes would have to be made for the program to be executed properly?

6.4 Write a program like the one developed in this section but have all scores greater than the average printed first, along with students' names, and followed by grades less than or equal to the average, along with those students' names.

6.5 A subscript must be an integer. If a variable used as a subscript does not have an integer for a value, some versions of BASIC truncate the value, while others round the value to the nearest integer.

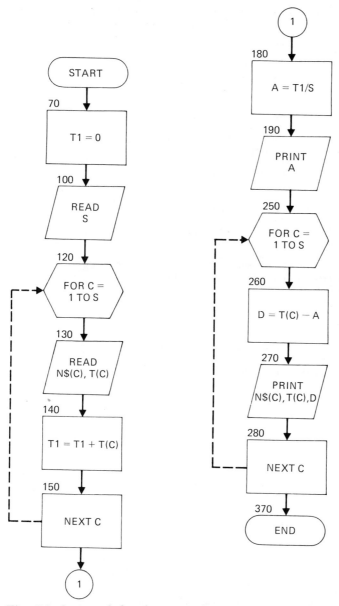

Fig. 6.3. Improved flowchart to print average test score and difference from average.

```
10 REM CALCULATE AVERAGE TEST SCORE AND DIFFERENCES
20 REM IF MORE THAN 40 STUDENTS ARE TO BE PROCESSED
30 REM THE DIM STATEMENT MUST BE CHANGED
40 REM PROGRAMMER. M. TROMBETTA
50 DIM N$(40),T(40)
55 REM
60 REM INITIALIZE THE ACCUMULATOR
70 LET T1 = 0
80 REM
90 REM READ THE NUMBER OF STUDENTS
100 READ S
110 REM READ NAMES AND SCORES AND ACCUMULATE THE SCORES
120 FOR C = 1 TO S
130    READ N$(C),T(C)
140    LET T1 = T1 + T(C)
150 NEXT C
160 REM
170 REM CALCULATE AVERAGE
180 LET A = T1/S
190 PRINT "AVERAGE TEST SCORE IS ";A
200 REM
220 REM CALCULATE DIFFERENCES
230 REM AND PRINT NAMES, SCORES AND DIFFERENCES
240 PRINT "NAME","SCORE","DIFFERENCE"
250 FOR C = 1 TO S
260    LET D = T(C) - A
270    PRINT N$(C),T(C),D
280 NEXT C
290 REM
300 REM THE NUMBER OF STUDENTS FOLLOWS
310 DATA 4
320 REM THE NAME AND TEST SCORE OF EACH STUDENT FOLLOWS
330 DATA "MELITA",90
340 DATA "BENITO",80
350 DATA "ANGELA",86
360 DATA "MICKEY",74
370 END


RUN

FIG6#4      17:45   11/14/79

AVERAGE TEST SCORE IS  82.5
NAME              SCORE            DIFFERENCE
MELITA             90                7.5
BENITO             80               -2.5
ANGELA             86                3.5
MICKEY             74               -8.5

TIME 0.0 SECS.
```

Fig. 6.4. Program to calculate average test scores and differences.

Write a short program that shows what your BASIC does with noninteger subscripts. The program should print either MY BASIC ROUNDS or MY BASIC TRUNCATES.

6.6 Write a program to analyze the student body at a college. The program should read four numbers that represent the number of freshmen, sophomores, juniors, and seniors. The program should then calculate and print the percentage of the student body that consists of freshmen, of sophomores, of juniors, and of seniors. Use an array in your program.

6.7 The Mamma Mia Pizzeria sells three kinds of pizza—cheese, sausage, and anchovy. The owner uses a computer to analyze sales. At the end of each week she types three DATA statements, each of which contains seven numbers. The seven numbers in the first DATA statement are the daily sales of cheese pizza during the past week. Similarly, the seven numbers in the second DATA statement are the daily sales of sausage pizza, and those in the third DATA statement are the daily sales of anchovy pizza. a) Write a program that will read the data and print the total number of pizzas sold each day of the week and the total number of each of the three kinds of pizza sold during the week. b) Suppose cheese pizza costs 4 dollars and 50 cents; sausage pizza costs 5 dollars and 50 cents; and anchovy pizza costs 6 dollars. Modify the program so that it calculates the total sales, the total number of each of the three kinds of pizzas sold each day of the week, and the totals for the week.

THE BUBBLE SORT

In Chapter 3 we wrote a program to sort three numbers. There I mentioned that using the same method to sort 10 numbers would require 3,628,799 IF statements. Even the smarter sort in Exercise 3.9 requires $n - 1$ IF statements to sort n numbers. That's a big improvement, but it is not a reasonable method if we want to sort many numbers.

In this section I will show you the "bubble sort." The bubble sort requires only two IF statements, no matter how many numbers are being sorted. Many other sorting methods can perform a sort in less computer time than the bubble sort, but the bubble sort is easy to understand and to program, and unless more than several hundred numbers are being sorted, the differences in execution time are negligible.

Suppose we have an array, A, with members in any mixed-up order. The problem is to sort A so that the members are in ascending order. When A is sorted, each member will be less than or equal to the next member: $A(1) <= A(2)$ and $A(2) <= A(3)$, and so on.

In the bubble sort we compare adjacent members of the array. If the first member is greater than the second member—that is, if the two members are in the "wrong" order—we swap the two members. If the first member is less than or equal to the second member—that is, if the two members are in the "right" order—we leave the two members alone. Every time we swap two members, the array gets a little closer to being sorted, and we feel intuitively that if we continue swapping long enough eventually the whole array will be sorted.

Let's clarify this procedure by applying it to an actual example. The procedure works for arrays of any size, but to keep this discussion to a reasonable length let's assume that A contains only five members and that initially they have the values shown in Fig. 6.5(a). We begin by comparing A(1) with A(2). Since A(1), which is 3, is less than A(2), which is 7, these members are in the "right" order, so we leave them alone. Next we compare A(2) with A(3). Since A(2), which is 7, is greater than A(3), which is 1, these members are in the "wrong" order so we

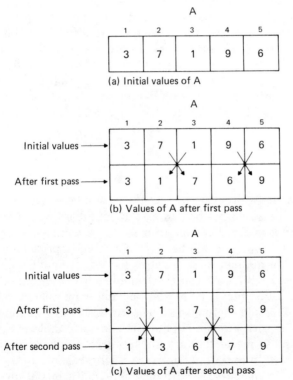

Fig. 6.5. Sorting using bubble sort method.

swap them, as shown in Fig. 6.5(b). We next compare A(3) with A(4). Because of the swap A(3) is now 7, and since A(4) is 9, these members are in the "right" order, so we leave them alone. Finally, we compare A(4), which is 9, and A(5), which is 6, and since these members are in the "wrong" order, we swap them. After the first pass A has the values shown in Fig. 6.5(b).

It seems that we have done a lot of work and have little to show for it, since A is still pretty mixed up. But if we go through the whole procedure again, we get the results shown in Fig. 6.5(c). We see that A has been sorted. (You should make sure you understand how Fig. 6.5(c) is obtained from Fig. 6.5(b).) In this case sorting A required only two passes, but that will not always be the case. In general the number of passes required to sort an array depends on the size of the array and how mixed up it was when we started.

The bubble sort involves repeated passes through the array, swapping members that are in the "wrong" order until the array is sorted. Exactly how we determine that the array is sorted will be clear when we draw the flowchart.

The variables we will need are

Input variables

Array to be sorted	A
Number of members of A to be sorted	N

Internal variables

Subscript	K
Flag to indicate sort is finished. (YES means it is; NO means it is not.)	F$

Output variable

Sorted array	A

We do not have to calculate an answer to this problem since by observation we can tell whether the sort was successful.

Flowcharts

The beginning of the flowchart is shown in Fig. 6.6. We start by reading N, the number of members of A that are to be sorted. The first FOR-NEXT loop simply assigns values to the first N members of A. Now we are ready to begin the actual sorting.

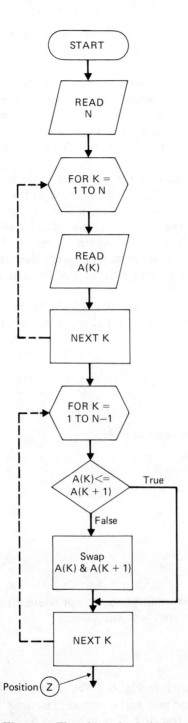

Fig. 6.6. Flowchart for bubble sort showing comparison and swap steps.

The bubble sort requires that we compare adjacent members of A. That is, we want to compare

A(1) with A(2)

A(2) with A(3)

A(3) with A(4)

.

.

.

A(N − 1) with A(N)

How can we perform all these comparisons? Naturally we don't want to write individual IF statements; if we did, our program would be no better than the ones we wrote in Chapter 3. We can use only one IF statement if we compare

A(K) with A(K + 1)

We can put this IF statement inside a FOR-NEXT loop in which K is the counter variable. When K is 1, we will compare A(1) with A(2). When K is 2, we will compare A(2) with A(3), and so on.

Notice, however, that the highest value K should have is N − 1. When K = N − 1, the value of the subscript K + 1 is N − 1 + 1 = N. So when K = N − 1, we will compare A(N − 1) with A(N). If by mistake we allow K to have the value N, then we will compare A(N) with A(N + 1). Since we are sorting N members of A, a reference to A(N + 1) is incorrect. The flowchart with the second FOR-NEXT loop and the IF statement is shown in Fig. 6.6.

If the condition A(K) <= A(K + 1) is true, we want to leave those two members alone, so we branch directly to the NEXT statement. If, on the other hand, the condition is false, we want to swap A(K) and A(K + 1). How can we swap A(K) and A(K + 1)? Your first thought might be that the following two LET statements could perform the swap:

LET A(K) = A(K + 1)

LET A(K + 1) = A(K)

Let's trace these two LET statements to see why they do not work. Suppose K = 2, A(2) = 7, and A(3) = 1. Since A(2) is greater than A(3), we want to swap these two members. With K = 2, the two statements are equivalent to

LET A(2) = A(3)

LET A(3) = A(2)

When the first LET statement is executed, the 1 in A(3) is put into A(2), and the 7 that was in A(2) is erased. That's correct, but look what happens when the second LET statement is executed. The 1 that is now in A(2) is put into A(3), and the 1 that is in A(3) is erased. In other words, the second LET statement accomplishes nothing! The 7 that was originally in A(2) has been lost! To save that 7 we must store it in a temporary area.

Let's call the temporary area T. The series of statements that will swap the values in A(K) and A(K + 1) are

LET T = A(K)

LET A(K) = A(K + 1)

LET A(K + 1) = T

You should trace these three statements to convince yourself that they do cause the values of A(K) and A(K + 1) to be swapped.

Use of a Flag

We have one last problem to solve: how do we know when to stop? Suppose we are at position Ⓩ on the flowchart in Fig. 6.6. If all the pairs of members of A are in the "right" order, the sort is finished, and we can go on to the next step. If even one pair of members of A is in the "wrong" order, the sort is not finished, and we must branch back to the start of the FOR-NEXT loop and execute another pass through A.

So now we are faced with the question: when we arrive at position Ⓩ, how do we know that all the pairs of members are in the "right" order? Let's look at the condition A(K) < = A(K + 1). If, during a particular pass, the condition were true whenever we evaluated it, it would mean that A(1) < = A(2) and A(2) < = A(3), and so on up to A(N − 1) < = A(N). In other words, if the condition were always true, all the pairs of members would be in the "right" order, and the sort would be complete.

We seem to be making progress very slowly, because now we are faced with another question, which hardly seems easier than the first: when we arrive at position Ⓩ, how do we know that on the previous pass the condition was always true? To answer this question we introduce a **flag**. A flag is a variable that is introduced into a program for the sole purpose of controlling the execution of the program, depending on the presence or absence of some condition. That definition sounds complicated, but a flag is not so very different from trailer data. When we use trailer data, we set one of the program's variables to a particular value to indicate that we have reached the end of the data. When we use a flag, we introduce a new variable and set it to a particular value to indicate some condition.

Let's call the flag F$, and let it have the value YES if the sort is finished and NO if it is not. We set F$ to YES just before the FOR-NEXT loop; we set it to NO in the false branch of the decision, and we test it after the NEXT statement as shown by positions Ⓧ, Ⓨ, and Ⓩ in Fig. 6.7.

Suppose that on a pass through A the condition A(K) <= A(K + 1) is false, even once. Then the LET statement at position Ⓨ will set F$ to NO. When we get to position Ⓩ and test F$, we will find that it has the value NO, and we will know that the sort is not yet finished. If the sort is not finished, we branch back to position Ⓧ to reset F$ to YES and execute another pass through the array.

After a number of passes the array will finally be sorted. When the array is sorted, the condition A(K) <= (K + 1) will be true every time we test it. On that pass through A the LET statement at position Ⓨ will not be executed. When we get to position Ⓩ and test F$, we will find that it has the value YES that we assigned to it at position Ⓧ. If that is the case, we know the sort is finished, and we can go on to the next step, as shown in Fig. 6.8, and print the sorted array.

The bubble sort is the most difficult program we have developed so far. In particular, swapping and using the flag is not easy. I hope you can write a BASIC program based on the flowchart in Fig. 6.8.

Exercises

6.8 In the bubble sort we swapped members of the A array using the statements

LET T = A(K)
LET A(K) = A(K + 1)
LET A(K +1) = T

These are not the only statements that can be used to swap members of A. Another set begins as follows:

LET T = A(K + 1)

Complete this set of statements.

6.9 Write a bubble sort program based on the flowchart shown in Fig. 6.8. Define A to have 20 members. As the flowchart shows, you should first read N, the number of members to be sorted (N must not be greater than 20). Then read N data values into A. Finally, sort and print A.

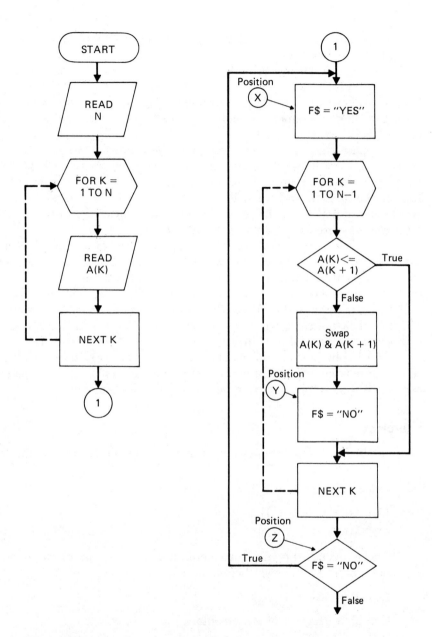

Fig. 6.7. Flowchart for bubble sort showing use of flag.

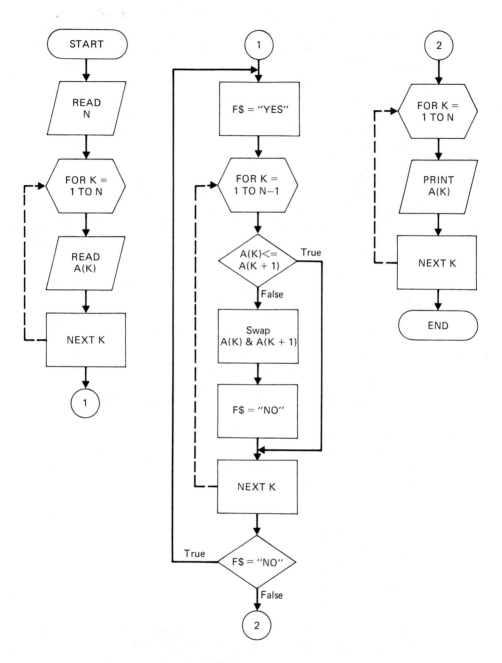

Fig. 6.8. Complete flowchart for bubble sort.

Does not work – not possible

6.10 If we make a more careful analysis, we can improve the bubble sort. In the algorithm we developed we compare all the adjacent members of A on each pass. Some of these comparisons are unnecessary. Let's introduce a new variable H. Every time we swap A(K) and A(K + 1), we set H equal to K. Since K starts from one and gets larger, when we finish a pass through A, H will be equal to the highest value of K for which A(K) and A(K + 1) were swapped. For example, suppose A has 20 members and on a particular pass members 7 and 8, 10 and 11, and 13 and 14 were swapped. Then on this pass H will be set to 13. A little thought will show that all the members of A greater than or equal to 13 are now sorted. (That is why we did not have to swap any of them.) Therefore on the next pass through A we do not have to compare all the adjacent members of A; we can stop at the comparison between A(12) and A(13).

The easiest way to do this is to allow the final value of the FOR statement to vary, instead of holding it constant at N − 1. Let the final value of the FOR statement be the variable U. On each pass set U equal to H − 1. (Of course on the first pass it is necessary that U equal N − 1.) Furthermore we do not need a separate flag; we can use H as the flag. As we start each pass through A, we set H equal to 0. If at the end of the pass H is less than or equal to 1, the sort is finished.

Draw a flowchart and write a program for this improved bubble sort.

6.11 The bubble sort we developed is all right as far as it goes, but it could be improved considerably. Suppose you were given the following list of baseball players and the number of home runs they hit during their careers:

Aaron	755
Killebrew	573
Mantle	536
Mays	660
Robinson	586
Ruth	714

We could use the bubble sort to sort the number of home runs in descending order (highest first), and the output would be

755

714

660

586

573

536

But from this list we cannot tell which player hit which number of home runs. It would be much nicer if our output were

Aaron	755
Ruth	714
Mays	660
Robinson	586
Killebrew	573
Mantle	536

Write a program that will produce this output. (*Hint:* Read the names into one array and the number of home runs into another array. As you go through the sort and swap members of the home run array, you must also swap the same two members of the name array. In this way you will maintain the correspondence between the name and home run arrays.)

6.12 Closely related to sorting is merging. When merging we start with two arrays that are already sorted and combine them to form a new, larger array that is also sorted.

Assume that we start with two five-member arrays, A and B, which have the values shown:

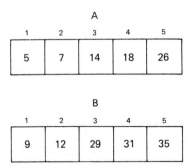

Notice that the members of A and B are already sorted. We want to merge them to form the array C[3]:

---

3. The members of C that came from B are shaded.

C

1	2	3	4	5	6	7	8	9	10
5	7	9	12	14	18	26	29	31	35

This problem requires three subscripts. I is the subscript for the A array; J is the subscript for the B array; and K is the subscript for the C array. The basic strategy of the merge is to compare A(I) with B(J), and to set C(K) equal to the smaller value. Initially we set I, J, and K equal to 1. The first time A(I) is compared with B(J) we will be comparing A(1) and B(1). Since A(1) is less than B(1), we set C(1) equal to A(1), and increment K and I. The second time A(I) is compared with B(J) we will be comparing A(2) and B(1). After each comparison we increment K and either I or J. If A(I) was less than B(J), we increment I, but if B(J) was less than A(I), we increment J.

By following this procedure we will eventually have I or J incremented to 6. Since A and B have only five members, a subscript of 6 does not make sense. The simplest way to get around this problem is to add a sixth member to A and B and to set it equal to a value larger than any value that can occur in the first five members, say 9999. Suppose, for example, that I becomes 6 while J is still 3. On subsequent comparisons B(J) will be less than A(I) because A(6) is 9999), so C(K) will be set equal to B(J), and K and J will be incremented. Eventually the remaining members of C will be set equal to the remaining members of B.

Now write a program to implement this merge algorithm. Read values for the A and B arrays, merge them, and print the resulting C array.

SEARCHING AN ARRAY

Data are frequently stored in an array and are retrieved and used during execution of a program. A simple example of retrieving data from an array is shown in Fig. 6.9. Here we have set up an array, M$, that contains the names of the 12 months. When a value is entered for the month number, N, we can print the name of that month by simply printing M$(N).

The program shown in Fig. 6.9 is particularly simple because, when we are given N, we know we want to print the Nth member of M$. Very often the situation is not as simple as this, and then we must search an array to find the desired member.

```
10 REM PRINTING THE NAMES OF THE MONTHS
20 REM PROGRAMMER M. TROMBETTA
30 DIM M$(12)
40 REM READ MONTH NAMES INTO M$
50 FOR K = 1 TO 12
60    READ M$(K)
70 NEXT K
80 PRINT "ENTER A MONTH NUMBER AND I'LL"
90 PRINT "TELL YOU THE NAME OF THE MONTH"
100 PRINT "ENTER ZERO TO STOP"
110 INPUT N
120    IF N = 0 THEN 150
130    PRINT "MONTH NO ";N;"IS ";M$(N)
140 GO TO 110
150 STOP
160 DATA "JANUARY","FEBRUARY","MARCH","APRIL"
170 DATA "MAY","JUNE","JULY","AUGUST","SEPTEMBER"
180 DATA "OCTOBER","NOVEMBER","DECEMBER"
190 END


RUN

FIG6#7        17:57    11/14/79

ENTER A MONTH NUMBER AND I'LL
TELL YOU THE NAME OF THE MONTH
ENTER ZERO TO STOP
?5
MONTH NO  5     IS MAY
?8
MONTH NO  8     IS AUGUST
?0

TIME 0.0 SECS.
```

Fig. 6.9. Searching an array to print the name of the month.

The Album-lending Problem

Before I show you how to search an array, I will describe a problem that requires searching an array. Suppose you have a large record album collection and that you want to use a computer to keep track of which records you have lent to which friends.

We want to write a program that will accept the name of an album, a one-letter code to indicate whether the album is being borrowed or returned, and, if the album is being borrowed, the name of the person borrowing it. The program should keep track of which albums are lent and which are not, and for those that are lent, the names of the friends who borrowed them.

We will solve this problem by setting up two related arrays. The first array, A$, will contain the names of all the albums you own. The second array, B$, will contain the names of the friends who have borrowed the albums. We arrange the A$, and B$ so that they correspond in the following way: suppose "Grease" is one of your albums, and Jane borrowed it. If "Grease" happens to be the fifth member of A$, then we will make "Jane" the fifth member of B$. If no one has borrowed a particular album, we will make its corresponding name in B$ be "Free".

We will use the following variable names:

Input variables

Album names' array	A$
Borrower names' array	B$
Code (R means returned; B means borrowed.)	C$
Name of friend who wants to borrow an album	F$
Number of albums in your collection	N
Name of album being borrowed or returned	N$

Internal variables

Searching subscript	J
Reading subscript	K
Flag to indicate whether search was successful (YES means search was successful; NO means it was not.)	S$

Output variables

Album names' array	A$
Borrower names' array	B$

The basic algorithm we will use is

1. Read N and fill the A$ and B$ arrays.
2. Accept N$ and C$.
3. If the value entered for N$ is END, go to step 8.

4. Search A$ for a member equal to N$.

5. If the album is being returned, set the corresponding member of B$ to FREE.

6. If the album is being borrowed, accept F$ and set the corresponding member of B$ to F$.

7. Repeat steps 2–6 for all sets of N$ and C$.

8. Print the status of the albums.

Exactly how the search step, step 4, is carried out and how we set the "corresponding" member of B$ to either FREE or F$ will be explained when we examine the flowchart.

The data in the A$ and B$ arrays indicate the status of our album collection and are called the **master data.** Master data are data that show the current status of a business or activity. The pairs of N$ and C$ that are entered in step 2 and indicate which albums are being borrowed and which are being returned are called **transaction data.** Transaction data are any data that cause a change in the master data. We will indicate that all the transactions have been entered by entering a value of END for N$.

Before we get to the flowchart, we must discuss an abnormal or error condition. Our search of A$ may be unsuccessful; there may not be a member of A$ that equals N$. This simply means that we misspelled the album name. If that happens, we should print a message that says that the name was misspelled and go on to the next transaction.

Flowcharts

The flowchart is shown in Fig. 6.10. You will notice that this flowchart shows that a subroutine is used for the search. The flowchart for the SEARCH subroutine is shown in Fig. 6.11, which we will discuss later.

In the main program, we start by reading N, the number of albums in our collection. We then use a FOR-NEXT loop to read data into the A$ and B$ arrays. We are now ready to process the individual album requests.

We accept the album name, N$, and one-letter code, C$. If C$ = R, it means the album is being returned, and if C$ = B, it means the album is being borrowed. We next execute the subroutine that searches the A$ array. At this point all we need to know about that subroutine is that, if the search is successful, S$ will be equal to YES, and J will be equal to the number of the member of A$ that is equal to N$: A$(J)

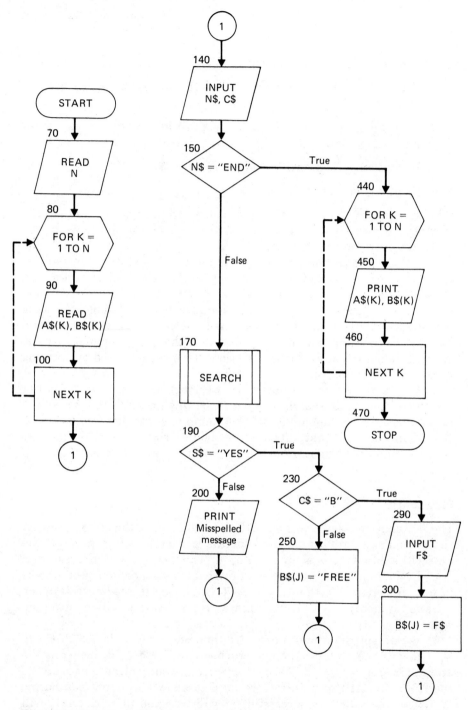

Fig. 6.10. Flowchart for album-lending problem.

= N\$. If the search is not successful, S\$ will be equal to NO, and it does not matter what the value of J is.

If the search is not successful, we print a message and return to accept the next transaction. If the search is successful, we must determine whether the album is being borrowed or returned by testing C\$.

If C\$ = B someone wants to borrow the album, so we request that the borrower's name, F\$, be entered. Recall that the B\$ array contains the names of the borrowers. Since the search has indicated that the album being borrowed is the Jth member of A\$, we remember the name of the friend who borrowed it by setting the Jth member of B\$ equal to F\$. We then return to accept the next transaction. If C\$ = R, the album is being returned, so we set B\$(J) equal to FREE and return to accept the next transaction.

The Sequential Search Subroutine

Now that we understand the flowchart for the main program, we may examine the flowchart for the search subroutine shown in Fig. 6.11. The search method shown in Fig. 6.11 is called a sequential search. Later we will see a different search method called the binary search.

The logic of the sequential search is straightforward. In a FOR-NEXT loop we compare each member of A\$ with N\$. If we find a match, the search has been successful, so we set the flag S\$ to YES and return to the main program. Notice that J automatically contains the value for which A\$(J) = N\$ is true. We say that J points to the member of A\$ that is equal to N\$.

If we fall through the FOR-NEXT loop, it means that none of the members of A\$ equals N\$. In this case the search has been unsuccessful, so we set S\$ to NO and return to the main program.

The program for the album-lending problem is shown in Fig. 6.12. The program follows directly from the flowchart and uses only statements you already know, so I think you will not have any trouble understanding it.

With a little thought you can probably think of ways to improve the speed of the sequential search we used in this problem. I will suggest an improvement in one of the programming exercises at the end of this section. Now I will show you a different, much faster search method.

The Binary Search*

When the array that is to be searched is arranged in numeric or alphabetical order, we can devise a much faster search method.

---

*This section may be omitted without loss of continuity.

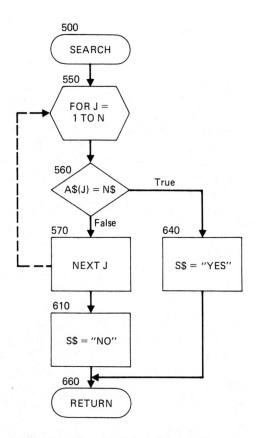

Fig. 6.11. Flowchart for sequential search subroutine.

Imagine you are looking for a name in a telephone book. If you followed the logic of the sequential search, you would start looking for the name on page one, and look at each page in turn until you found the name you were looking for. Of course, you would never do that; it would be too slow. What you would actually do is open the book where you think the name might be. If you found that you had overshot the name, you would next look closer to the front of the book, and if you found that you had undershot the name, you would next look closer to the back of the book. The reason this logic works is that the telephone book is arranged in alphabetical order. Similarly, the binary search will work only if the members of the array being searched are arranged in alphabetical or numeric order.

Let's take a second to analyze more carefully what we mean by saying we overshot or undershot the name. If we are looking for the name "Jackson" and we opened the telephone book to the name "Miller," we would say we overshot the name we were looking for because in an

```
10 REM ALBUM-LENDING PROGRAM
20 REM PROGRAMMER, M. TROMBETTA
30 REM FOR MORE THAN 100 ALBUMS, CHANGE THE DIM STATEMENT
40 DIM A$(100),B$(100)
50 REM
60 REM READ NO OF ALBUMS AND FILL A$ AND B$ ARRAYS
70 READ N
80 FOR K = 1 TO N
90    READ A$(K),B$(K)
100 NEXT K
110 REM
120 PRINT "ENTER ALBUM NAME AND B FOR BORROWED OR R FOR RETURNED"
130 PRINT "ENTER END FOR ALBUM NAME TO STOP"
140 INPUT N$,C$
150 IF N$ = "END" THEN 400
160 REM SEARCH FOR MEMBER OF A$ EQUAL TO N$
170 GO SUB 500
180 REM CHECK IF SEARCH WAS SUCCESSFUL
190 IF S$ = "YES" THEN 220
200 PRINT "YOU MUST HAVE MISSPELLED "; N$
210 GO TO 120
220 REM CHECK IF ALBUM IS BEING BORROWED
230 IF C$ = "B" THEN 270
240 REM ALBUM IS BEING RETURNED
250 LET B$(J) = "FREE"
260 GO TO 120
270 REM SOMEONE WANTS TO BORROW THE ALBUM - GET BORROWER'S NAME
280 PRINT "ENTER NAME OF BORROWER"
290 INPUT F$
300 LET B$(J) = F$
310 GO TO 120
400 REM
410 REM PRINT STATUS OF ALBUMS
420 PRINT "CURRENT STATUS OF ALBUMS"
430 PRINT "ALBUM NAME","BORROWER'S NAME"
440 FOR K = 1 TO N
450    PRINT A$(K),B$(K)
460 NEXT K
470 STOP
500 REM
510 REM SEQUENTIAL SEARCH ROUTINE
520 REM SEARCH A$ ARRAY FOR MEMBER EQUAL TO N$
530 REM IF SEARCH IS SUCCESSFUL S$ CONTAINS YES
540 REM AND J CONTAINS THE NUMBER OF THE MEMBER OF A$ EQUAL TO N$
550 FOR J = 1 TO N
560    IF A$(J) = N$ THEN 640
570 NEXT J
580 REM
590 REM IF WE DROP THROUGH FOR-NEXT LOOP SEARCH WAS UNSUCCESSFUL
600 REM SET SWITCH AND RETURN
610 LET S$ = "NO"
620 GO TO 660
630 REM
640 REM SEARCH WAS SUCCESSFUL - SET SWITCH AND RETURN
650 LET S$ = "YES"
660 RETURN
700 REM THE NUMBER OF ALBUMS FOLLOWS
710 DATA 13
720 REM THE NAME OF THE ALBUM AND NAME OF THE BORROWER FOLLOW
730 DATA "CANDY-O","BECKY"
```

Fig. 6.12. Album-lending program.

```
740 REM THE FOLLOWING ALBUM WAS A GIFT FROM AUNT MARY
750 DATA "DANCE-LOMBARDO","FREE"
760 DATA "GREASE","DEBBIE"
770 DATA "HOUSE OF THE HOLY", "ANDREA"
780 DATA "PHYSICAL GRAFFITI","BENJI"
790 DATA "RUMORS","FREE"
800 DATA "RUST NEVER SLEEPS","JEFFREY"
810 REM THE FOLLOWING ALBUM BELONGS TO YOUR KID SISTER
820 DATA "SESAME ST STORIES", "KID SISTER"
830 DATA "SO FAR","SUSI"
840 DATA "SOME GIRLS","CAROLE"
850 DATA "STEAL YOUR FACE","MARGARET"
860 DATA "STRANGER IN TOWN","LISA"
870 DATA "STREET LEGAL","FREE"
999 END


RUN

FIG6#10      15:42    02/25/80

ENTER ALBUM NAME AND B FOR BORROWED OR R FOR RETURNED
ENTER END FOR ALBUM NAME TO STOP
?CANDY-O,R
ENTER ALBUM NAME AND B FOR BORROWED OR R FOR RETURNED
ENTER END FOR ALBUM NAME TO STOP
?STREET LEGAL,B
ENTER NAME OF BORROWER
?CORA
ENTER ALBUM NAME AND B FOR BORROWED OR R FOR RETURNED
ENTER END FOR ALBUM NAME TO STOP
?SO FAR,R
ENTER ALBUM NAME AND B FOR BORROWED OR R FOR RETURNED
ENTER END FOR ALBUM NAME TO STOP
?GREESE,R
YOU MUST HAVE MISSPELLED GREESE
ENTER ALBUM NAME AND B FOR BORROWED OR R FOR RETURNED
ENTER END FOR ALBUM NAME TO STOP
?GREASE,R
ENTER ALBUM NAME AND B FOR BORROWED OR R FOR RETURNED
ENTER END FOR ALBUM NAME TO STOP
?END,B
CURRENT STATUS OF ALBUMS
ALBUM NAME              BORROWER'S NAME
CANDY-O                 FREE
DANCE-LOMBARDO          FREE
GREASE                  FREE
HOUSE OF THE HOLY ANDREA
PHYSICAL GRAFFITI BENJI
RUMORS                  FREE
RUST NEVER SLEEPS JEFFREY
SESAME ST STORIES KID SISTER
SO FAR                  FREE
SOME GIRLS              CAROLE
STEAL YOUR FACE   MARGARET
STRANGER IN TOWN  LISA
STREET LEGAL            CORA

TIME 0.0 SECS.
```

Fig. 6.12 (cont'd.). Album-lending program.

alphabetical arrangement Miller comes after Jackson. Another way of saying this is that, in an alphabetical sense, Miller is greater than Jackson. So if the name we found were greater than the name we were looking for, we would next look closer to the front of the book. Similarly, if the name we found were less than the name we were looking for, we would look closer to the back of the book.

The binary search works in much the same way. Suppose we are given an array, called N$, of 12 names in alphabetical order, as shown in Fig. 6.13. We are given the name "Fell" and we want to search N$ to determine the subscript of the member that contains that name. We will compare Fell with a particular member. If the member is greater than Fell, we next look closer to the beginning of N$. If the member is less than Fell, we next look closer to the end of N$.

As the search proceeds, we will discover that some sections of the array could not possibly contain the name we are looking for, so we will eliminate those sections from the search. It will be helpful to introduce two new variables: L and H. L is the subscript of the lowest member of N$ that is still in the search, and H is the subscript of the highest member that is still in the search. At the start L = 1, and H = 12, since the whole array has to be searched. As in the sequential search we will use J as the subscript of the member we are currently comparing against the given name, Fell.

We begin by comparing Fell against the middle member of the array. Right away we run into a problem. There is no middle member of this array. Six is not the subscript of the middle member because there are five members below it (1–5) and six members above it (7–12). Similarly, seven is not the subscript of the middle member.

		1st comparison	2nd comparison	3rd comparison
		L = 1, H = 12	L = 1, H = 5	L = 4, H = 5
Position	Member	J = 6	J = 3	J = 4
1	Alleyn			ELIMINATED
2	Appleby		J = 3	
3	Campion			
4	Fell			J = 4
5	Fen			
6	Holmes	J = 6		
7	Marple		ELIMINATED	ELIMINATED
8	Poirot			
9	Queen			
10	Stout			
11	Wimsey			
12	Wolfe			
		(a)	(b)	(c)

Fig. 6.13. Successful binary search for "Fell."

You can always calculate the subscript of the middle member by the equation

$$J = (L + H) / 2$$

If we use this equation, we find that J = 6.5, but a subscript must be an integer. The simplest way to ensure that J is an integer is to use the INT function. So the equation we will use to calculate J is

$$J = INT ((L + H) / 2)$$

The first value of J calculated by this equation is 6. So we compare the sixth member of N$, Holmes, against Fell, as shown in Fig. 6.13(a). Since Holmes is greater than Fell (in the alphabetical sense), we know that Fell must be in the lower half of N$. With one comparison we have eliminated half of N$! Now we can concentrate on the first five members of N$.

To search the lower half of N$ we move the upper limit H down to J − 1, or 5, as shown in Fig. 6.13(b). Then we use our equation to calculate a new J. With L = 1 and H = 5, the equation gives J = 3. So we now compare the third member of N$, Campion, against Fell. Since Campion is less than Fell, we know that Fell must be in the upper half of the array we are searching; it must be between J + 1 and H.

To search this section of N$ we move the lower limit L up to J + 1, or 4, as shown in Fig. 6.13(c). With L = 4 and H = 5, the equation gives J = 4. So we now compare the fourth member of N$, and since it is Fell, we have found a match, and the search is over.

We must now investigate what happens when we search for a name that is not in the array. Suppose we are given the name "Thatcher," and we want to find the matching member in N$. We begin, as before, by comparing the sixth member of N$, Holmes, against Thatcher, as shown in Fig. 6.14(a). Since Holmes is less than Thatcher we know that, if Thatcher is anywhere in N$, it must be in the upper half.

To search the upper half of N$ we move the lower limit L up to J + 1 or 7, as shown in Fig. 6.14(b). With L = 7 and H = 12, we find J = 9. So we next compare the ninth member of N$, Queen, against Thatcher. Since Queen is less than Thatcher, we know that, if Thatcher is anywhere in our array, it must be between J + 1 and H. To search this section of N$ we move the lower limit L to J + 1 or 10, as shown in Fig. 6.14(c).

With L = 10 and H = 12, we find J = 11, so we next compare the eleventh member of N$, Wimsey, against Thatcher. Since Wimsey is greater than Thatcher, we move the upper limit H down to J − 1 or 10, as shown in Fig. 6.14(d).

Position	Member	1st comparison $L = 1, H = 12$ $J = 6$	2nd comparison $L = 7, H = 12$ $J = 9$	3rd comparison $L = 10, H = 12$ $J = 11$	4th comparison $L = 10, H = 10$ $J = 10$
1	Alleyn		E L I M I N A T E D	E L I M I N A T E D	E L I M I N A T E D
2	Appleby				
3	Campion				
4	Fell				
5	Fen				
6	Holmes	$J = 6$			
7	Marple				
8	Poirot				
9	Queen				
10	Stout		$J = 9$		$J = 10$
11	Wimsey			$J = 11$	ELIMINATED
12	Wolfe				
		(a)	(b)	(c)	(d)

Fig. 6.14. Unsuccessful binary search for "Thatcher."

With L = 10 and H = 10, clearly J = 10, so we now compare the tenth member of N$, Stout, against Thatcher. Since Stout is less than Thatcher, we must move the lower limit L up to J + 1 or 11. But here we have run into an impossibility: the lower limit is 11, while the upper limit is 10! This "crossing" of the upper and lower limits tells us that we have searched the complete array and that the name we were searching for is not in the array. So the binary search ends either when we find a match, which means the search was successful, or when the upper and lower limits cross, which means that the search was unsuccessful.

It may seem that the binary search is quite complicated and that we have achieved only a small improvement in speed over the sequential search. The improvement only seems small because I have demonstrated the binary search on a small array of only 12 members. The binary search really shows its superiority to the sequential search when the arrays get large, 100 members or more. Remember that in the binary search each comparison eliminates half of the remaining array. Using that fact it is possible to calculate the maximum number of comparisons required completely to search arrays of different sizes. The results are

Size of array	*Maximum number of comparisons*
10	4
100	7
1000	10

A sequential search of a 1000-member array would require, on the average, 500 comparisons. There you can see the enormous advantage of the binary search.

The Binary Search Subroutine

Figure 6.15 shows a flowchart for a binary search subroutine. The flowchart follows the logic we have just demonstrated. We begin by setting L equal to 1 and H equal to N. We then set J equal to the midpoint of the array. If A$(J) = N$, the search was successful, so we set the flag S$ equal to YES and return. If A$(J) is not equal to N$, we determine whether it is larger or smaller than N$. IF A$(J) is larger than N$, we lower H to J − 1. If A$(J) is greater than N$, we raise L to J + 1. Finally we determine whether L and H have crossed. If L is greater than H, the search was unsuccessful, so we set the flag S$ equal to NO and return. If L is not greater than H, we loop back to continue the search.

Just because I have illustrated the sequential and binary searches by searching an array of names, you should not assume that only arrays containing names or other alphabetical data can be searched. Any kind of array can be searched. If we wanted to search an array containing telephone numbers, the logic of these sequential and binary searches would work perfectly.

The BASIC program for our album-lending problem using a binary search is shown in Fig. 6.16. If you compare this program with the one shown in Fig. 6.12, which uses a sequential search, you will see that the only differences involve the search subroutine beginning at line 500. This is a dramatic illustration of the advantages of using subroutines. When I wanted to change the search method used in the program, I simply replaced the sequential search subroutine by the binary subroutine, and it was not necessary to make any changes to the main program. The GOSUB 500 statement now executes a binary search instead of a sequential search.

There is one artificial aspect to our album-lending programs. As we enter transactions, the program keeps track of which albums are borrowed and which are returned, and at the end of a session, when we enter END, the program prints a report giving the current status of our albums. But when we turn the computer off, that current status is "forgotten." At our next session, before we can use the program, we must change the DATA statements to reflect the status as it was at the end of the previous session. Changing the DATA statements is a lot of trouble, and what we would like is to have the computer remember the status

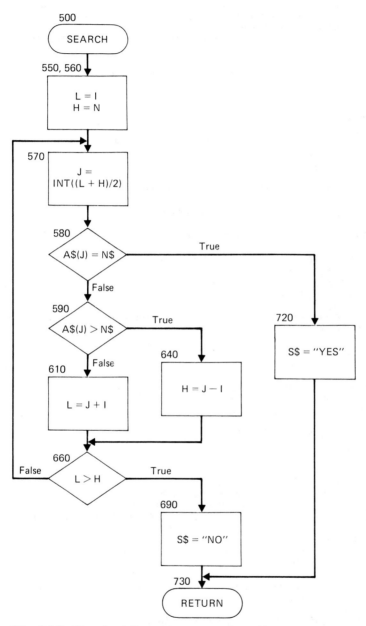

Fig. 6.15. Flowchart for a binary search routine.

```
10 REM ALBUM-LENDING PROGRAM
20 REM PROGRAMMER, M. TROMBETTA
30 REM FOR MORE THAN 100 ALBUMS, CHANGE THE DIM STATEMENT
40 DIM A$(100),B$(100)
50 REM
60 REM READ NO OF ALBUMS AND FILL A$ AND B$ ARRAYS
70 READ N
80 FOR K = 1 TO N
90    READ A$(K),B$(K)
100 NEXT K
110 REM
120 PRINT "ENTER ALBUM NAME AND B FOR BORROWED OR R FOR RETURNED"
130 PRINT "ENTER END FOR ALBUM NAME TO STOP"
140 INPUT N$,C$
150 IF N$ = "END" THEN 400
160 REM SEARCH FOR MEMBER OF A$ EQUAL TO N$
170 GO SUB 500
180 REM CHECK IF SEARCH WAS SUCCESSFUL
190 IF S$ = "YES" THEN 220
200 PRINT "YOU MUST HAVE MISSPELLED "; N$
210 GO TO 120
220 REM CHECK IF ALBUM IS BEING BORROWED
230 IF C$ = "B" THEN 270
240 REM ALBUM IS BEING RETURNED
250 LET B$(J) = "FREE"
260 GO TO 120
270 REM SOMEONE WANTS TO BORROW THE ALBUM - GET BORROWER'S NAME
280 PRINT "ENTER NAME OF BORROWER"
290 INPUT F$
300 LET B$(J) = F$
310 GO TO 120
400 REM
410 REM PRINT STATUS OF ALBUMS
420 PRINT "CURRENT STATUS OF ALBUMS"
430 PRINT "ALBUM NAME","BORROWER'S NAME"
440 FOR K = 1 TO N
450    PRINT A$(K),B$(K)
460 NEXT K
470 STOP
500 REM
510 REM BINARY SEARCH ROUTINE
520 REM SEARCH A$ ARRAY FOR MEMBER EQUAL TO N$
530 REM IF SEARCH IS SUCCESSFUL S$ CONTAINS YES
540 REM AND J CONTAINS THE NUMBER OF THE MEMBER OF A$ EQUAL TO N$
550 LET L = 1
560 LET H = N
570 LET J = INT ((L + H) / 2)
580    IF A$(J) = N$ THEN 710
590    IF A$(J) > N$ THEN 630
600 REM A$(J) TO LOW, SEARCH HIGHER IN A$ ARRAY
610    LET L = J + 1
620    GO TO 660
630 REM A$(J) TO HIGH, SEARCH LOWER IN A$ ARRAY
640      LET H = J - 1
650 REM IF L AND H CROSS THE SEARCH WAS UNSUCCESSFUL
660    IF L > H THEN 680
```

Fig. 6.16. Album-lending program—binary search.

```
670 GO TO 570
680 REM SEARCH WAS UNSUCCESSFUL. SET S$ AND RETURN
690 LET S$ = "NO"
700 GO TO 730
710 REM SEARCH WAS SUCCESSFUL. SET S$ AND RETURN
720 LET S$ = "YES"
730 RETURN
800 REM THE NUMBER OF ALBUMS FOLLOWS
810 DATA 13
820 REM THE NAME OF THE ALBUM AND NAME OF THE BORROWER FOLLOW
830 DATA "CANDY-O","BECKY"
840 REM THE FOLLOWING ALBUM WAS A GIFT FROM AUNT MARY
850 DATA "DANCE-LOMBARDO","FREE"
860 DATA "GREASE","DEBBIE"
870 DATA "HOUSE OF THE HOLY", "ANDREA"
880 DATA "PHYSICAL GRAFFITI","BENJI"
890 DATA "RUMORS","FREE"
900 DATA "RUST NEVER SLEEPS","JEFFREY"
910 REM THE FOLLOWING ALBUM BELONGS TO YOUR KID SISTER
920 DATA "SESAME ST STORIES", "KID SISTER"
930 DATA "SO FAR","SUSI"
940 DATA "SOME GIRLS","CAROLE"
950 DATA "STEAL YOUR FACE","MARGARET"
960 DATA "STRANGER IN TOWN","LISA"
970 DATA "STREET LEGAL","FREE"
980 END
```

Fig. 6.16 (cont'd.). Album-lending program—binary search.

from one session to the next. This indeed can be done by using files. We will learn about files in the next chapter.

Exercises

6.13 The program in Fig. 6.9 has one major shortcoming. A user who enters a number less than 1 or greater than 12 will get a SUBSCRIPT OUT OF BOUNDS error. Modify the program to verify that the number entered is between 1 and 12. If it is not between 1 and 12, print it and a message like 14 IS NOT A VALID MONTH NUMBER and branch back to the INPUT statement to accept another value.

6.14 The program in Fig. 6.12 uses K as the subscript for reading data and J as the subscript for searching the array. Could the same subscript, say K, be used for both functions?

6.15 The album names used in the program in Fig. 6.12 are in alphabetical order. Would the sequential search work properly if the album names were not in alphabetical order?

6.16 Since the album names used in Fig. 6.12 are in alphabetical order, we can improve the sequential search a little. If during the search we arrive at a member of A\$ that is greater than N\$, the search has ended unsuccessfully since N\$ cannot be any further back in the A\$ array. Modify the program to include this improvement.

6.17 Trace the binary search algorithm, showing the values taken by L, H, and J, using Marple and King as the search names.

6.18 In our unsuccessful binary search for Thatcher the last comparison we made was against the tenth member of N\$, Stout. Explain exactly what would have happened if the tenth member of N\$ were Victor instead of Stout.

TWO-DIMENSIONAL ARRAYS

Many problems require arrays that have two subscripts. For example, a bowling team might want to keep track of the scores of each of its members for each game that they bowl. If we let S be the array of scores, then S(3,2) could be the score of player number 3 for game number 2. Arrays that have two subscripts are called **two-dimensional arrays** to distinguish them from arrays that have only one subscript and are therefore called one-dimensional arrays.

Like one-dimensional arrays, two-dimensional arrays must be declared in a DIM statement. If our bowling team had four members, and we wanted to keep track of the scores for a five-game tournament, S would be declared in the following DIM statement.

DIM S(4,5)

Notice the comma that is required between 4 and 5.

The members of S are arranged as shown in Fig. 6.17(a). The first subscript gives the row number, and the second subscript gives the column number. In this example the rows correspond to the players, and the columns correspond to the games. Row 1 contains the scores for player 1; row 2 contains the scores for player 2, and so on. Column 1 contains the scores for game 1; column 2 contains the scores for game 2, and so on. The S array is shown with the players' scores in Fig. 6.17(b). What score did player 3 get in game 2? What score did player 2 get in game 3? The answers are given at the end of the chapter.

Just as FOR-NEXT loops are the natural way to process one-dimensional arrays, so nested FOR-NEXT loops are the natural way to process two-dimensional arrays. Suppose the players' scores were given by the following DATA statements:

DATA 186, 174, 163, 191, 206

DATA 158, 193, 168, 177, 181

	Game 1 Column 1	Game 2 Column 2	Game 3 Column 3	Game 4 Column 4	Game 5 Column 5
Player 1, Row 1 ⟶	1, 1	1, 2	1, 3	1, 4	1, 5
Player 2, Row 2 ⟶	2, 1	2, 2	2, 3	2, 4	2, 5
Player 3, Row 3 ⟶	3, 1	3, 2	3, 3	3, 4	3, 5
Player 4, Row 4 ⟶	4, 1	4, 2	4, 3	4, 4	4, 5

(a) Members of the S array

	Game 1	Game 2	Game 3	Game 4	Game 5
Player 1 ⟶	186	174	163	191	206
Player 2 ⟶	158	193	168	177	181
Player 3 ⟶	202	226	214	258	197
Player 4 ⟶	136	141	157	132	154

(b) The S array showing the players' scores

Fig. 6.17. (a) The members of the S array. (b) The S array showing the players' scores.

DATA 202, 226, 214, 258, 197

DATA 136, 141, 157, 132, 154

The data can be entered into the S array using the following nested FOR-NEXT loops:

FOR J = 1 TO 4

FOR K = 1 TO 5

READ S(J,K)

NEXT K

NEXT J

To understand how these nested FOR-NEXT loops work consider the READ statement

READ S(J,K)

Recall that the S array has been set up with rows corresponding to players and columns corresponding to games. Therefore the first subscript, J, corresponds to the players, and the second subscript, K, corresponds to the games.

The outer FOR-NEXT loop sets J equal to 1, and the inner loop sets K equal to 1 through 5. The READ statement is executed five times as follows:

READ S(1,1), which corresponds to player 1, game 1

READ S(1,2), which corresponds to player 1, game 2

READ S(1,3), which corresponds to player 1, game 3

READ S(1,4), which corresponds to player 1, game 4

READ S(1,5), which corresponds to player 1, game 5

This is the order in which the scores are given in the first DATA statement.

Then J is set equal to 2 by the outer loop, and as the inner loop sets K equal to 1 through 5, we read the five scores for player 2. This is the order in which the scores are given in the second DATA statement. The outer loop then sets J equal to 3, and we read the five scores for player 3 from the third DATA statement. Finally the outer loop sets J equal to 4, and we read the five scores for player 4 from the fourth DATA statement.

The Bowling Tournament Problem

To illustrate the use of two-dimensional arrays, I will develop a program to calculate the average score of each player and the average score of each game. As in the BASIC statements used to read the data, J will be the player subscript, and K will be the game subscript.

The variable names we will use are:

Input variable

Score array   S

Internal variables

Accumulator   S1

Player subscript   J

Game subscript   K

Output variable

Average   A

The algorithm is

1. Read the scores into the S array.

2. Calculate and print the average for each player.

3. Calculate and print the average for each game.

As usual we will fill in the details when we draw the flowchart.

Flowchart

The flowchart that carries out the algorithm is shown in Fig. 6.18. The flowchart consists of three independent nested FOR-NEXT loops. The first nested loop reads the data into S, using the technique I have already explained. The second nested loop has the same structure as the first. I have added a statement that initializes the accumulator, S1. Inside this inner loop the S array is accumulated, one row at a time, instead of being read, one row at a time, as it is in the first inner loop. When we drop through the inner loop, we calculate and print the average for a player. It would not be difficult to incorporate the calculation of the players' averages into the first loop and eliminate this second nested loop altogether. Eliminating the second loop would make our program a little shorter, but also a little more complicated and harder to understand. I prefer to keep it longer and easier to understand.

The third set of nested loops is entirely different. To calculate the average score for each game, we must process the S array column by column. To do this we interchange the J and K loops, making the K loop the outer loop and the J loop the inner loop. The first time we execute this section, the outer loop will set K equal to 1. Then the inner loop will set J to 1 through 4. In the accumulation step, therefore, we will add first S(1,1) then S(2,1), then S(3,1), and finally S(4,1). These are the four scores for game 1, so when we divide by 4 we will have the average for game 1. When K = 2, we will calculate the average for game 2, and so on.

The BASIC program shown in Fig. 6.19 follows directly from the flowchart. You should have no trouble understanding it.

Exercises

6.19 In the program in Fig. 6.19 interchange lines 220 and 230. What value would be printed for the average score for the first player? What value would be printed for the average score for the second player?

6.20 Suppose in the bowling team problem the data were given by game rather than by player. In that case the DATA statements would be

DATA 186, 158, 202, 136

DATA 174, 193, 226, 141

DATA 163, 168, 214, 157

DATA 191, 177, 258, 132

DATA 206, 181, 197, 154

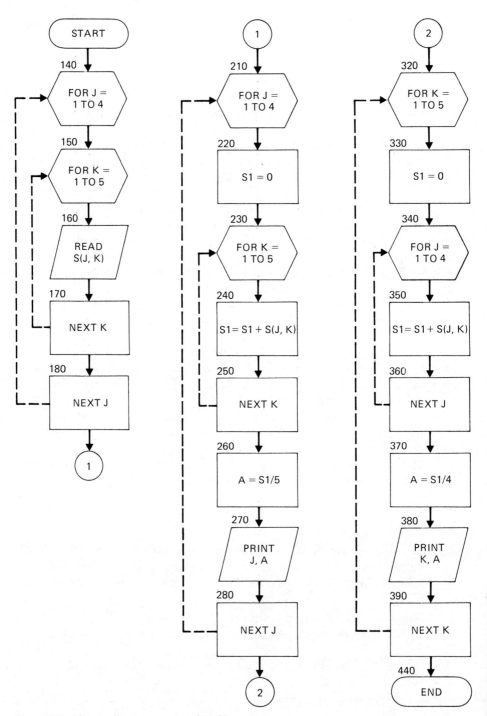

Fig. 6.18. Flowchart for average bowling scores.

```
100 REM AVERAGE BOWLING TEAM SCORES
110 REM PROGRAMMER M. TROMBETTA
120 DIM S(4,5)
130 REM READ SCORES INTO S ARRAY
140 FOR J = 1 TO 4
150   FOR K = 1 TO 5
160     READ S(J,K)
170   NEXT K
180 NEXT J
190 REM
200 REM CALCULATE AVERAGE SCORE FOR EACH PLAYER
210 FOR J = 1 TO 4
220   LET S1 = 0
230   FOR K = 1 TO 5
240     LET S1 = S1 + S(J,K)
250   NEXT K
260   LET A = S1 / 5
270   PRINT "AVERAGE SCORE FOR PLAYER ";J;"IS ";A
280 NEXT J
290 REM
300 PRINT
310 REM CALCULATE AVERAGE SCORE FOR EACH GAME
320 FOR K = 1 TO 5
330   LET S1 = 0
340   FOR J = 1 TO 4
350     LET S1 = S1 + S(J,K)
360   NEXT J
370   LET A = S1 / 4
380   PRINT "AVERAGE SCORE FOR GAME ";K;"IS ";A
390 NEXT K
400 DATA 186,174,163,191,206
410 DATA 158,193,168,177,181
420 DATA 202,226,214,258,197
430 DATA 136,141,157,132,154
440 END


RUN

FIG6#17     11:45   07/14/80

AVERAGE SCORE FOR PLAYER  1     IS   184
AVERAGE SCORE FOR PLAYER  2     IS   175.4
AVERAGE SCORE FOR PLAYER  3     IS   219.4
AVERAGE SCORE FOR PLAYER  4     IS   144

AVERAGE SCORE FOR GAME  1     IS   170.5
AVERAGE SCORE FOR GAME  2     IS   183.5
AVERAGE SCORE FOR GAME  3     IS   175.5
AVERAGE SCORE FOR GAME  4     IS   189.5
AVERAGE SCORE FOR GAME  5     IS   184.5

TIME 0.0 SECS.
```

Fig. 16.19. Program to calculate average bowling scores.

Modify the program in Fig. 6.19 to accept the data in this form.

6.21 A group of investors is planning to build a ski resort. They have three possible sites under study. Naturally they are interested in the snowfall at these sites. They have collected snowfall data for the three sites for each of the last five years. The data are

		Year Number			
Site Number	1	2	3	4	5
1	106	147	139	153	126
2	143	151	117	134	139
3	136	143	130	142	145

Write a program that will calculate and print the average snowfall over the past five years for each site. Also calculate and print the grand average snowfall for all three sites. Finally, sort and print the average snowfall for the three sites in descending order.

SUMMARY

In this chapter you have learned

- How to use the DIM statement to define one- and two-dimensional arrays
- How to use FOR-NEXT loops to process one- and two-dimensional arrays.
- How to sort an array
- How to search an array by using a sequential search or a binary search
- How to use a flag
- Answers to problems in this chapter

1. The value assigned to P(9) is 12.

2. The value assigned to Y is 6.

3. In game 2 player 3 bowled 226.

4. In game 3 player 2 bowled 168.

files

OBJECTIVES

In this chapter you will learn
- How to create and list a sequential file
- How to process a transaction file against a master file
- The rules for the BASIC statements

    1. OPEN

    2. PRINT

    3. INPUT

    4. CLOSE

    5. SCRATCH (or RESTORE)

How to use the END condition

In addition you should learn the meanings of the following terms:

End-of-file mark	Field
Key	File, sequential and direct
Master file	Record
Transaction file	

      Up to now we have not been able to have the computer "remember" the results of a program from one session to another. The discussion of the album-lending problem, for example, showed that it was necessary to retype all the DATA statements at the start of each session, to reflect the current status of the albums. Retyping all the DATA statements at the start of each session, however, is so much work that it greatly reduces the usefulness of the program. It is particularly annoying because the computer "knew" the status of all the albums at the end of the previous session, and in fact it even printed the status. What we need is some way to have the computer remember the status from one session to another. The way to do that is by using files.

FILES

Let's start with some definitions. A **field** is an item of data. A name, for example, is a field. Similarly, a social security number, a selling price, and a rate of pay are all examples of fields. A **record** is a group of related fields that refer to one item. In a payroll system, for example, a record might consist of the employee's name, the social security number, and the rate of pay, each of which is a field. There is one record for each employee. In the album-lending problem a record consists of two fields—the album name and the borrower's name. Again there is one record for each album.

One of the fields in a record is singled out to be the identifying field. That field is called the **key** field. When we want to refer to a particular record, we specify the key. No two records should have the same key, so that, when we specify the key, there is no confusion over which record we are talking about. In a payroll system the social security number is a logical choice for the key field because no two employees have the same social security number. The employee's name field would not be a good choice for the key field because we might have two employees with the same name. In that case, if we told either a computer or another human being we wanted to see the record for employee John Smith, it would not be clear which record we wanted. In the records for the album-lending problem the album name is the key field. (We hope that no two albums will have the same name.)

Now that you know what a record is the definition of a **file** is easy. A file is a collection of related records. In a payroll system the collection of all the employee records is called the payroll file. In the album-lending problem the collection of all the records is called the album file.

The files we will be concerned with have one additional characteristic: they are stored in a form that is easy for the computer to read. For example, the listing produced by the album-lending program, showing all the albums and the names of their borrowers, is a file. (It is a file because it satisfies our definition of a file as a collection of related records.) But the only way we can get the data from that file back into the computer is to retype it. That is not the kind of file we will discuss in this chapter.

For a file to be in a form that is easy for the computer to read, it must be stored on a secondary storage device, either magnetic tape or magnetic disk. In fact, when you saved your programs, the computer stored them on tape or disk. In those cases you created program files. In this chapter you will learn how to create and use data files.

There are two different types of data files: **sequential files** and **direct files**. In a sequential file the records are stored by key in sequential order. Furthermore sequential files are created and processed sequentially. This means that when processing a sequential file it is necessary to read the first record, then the second record, then the third, and so on until the last record is read. Direct files, in contrast, permit records to be read in any order. Direct files are very useful, but they are rather complicated, and only the more powerful versions of BASIC permit them. In this book we will discuss sequential files only.

To keep the examples in this book to a reasonable length, the files will contain only a few records. You should realize, however, that a file may contain hundreds or even thousands of records. The ability of a computer to process files with enormous numbers of records is one of the reasons computers are so useful.

ELEMENTARY FILE PROCESSING

Unfortunately file processing is one of the least standard areas of BASIC. In this chapter I will show you the file statements used by Dartmouth BASIC, Edition 7. I chose to demonstrate Dartmouth BASIC because its file statements are similar to those in the proposed standard BASIC. During the next several years many versions of BASIC will be modified so that their file statements will be more like those in standard BASIC. Your instructor will tell you the file statements used in your version of BASIC, and you should write them on the inside front cover of this book. Fortunately the fundamental principles of file processing apply to all versions of BASIC.

Creating a Sequential File

Let's imagine that we want to create a charge account file for a department store. In a real application the records in such a file would contain a lot of data: the charge account number, the customer's name and address, the amount of money the customer owes, and perhaps additional data. If we included all this data in our sample problem, however, the fundamental principles might get lost in the details. So to simplify the problem, assume that the file we want to create contains just the charge account number, which will be the key, and the amount of money the customer owes. Let's let K (for key) stand for the charge account number and B stand for the amount of money the customer owes. (B can also be called the balance due on the account.)

The OPEN, PRINT, and CLOSE Statements

A program that creates the charge account file is shown in Fig. 7.1. The program simply reads the data and writes it to the file. The records that are to be used to create the file are given in the DATA statements. Notice

```
10 REM CREATING THE CHARGE ACCOUNT FILE
20 OPEN #1: "CHARGE"
30 READ K,B
40   IF K = 0 THEN 70
50     PRINT #1: K,B
60 GO TO 30
70 CLOSE #1
80 PRINT "THE CHARGE ACCOUNT FILE HAS BEEN CREATED"
90 DATA 146, 45.46
100 DATA 175, 33.07
110 DATA 212, 9.22
120 DATA 334, 108.42
130 DATA 348, 26.17
140 DATA 397, 56.84
150 REM TRAILER DATA FOLLOWS
160 DATA 0,0
170 END


RUN

FIG7#1      11:56      01/03/80

THE CHARGE ACCOUNT FILE HAS BEEN CREATED

TIME 0.0 SECS.
```

Fig. 7.1. Program to create the charge account file.

that the records are arranged by key in ascending order. Remember that in a sequential file the records are stored by key in sequential order.

The program in Fig. 7.1 contains several new BASIC statements. An OPEN statement is shown in line 20. An OPEN statement associates a file number with a file name. In line 20 the file number is 1 and the file name is CHARGE. The name CHARGE is associated with the file when it is stored on tape or disk. Later, when we want to use this file, we simply specify the name CHARGE.

An OPEN statement must be executed for a file before data may be read from or written to the file. The file name is used only in the OPEN statement, in all other statements that refer to that file the file number is used. The format of the OPEN statement is

OPEN #file number: "file name"

Notice that a number sign precedes the file number, a colon separates the file number and file name, and the file name is enclosed in quotation marks. The program in Fig. 7.1 uses only one file, but in programs that use more than one file every file must have a separate OPEN statement. Furthermore each file must have a different file number.

The format of the OPEN statement varies from one version of BASIC to another, and many BASICs do not use any OPEN statement at all. In those versions the first statement that reads or writes to a file automatically opens it. Your instructor will tell you the format of the OPEN statement used in your version of BASIC, and you should write it on the inside front cover of this book.

Different versions of BASIC have different rules for legal file numbers and file names. File numbers 1–4, however, and file names consisting of up to six letters are legal in most versions of BASIC.

The PRINT statement in line 50 actually puts the data in the file. The format of the file PRINT statement is

PRINT #file number: variable, variable, variable

Notice again the use of the number sign and the colon. As with the ordinary PRINT statement you may list as many variables as you like. Again your instructor will tell you the format of the statement used by your BASIC to write data to a file, and you should write it on the inside front cover of this book.

The purpose of the CLOSE statement in line 70 is to tell the computer we are finished with the file. In programs that use more than one file each file requires its own CLOSE statement. The format of the CLOSE statement is

CLOSE #file number

As was the case with the OPEN statement, the format of the CLOSE statement is different in different versions of BASIC, and some BASICs do not use a CLOSE statement at all. Your instructor will tell you the format of the CLOSE statement used in your BASIC, and you should write it in the inside front cover of this book.

A program like the one in Fig. 7.1, which reads data from DATA statements and creates a file, does not produce any output that can be seen. To indicate that the program executed properly and that the file was created properly, I included the PRINT statement in line 80.

Reading a Sequential File

The CHARGE file that was created by the program in Fig. 7.1 may be read by another program. A program that reads and prints the data from the CHARGE file is shown in Fig. 7.2. The output in Fig. 7.2 shows that the data written on the file by the program in Fig. 7.1 were read and printed.

The INPUT Statement and END Condition

Now let's look at the BASIC statement used to read a file. The OPEN and CLOSE statements in the program in Fig. 7.2 are used exactly as they were in the program in Fig. 7.1. I used 2 as the file number in this program instead of 1, which was used in Fig. 7.1, to emphasize that, when you read a file, you do not have to use the same file number that was used when the file was created.

The INPUT statement in line 40 is used to read the data from the file. The format of the INPUT statement is

INPUT #file number: variable, variable, variable

In its use of the number sign and the colon the INPUT statement is similar to the PRINT statement. As in the ordinary INPUT statement, you may list as many variables as you like. Your instructor will tell you the format of the statement used by your BASIC to read a file, and you should write it on the inside front cover of this book.

The IF statement in line 30 is used to determine the time when we have read all the data in the file. When a file is created, the computer system writes a special symbol called the **end-of-file mark** after the last record in the file. The IF statement in line 30 is used to determine whether the next INPUT statement will encounter the end-of-file mark. If the next INPUT statement will encounter the end-of-file mark, the END #2 condition is set to true; otherwise it is set to false.

```
10 REM READING THE CHARGE ACCOUNT FILE
20 OPEN #2: "CHARGE"
30 IF END #2 THEN 70
40    INPUT #2: K,B
50    PRINT K,B
60 GO TO 30
70 CLOSE #2
80 END


RUN

FIG7#2      17:44      01/05/80

   146         45.46
   175         33.07
   212          9.22
   334        108.42
   348         26.17
   397         56.84

TIME 0.0 SECS
```

Fig. 7.2. Program to read the charge account file.

As long as more data remain in the file, we will fall through the IF statement and continue the loop. Eventually all the data in the file will have been read, and we will reach the end-of-file mark. When that happens, the system sets the END #2 condition to true. The IF statement then causes a branch to the CLOSE statement in line 70.

A useful way to think about this is that the end-of-file mark serves as automatic trailer data. The IF statement is a way to determine whether we are about to read this automatic trailer data. If the ordinary READ and DATA statements had this feature, we would never have had to include a DATA statement with trailer data in our earlier programs. We must keep in mind that, when we use trailer data, we test after the READ statement to see whether we have just read the trailer data, but when we use the END condition, we test before the INPUT statement to see whether we are about to read the end-of-file mark.

Unfortunately not all BASICs support the END condition. In BASICs that do not have the END condition it is necessary to put trailer data in the file to signal the end of the file. Your instructor will tell you how your BASIC signals the end of the file, and you should write it on the inside front cover of this book.

Using a File for the Album-lending Program

Now that you understand how to read from and write to a file, let's see how a file could be used with the album-lending program. You would first have to write a program to create the file. The first record on the file should contain a single number, the number of albums you own. The remaining records consist of pairs of strings, the first giving the album's name and the second giving the borrower's name.

The program to create the file would read values from DATA statements and write these values on the file. The program would be so similar to the program in Fig. 7.1 that you can write it as as programming exercise.

Once the file has been created, we have to write a program that will use it. Such a program is shown in Fig. 7.3. The program in Fig.

```
10 REM ALBUM-LENDING PROGRAM
20 REM PROGRAMMER. M. TROMBETTA
30 REM FOR MORE THAN 100 ALBUMS, CHANGE THE DIM STATEMENT
40 DIM A$(100),B$(100)
50 REM
60 REM READ NO OF ALBUMS AND FILL A$ AND B$ ARRAYS FROM ALBUM FILE
65 OPEN #1: "ALBUM"
```

Fig. 7.3. The album-lending program with files.

```
70  INPUT #1: N
80  FOR K = 1 TO N
90     INPUT #1: A$(K), B$(K)
100 NEXT K
105 CLOSE #1
110 REM
120 PRINT "ENTER ALBUM NAME AND B FOR BORROWED OR R FOR RETURNED"
130 PRINT "ENTER END FOR ALBUM NAME TO STOP"
140 INPUT N$,C$
150 IF N$ = "END" THEN 400
160 REM SEARCH FOR MEMBER OF A$ EQUAL TO N$
170 GO SUB 500
180 REM CHECK IF SEARCH WAS SUCCESSFUL
190 IF S$ = "YES" THEN 220
200 PRINT "YOU MUST HAVE MISSPELLED "; N$
210 GO TO 120
220 REM CHECK IF ALBUM IS BEING BORROWED
230 IF C$ = "B" THEN 270
240 REM ALBUM IS BEING RETURNED
250 LET B$(J) = "FREE"
260 GO TO 120
270 REM SOMEONE WANTS TO BORROW THE ALBUM - GET BORROWER'S NAME
280 PRINT "ENTER NAME OF BORROWER"
290 INPUT F$
300 LET B$(J) = F$
310 GO TO 120
400 REM
410 REM PRINT STATUS OF ALBUMS
420 PRINT "CURRENT STATUS OF ALBUMS"
430 PRINT "ALBUM NAME","BORROWER'S NAME"
440 FOR K = 1 TO N
450    PRINT A$(K),B$(K)
460 NEXT K
462 REM WRITE THE CURRENT STATUS BACK TO THE ALBUM FILE
463 OPEN #1: "ALBUM"
464 SCRATCH #1
465 PRINT #1: N
466 FOR K = 1 TO N
467    PRINT #1: A$(K), B$(K)
468 NEXT K
469 CLOSE #1
470 STOP
500 REM
510 REM SEQUENTIAL SEARCH ROUTINE
520 REM SEARCH A$ ARRAY FOR MEMBER EQUAL TO N$
530 REM IF SEARCH IS SUCCESSFUL S$ CONTAINS YES
540 REM AND J CONTAINS THE NUMBER OF THE MEMBER OF A$ EQUAL TO N$
550 FOR J = 1 TO N
560    IF A$(J) = N$ THEN 640
570 NEXT J
580 REM
590 REM IF WE DROP THROUGH FOR-NEXT LOOP SEARCH WAS UNSUCCESSFUL
600 REM SET SWITCH AND RETURN
610 LET S$ = "NO"
620 GO TO 660
630 REM
640 REM SEARCH WAS SUCCESSFUL - SET SWITCH AND RETURN
650 LET S$ = "YES"
660 RETURN
999 END
```

Fig. 7.3 (cont'd.). The album-lending program with files.

7.3 is very similar to the original album-lending program in Fig. 6.10. The differences are (1) that initially the values of N and the A$ and B$ arrays are obtained from the ALBUM file, rather than from DATA statements and (2) that after the updated status of the albums is printed, it is also written back to the ALBUM file. Let's see how these differences show up in the program.

In Fig. 7.3 line 65, where the ALBUM file is opened, did not have a corresponding line in the original program. Lines 70 and 90 have been changed from READ statements in the original program to INPUT #1: statements here. Line 105, where the ALBUM file is closed after all the data have been read from it, also had no corresponding line in the original program. These are the only changes required to obtain the values of N, A$, and B$ from the ALBUM file rather than from DATA statements. Notice also that the DATA statements that occupied lines 700–870 have been eliminated.[1]

The new statements required to write the updated status of the albums back to the ALBUM file are shown in lines 462–469. First we open the file, and then we "scratch" it. The purpose of the SCRATCH statement is to erase the old data from the ALBUM file. Some versions of BASIC use the RESTORE statement instead of the SCRATCH statement, and still other versions use neither. In these versions of BASIC the very act of writing new data to a file automatically erases the old data.

If you were using a personal computer like the TRS-80 with a cassette recorder you would use a STOP statement instead of using the SCRATCH or RESTORE statements to interrupt execution of the program. You would physically rewind the tape, set the recorder to record mode, and resume execution by typing the CONT command.

The remaining statements required to write the updated status of the albums back to the ALBUM file are similar to the statements used to read the data from the file. We just replace the INPUT statement, which is used to read the file, by the PRINT statement, which is used to write to the file.

When we discussed the album-lending program in Chapter 6, we said that A$ and B$ were master data. You remember that master data show the current status of a business or activity. When such data are stored on a file, we call the file a **master file.** Similarly in Chapter 6 we called N$ and C$ transaction data. You recall that transaction data are any data that cause a change to master data. When such data are stored on a file, we call that file a **transaction file.** This is the first

---

1. The END condition was not used in this problem because we know that N is the number of records the file contains. We set up a FOR-NEXT loop to read exactly N records, so we do not have to test for the end of file.

program we have seen that uses a transaction file to update a master file. Updating master files is an important data-processing application for business, and we will see other examples later in this chapter.

Exercises

7.1 The Mighty Good Ice Cream Company wants to use a computer to keep track of its inventory. You have been asked to create the master inventory file. There will be one record for each of the 31 flavors available. The record will contain the name of the flavor, which is the key, and the number of gallons on hand. Write a program to create this file. Make up your own data.

7.2 Write a program to read and print the ice cream inventory file created in Exercise 7.1.

7.3 Write a program to create the ALBUM file. You can use the data given in Fig. 6.10 or make up your own data.

ADVANCED FILE PROCESSING

The program shown in Fig. 7.3 is unusual in one very important respect: the album file is so small that the whole file may be read into the computer's primary storage. Typically files contain hundreds or even thousands of records, and the whole file cannot be read into the computer's primary storage at one time. In these cases a record is read into storage; it is processed, and then the next record is read.

We could imagine a program in which we would read through the charge account file and print those records that have a balance greater than 1000 dollars. The logic of such a program is exactly the same whether the data are stored on a file or given in DATA statements. Since that kind of program does not involve any new concepts, I will not demonstrate such a program. Instead let's look at some programs that involve concepts we have not met before.

The logic of sequential file processing can get rather complicated. To help you to understand the logic of sequential file processing, we will study a series of problems of increasing difficulty. In all of these problems we will be working with the charge account file that was created in Fig. 7.1. The charge account file will be our master file.

Listing Selected Records

Let's write a program to solve the following problem. We want to list selected records from the master file. The keys—that is, the charge account numbers of the records we want to list—have been stored on a file, the transaction file. The records in the transaction file contain only one field, and that is the key of a record in the master file that we want to list. The transaction file could be created by a program similar to the one shown in Fig. 7.1, which created the master file.

It is not necessary that the keys of the records we want to list be contained in a file. It is possible to enter the transaction data using an INPUT statement or READ-DATA statements. No matter how the keys of the records we want to list are entered, the basic logic of the program remains the same. I have mentioned several times that the records in the master file must be by key in sequential order. It is also necessary that the records in the transaction file be by key in sequential order.

To explain exactly what we want the program to do, let's imagine that the first few master records and transaction records have the keys shown in Fig. 7.4.

File	Keys			
Master	146	175	212	334
Transaction	146	152	175	334

Fig. 7.4. Keys of initial master and transaction records.

Comparing the keys of the two files, we see that master records 146, 175, and 334 have matching transaction records, and therefore are to be listed. (Incidentally, although we speak of master records 146, 175, and 334, for complete accuracy we should say master records with keys 146, 175, and 334, but our meaning should be clear, and we will generally use the simpler expression.) Master record 212 has no matching transaction record and therefore is not to be listed. Finally, consider transaction record 152. According to the statement of the problem we are supposed to list master record 152, but no such master record exists! Clearly an error has been made, and it is most likely that transaction record 152 represents a typing error. We would like to know about such errors so that they can be corrected, so we will list transaction records that do not match any master record with the message, ERROR-NO MATCHING MASTER RECORD.

We will use the following variable names:

Input variables

Master record key	K1
Master record balance	B1
Transaction record key	K2

Internal variable

Flag to indicate end of file   F$

Output variables

Master record key   K1

Master record balance   B1

The algorithm we will use is

1. Compare the keys from the master and transaction records.

   a) Master records that have matching transaction records are listed.
   b) Master records that do not have matching transaction records are not listed.
   c) Transaction records that do not have matching master records are listed with error messages.

As usual the details of the algorithm will be developed when we draw the flowchart.

The beginning of the flowchart is shown in Fig. 7.5. Since this program is reasonably complicated, I will make extensive use of subroutines. After opening the files we read a master record and a transaction record. Reading the files will be a little complicated because we have to check for the end of file condition, so I will do the reading in subroutines, the details of which will be filled in later. After the two readings the subroutine that does the listing is envoked. Notice that the listing subroutine returns to the main program only after all the processing is done, so that the only things left for the main program to do are to close the files and to stop the run.

Now let's examine the listing subroutine. We will trace the flowchart assuming the keys are as given in Fig. 7.4. The keys of the first record of both files are 146. The listing subroutine begins by comparing the keys. If they are equal, as they are in our example, we have found a master record that should be listed. So we list it and read the next master and next transaction records.

The key of the next master record is 175 and of the next transaction record is 152. When we branch back to connector 1 and compare the keys, we find they are not equal. We therefore go on to the second comparison where we find that the master key is greater than the transaction key. What does this mean? We have just read master record 175. We may deduce that there is no master record 152 because, if there were a master record 152, we would have read it before we got to master

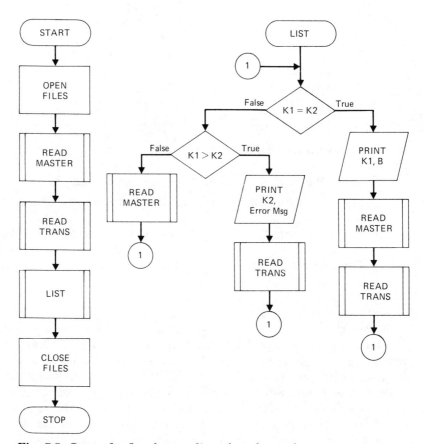

Fig. 7.5. Start of a flowchart to list selected records.

record 175. We conclude therefore that transaction record 152 has no matching master record. We are being asked to list a master record that does not exist. This transaction record is an error, so we list it with an error message. We then read the next transaction record and branch back to connector 1. We do not read the next master record since we have a perfectly good master record, number 175, and must still see whether it should be listed or not.

In our example the next transaction record is 175, so when the keys are compared, we find that they are equal, and we list master record 175. We read the next master and the next transaction record and then branch back to connector 1.

The next master is 212, and the next transaction is 334. Once again the keys are not equal, but this time when we get to the second comparison we find the master key is not greater than the transaction key.

What does this mean? Applying the same logic we used before, we know there is no transaction record 212 because, if there were, we would have read it before we read transaction record 334. We conclude that master record 212 has no matching transaction record and therefore should not be listed. We now read the next master record and branch back to connector 1. We do not read the next transaction record because we have yet to process our current transaction record, number 334. The program continues in this way until one of the files reaches its end.

End-of-File Processing—END Condition

To complete the solution to this problem, we must develop the correct end-of-file processing. Figure 7.6 shows the complete flowchart, including the READ MASTER and READ TRANS subroutines for versions of BASIC that have an END condition. Later we will show these subroutines for versions of BASIC that do not have an END condition.

As Fig. 7.6 shows, before reading a file we test END for that file to determine whether the next reading for that file will encounter the end-of-file mark. The end-of-file processing that is required depends on which file reaches its end first. Suppose the last few master records and transaction records have the keys shown in Fig. 7.7, where we have indicated the end of file by EOF.

The keys in Fig. 7.7 show that, after listing master record 786, master record 849 will be read, but the next reading of the transaction file will encounter the end-of-file mark. With these keys the transaction file reaches its end first. When we reach the end of the transaction file, the program is finished, and all that remains is to close the files and stop the program. Therefore when the end of the transaction file is detected, we set the flag F$ to YES as shown in the flowchart in Fig. 7.6. Also shown in Fig. 7.6 are the modification of the main program to include initializing F$ to NO and the modification of the LIST subroutine to include a test of F$ after the return from READ TRANS. If F$ is equal to YES, we branch to the RETURN statement to cause a return to the main program. If F$ is not equal to YES, we branch to connector 1 to continue processing.

Next consider the situation where the last few master and transaction records have the keys shown in Fig. 7.8.

These keys show that, after listing master record 877, the next reading of the master file will encounter the end-of-file mark. In this case the master file reaches its end first. The remaining transaction records, 896, 941, and 982, have no matching master records and should be listed with an error message.

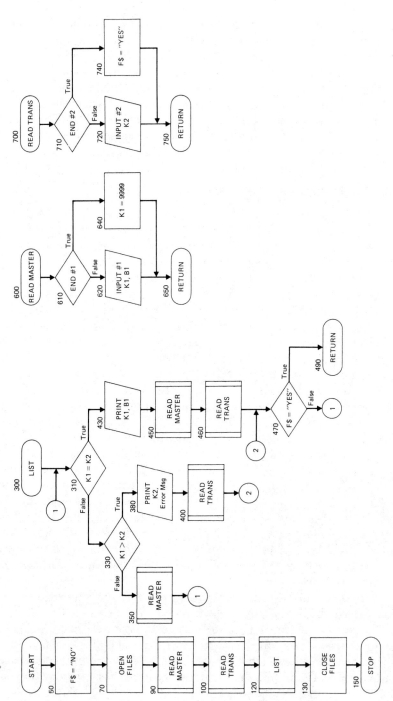

Fig. 7.6. Flowchart to list selected records.

The simplest way to have these remaining transaction records listed with an error message is to set the master key equal to the highest possible value. For example, if all the charge account numbers are three digits, we could set the master key equal to 9999, as shown in Fig. 7.6. By setting K1 equal to 9999 we ensure that, when the keys are compared, K1 will be greater than K2 so that the transaction record will be listed with an error message, and the next transaction record will be read. In this way all the transaction records remaining after the master file reaches its end will be listed with an error message.

A program based on the flowchart in Fig. 7.6 is shown in Fig. 7.9. The program follows the flowchart quite closely, and I think you will not have any trouble understanding it.

File	Keys			
Master	786	849	877	EOF
Transaction	786	EOF		

Fig. 7.7. Keys of final master and transaction records.

File	Keys				
Master	877	EOF			
Transaction	877	896	941	982	EOF

Fig. 7.8. Keys of final master and transaction records.

End-of-File Processing—No END Condition

The flowchart in Fig. 7.6 and the program in Fig. 7.9 cannot be used for those versions of BASIC that do not have END conditions. For those versions of BASIC we must modify the READ MASTER and READ TRANS subroutines as shown in Fig. 7.10.

For BASICs that do not have END conditions we simply add a trailer record to the master and transaction files. The key of this trailer record is 9999, the highest possible key. As Fig. 7.10 shows, under these circumstances the READ MASTER subroutine becomes very simple: we just

```
10 REM LISTING SELECTED RECORDS
20 REM   PROGRAMMER. M TROMBETTA
30 REM
40 REM INITIALIZE END-OF-JOB FLAG
50 LET F$ = "NO"
60 REM OPEN FILES AND READ FIRST MASTER AND TRANSACTION RECORD
70 OPEN #1: "MASTER"
80 OPEN #2: "TRANS"
90 GOSUB 600
100 GOSUB 700
110 REM EXECUTE LISTING SUBROUTINE
120 GOSUB 300
130 CLOSE #1
140 CLOSE #2
150 STOP
160 REM
300 REM LISTING SUBROUTINE
310 IF K1 = K2 THEN 420
320 REM KEYS ARE UNEQUAL, DETERMINE WHICH IS GREATER
330 IF K1 > K2 THEN 370
340 REM MASTER IS LOWER, READ NEXT MASTER
350 GOSUB 600
360 GO TO 300
370 REM MASTER IS GREATER, WRITE ERROR MESSAGE
380 PRINT "TRANSACTION ";K2; " HAS NO MATCHING MASTER"
390 REM READ NEXT TRANS AND TEST END-OF-JOB FLAG
400 GOSUB 700
410 GO TO 470
420 REM KEYS ARE EQUAL, LIST MASTER
430 PRINT "MASTER RECORD ";K1; " HAS BALANCE ";B1
440 REM READ NEXT MASTER AND TRANS AND TEST FOR END-OF-JOB FLAG
450 GOSUB 600
460 GOSUB 700
470 IF F$ = "YES" THEN 490
480 GO TO 300
490 RETURN
500 REM
600 REM SUBROUTINE TO READ MASTER FILE
610 IF END #1 THEN 640
620 INPUT #1: K1,B1
630 GO TO 650
640 LET K1 = 9999
650 RETURN
660 REM
700 REM SUBROUTINE TO READ TRANSACTION FILE
710 IF END #2 THEN 740
720 INPUT #2: K2
730 GO TO 750
740 LET F$ = "YES"
750 RETURN
760 END

RUN

FIG7#9      11:57   06/14/80

MASTER RECORD  146    HAS BALANCE  20
TRANSACTION  152   HAS NO MATCHING MASTER
MASTER RECORD  175    HAS BALANCE  30
MASTER RECORD  334    HAS BALANCE  50
MASTER RECORD  786    HAS BALANCE  60

TIME 0.0 SECS.
```

Fig. 7.9. A program that lists selected records.

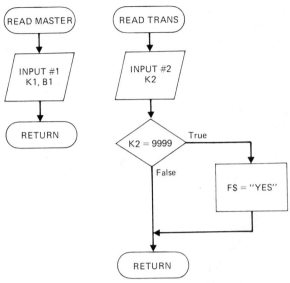

Fig. 7.10. READ MASTER and READ TRANS subroutines for BASICs that do not have an END condition.

read the master file. When we come to the end of the master file, K1 becomes 9999, and any remaining transaction records automatically are written with error messages.

In the READ TRANS subroutine we test after every reading to see whether we have just read the trailer record. If we have, we set F$ to YES, and return. No other changes are required. In particular the main program and the LIST subroutine do not have to be changed in any way.

Exercises

7.4 Suppose the keys of the master and transaction files were

File	Keys			
Master	36	82	EOF	
Transaction	47	82	96	EOF

Trace the program in Fig. 7.9 using these keys. Make a list, in order, of the line numbers that will be executed. To help you get started, here are the first few line numbers: 10, 20, 30, 40, 50, 60, 70, 80, 600, 610, 620, and so on.

7.5 Determine what would happen if the program in Fig. 7.9 were executed using the following data:

File	Keys		
Master	31	82	EOF
Transaction	36	36	EOF

Notice that by mistake two transaction records have a key equal to 36.

7.6 Examine the output shown in Fig. 7.9 to determine the contents of the transaction file. Can you also determine the contents of the master file?

7.7 Write a program to list selected records from the Mighty Good Ice Cream Company inventory file that was created in Exercise 7.1.

DELETING SELECTED RECORDS

The next problem to consider is the deletion of selected records from the master file. If some customers closed their accounts, we might want to delete their records from the master file. Once again a transaction file has been created; this time it contains the keys of the records we wish to delete.

In order to delete records from the master file we must create a new version of the master file, one that contains all the records from the original master file, except those we want to delete. This program therefore involves two master files: the original master file, which we call the old master file, which is used as an input file, and the new master file, which contains the records from the old master file that were not deleted, which is used as an output file.

Once again, any transaction records that do not have a matching master record are to be listed with error messages. Finally, the records that are deleted will be listed with an appropriate message, so that we will have a permanent record of the changes made to the master file.

We will use the following variable names:

Input variables

Old master record key	K1
Old master record balance	B1
Transaction record key	K2

Internal variable

Flag to indicate end of file	F$

Output variables

New master record key   K3

New master record   B3
balance

The algorithm we will use is

1. Compare the keys from the old master and transaction records.

   a) Old master records that have matching transaction records are listed with delete messages.

   b) Old master records that do not have matching transaction records are written to the new master file.

   c) Transaction records that do not have matching old master records are listed with error messages.

As usual the details of the algorithm will be developed when we draw the flowchart.

The flowchart is shown in Fig. 7.11. The structure of the flowchart is similar to the structure of the flowchart in Fig. 7.6. The flowchart consists of a main program and subroutines to do the deleting and to read the old master and transaction files. The main program is almost identical to the main program in Fig. 7.6, so we do not have to discuss it any further.

Let's examine the delete subroutine closely. If the keys are compared and found to be equal, it means the current old master record should be deleted. The current old master record is deleted from the old master file simply by not writing it on the new master file. Instead we list that old master record together with a delete message. We then read the next old master and transaction records and branch back to connector 1 to continue processing. (The test of F$ is related to end-of-file processing, which we will discuss later.)

If the keys are not equal, we determine which is larger. The logic is as before: if the transaction key is less than the old master key, we may conclude that this transaction record has no matching old master record. We are being asked to delete an old master record that does not exist. We conclude this transaction record is an error, so we list it with an error message. We then read the next transaction record and branch back to connector 1.

If the old master key is less than the transaction key, we conclude that this old master record has no matching transaction record. This means that this old master record is not to be deleted. So we create a

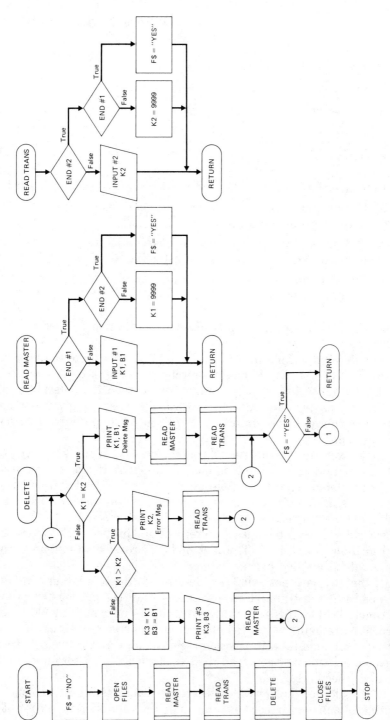

Fig. 7.11. Flowchart to delete selected records.

246

new master record from the old master record and write the new master record on the new master file. We then read the next old master record and branch back to connector 1.

End-of-File Processing—END Condition

Finally let's consider the end-of-file processing, which is where the greatest differences from the flowchart in Fig. 7.6 occur. In both flowcharts, if the old master file reaches its end before the transaction file, it means that transaction records are remaining in the file with keys higher than the highest key in the old master file. As before we conclude that these remaining transaction records are in error, and we must continue processing the transaction file until all the remaining transaction records are listed on the error report.

On the other hand, if the transaction file reaches its end first, it means there are no more master records to be deleted. We must continue processing the old master file so that the remaining records are written on the new master file.

In other words, processing must continue until both files reach their ends. Figure 7.11 shows how this is done. When the end of the file is detected for either file, a test is made to determine whether the other file has already reached its end. If it has, the run is over, and we set F$ equal to YES. If it has not, we set the key of the file that has reached its end to 9999 and continue processing.

We must also include in the delete subroutine a test of F$ on the return from READ MASTER and READ TRANS. As before, if F$ is equal to YES, we branch to the RETURN statement to cause a return to the main program. If F$ is not equal to YES, we branch to connector 1 to continue processing.

By tracing the flowchart you should convince yourself that setting the old master key equal to 9999 when the old master file reaches its end and that setting the transaction key equal to 9999 when the transaction file reaches its end will cause the correct branch to be taken when the keys are compared. Therefore any transaction records remaining after the old master file has reached its end are written with error messages, while any old master records remaining after the transaction file has reached its end are written on the new master file.

End-of-File Processing—No END Condition

For versions of BASIC that do not have END conditions the READ MASTER and READ TRANS subroutines must be modified, as they had to be when we were listing selected records.

Once again we assume that both files contain a trailer record whose key is 9999. As shown in Fig. 7.12, after each reading we test the key of the file just read to determine whether it is equal to 9999. If it is, we then test the key of the other file to determine whether it also is equal to 9999. If both keys are equal to 9999, it means both files are at their ends, so we set F$ to YES and return. If only one key is equal to 9999, we simply return without setting the flag. In this case the logic of the delete subroutine ensures that the correct end-of-file processing takes place, and the file that is not at its end will be read repeatedly until it too reaches its end.

One other modification is required to the flowchart in Fig. 7.11. When we return to the main program from the delete subroutine, but before the files are closed, it is necessary to write the trailer record to the new master file.

Exercises

7.8 Based on the flowchart in Fig. 7.11, write a program to delete records from the CHARGE file.

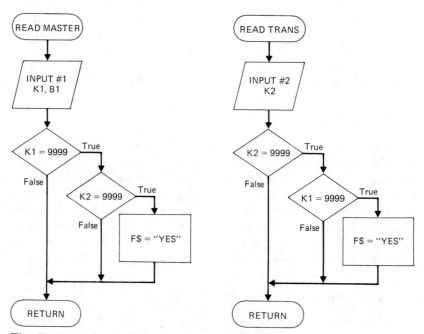

Fig. 7.12. READ MASTER and READ TRANS subroutines for BASICs that do not have END conditions.

7.9 Write a program to delete records from the Mighty Good Ice Cream
Company inventory file, which was created in Exercise 7.1.

ADDING RECORDS

The next problem to consider is adding records to an old master file.
Since in this problem each transaction record represents a record that
should be added to the master file, it must contain all the data contained
in the master record. In our charge account example this means that
each transaction record must contain the charge account number, which
is the key, and the balance in the account. Previously, when we were
listing and deleting records, the transaction records contained only the
key.

To add records to the master file, we must create a new master file
that contains both the records from the old master file and the new
records we are adding. The added records must, of course, be inserted
in their proper sequential positions.

We can use the same variable names we used for deleting records,
but we add the input variable "B2" to stand for the transaction record
balance.

In simplified form the algorithm we will use is

1. Compare the keys from the old master and transaction records.
   a) Transaction records that have matching master records are
      listed with error messages.
   b) If the keys are not equal, the record with the lower key is
      written on the new master file.

Notice we have a significant change from the previous problems. In the
previous problems transaction records with no matching master record
were in error, but now it is transaction records with matching master
records that are in error. This is true because, when the keys are equal,
we are supposed to add to the master file a new record that has the same
key as an existing record. Since keys should be unique, we conclude that
transaction records with matching master records are in error.

If the keys are not equal, the algorithm says that the record with
the lower key should be written on the new master file. By writing the
record with the lower key on the new master we ensure that the new
master file will be in sequential order.

The flowchart to add records is shown in Fig. 7.13. The flowchart
is similar to the flowchart shown in Fig. 7.11. Except that, when the

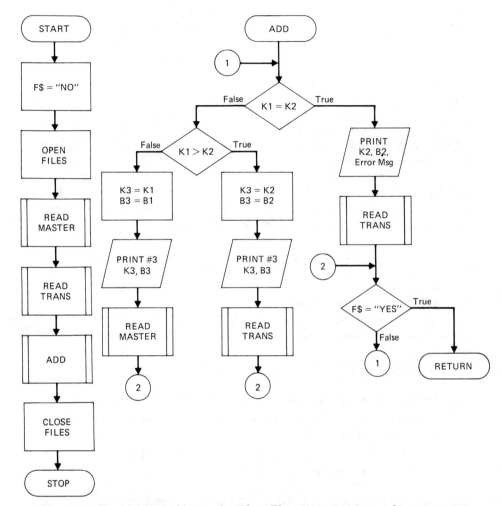

Fig. 7.13. Flowchart to add records. (*Note:* The READ MASTER and READ TRANS subroutines are identical to the ones shown in Fig. 7.11.)

transaction file is read, we must read K2 and B2, the READ MASTER and READ TRANS subroutines are identical to the versions shown in Fig. 7.11. Therefore I have not repeated them in Fig. 7.13. The main program is also essentially the same in the two flowcharts. The only thing that is new is the ADD subroutine. In the ADD subroutine, if the keys are equal, we list the transaction record with an error message. We then read the next transaction record and test F$.

If the keys are not equal, we write the record with the lower key on the new master file. If the record we just wrote were an old master record, we would read the next old master record, and if the record we just wrote were a transaction record, we would read the next transaction record.[2]

End-of-File Processing

Once again it is necessary to continue processing until both files reach their ends. The logic of the flowchart in Fig. 7.13 ensures that any old master records remaining after the transaction file has reached its end will be copied to the new master file. Likewise any transaction records remaining after the old master reaches its end will be added to the new master file.

For BASICs that do not have an END condition it is necessary to use the READ MASTER and READ TRANS subroutines in Fig. 7.12 instead of those in Fig. 7.11. For these BASICs it is also necessary to modify the main program so that, when we return from the ADD subroutine but before the files are closed, the trailer record is written to the new master file.

Exercises

7.10 Based on the flowchart in Fig. 7.13, write a program to add records to the CHARGE file.

7.11 Write a program to add records to the Mighty Good Ice Cream Company inventory file, which was created in Exercise 7.1.

7.12 Although we have been thinking of the flowchart in Fig. 7.13 as showing the logic of adding to the master file, the flowchart could also be interpreted as showing the logic required to merge two files, file 1 and file 2, to create a new file, file 3. With that in mind, write a program that will merge three files, file 1, file 2, and file 3, to produce a new file, file 4. To simplify the problem let's assume that there are no duplicate keys so that no two keys will ever be equal, and we never have to print a key with an error message.

UPDATING RECORDS

Finally let's consider a case in which some customers charged purchases against their accounts or made payments to their accounts. We want to

---

2. This is the same strategy we used in Exercise 6.12 when we merged two arrays.

update the master file so that it includes all the charges and payments that have been made since the master file was created or since it was last updated.

Each charge or payment is used to create a transaction record. The transaction records contain the charge account number, which is the key, the amount of the transaction, and a code that indicates whether the transaction is a charge or a payment. If the code is 1, the transaction is a charge, and if the code is 2, it is a payment.

The balance on the old master record will be updated by adding the charges and subtracting the payments. (This may sound backwards until you remember that the balance represents what the customer owes.) An important feature of this problem is that we must allow for the possibility that some customers may have made more than one charge or payment to their accounts since the master file was created or least updated. This means that there may be more than one transaction record that must be applied against a single old master record. After all the transactions have been applied to a particular old master, it is written on the new master file.

We can use the same data names we used for deleting records, with the addition of two input variables, C2 to stand for the transaction record code and A2 to stand for the transaction record amount.

In simplified form the algorithm we will use is

1. Compare the keys from the old master and transaction records.
   a) Master records that have matching transaction records are updated.
   b) Master records that do not have matching transaction records are copied to the new master file.
   c) Transaction records that do not have matching master records are listed with error messages.

The flowchart to update records is shown in Fig. 7.14. Once again the flowchart is similar to the flowcharts in Figs. 7.11 and 7.13. Except that, when we read the transaction file, we must read K2, C2, and A2, the READ MASTER and READ TRANS subroutines are identical to the versions shown in Fig. 7.11 and are not shown in Fig. 7.14. The main program is also essentially the same as in Figs. 7.11 and 7.13. The only thing that is new then is the UPDATE subroutine.

In the UPDATE subroutine, if the keys are equal, we check to see whether the code is 1. If it is, we add the amount from the transaction record to the old master balance. If the code is not 1, it must be 2, so in that case we subtract the amount from the old master balance. In either case we then read the next transaction record. We do not read

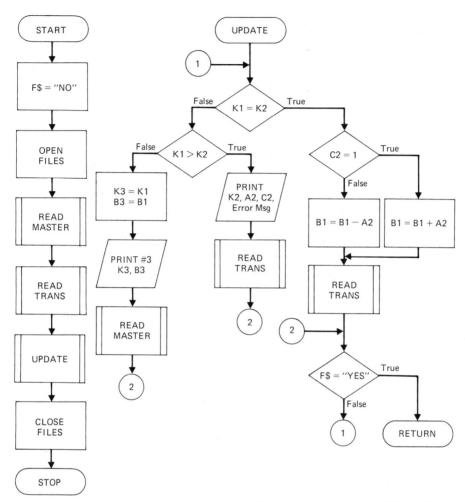

Fig. 7.14. Flowchart to update records. (*Note:* The READ MASTER READ TRANS subroutines are identical to the ones shown in Fig. 7.11.)

the next old master record since additional transaction records may be applied against the current old master record.

If the keys are not equal, we determine which is greater. If the master key is greater than the transaction key, it means that this transaction does not have a matching master record. We therefore list it together with an error message and read the next transaction record.

Suppose on the other hand the master key is less than the transaction key. This means that there are no more transactions to apply against the current old master. The current old master should therefore be written on the new master file. Notice that we do not know whether the current old master record was updated by an earlier transaction or whether it never had a matching transaction. It does not matter because in either case, when the transaction key is greater than the master key, the current old master record should be written on the new master file. After writing the current old master record on the new master file we read the next old master record.

End-of-File Processing

The end-of-file processing is identical to that required when we were deleting records: any old master records that remain after the transaction file has reached its end must be copied to the new master file. Any transaction records that remain after the master file has reached its end must be listed with error messages. The logic of the flowchart ensures that this is exactly what will happen.

For BASICs that do not have an END condition it is necessary to use the READ MASTER and READ TRANS subroutines in Fig. 7.12, instead of those in Fig. 7.11. For these BASICs too it is necessary to modify the main program so that, when we return from the UPDATE subroutine but before the files are closed, the trailer record is written to the new master file.

Exercise

7.13 Based on the flowchart in Fig. 7.14, write a program to update records in the CHARGE file.

7.14 Write a program to update the Mighty Good Ice Cream Company inventory file, which was created in Exercise 7.1. Your program should account for both receipts of ice cream from the manufacturing plant and shipments to customers.

7.15 A club maintains a master file of the annual dues due from each member. Each record in this file contains the member's identification number, which is the key, and the amount of that member's annual dues. Every January the treasurer of the club prepares a transaction record for each dues check received. These transaction records contain the member identification number and the amount of the check. On January 15 the treasurer sorts all the transaction records into order by key. Since you are a member of the club and also a BASIC expert, the treasurer has asked you to write a program that will read the master and transaction files and print a report listing the member identification numbers of all members who have not paid their dues in full and the amount they still owe. As usual, a transaction record without a matching master record is an error, but this problem involves a new condition: a master record without a matching transaction record indicates a member who paid no dues at all. These cases too should be listed, together with members who made only a partial payment.

SUMMARY

In this chapter you have learned

- How to create and list a sequential file
- How to use a file to have the computer remember data from one session to another
- The logic of sequential file processing, including how to use a transaction file to list, delete, add, and update records from a master file
- How to determine the processing required when either the master or the transaction file reaches its end

- The rules for the following BASIC statements
  1. OPEN
  2. PRINT
  3. INPUT
  4. CLOSE
  5. SCRATCH (or RESTORE)

- The rules for the END condition

strings

OBJECTIVES

In this chapter you will learn

- Advanced string processing, including how to take strings apart and how to put them together
- The rules for the BASIC functions

  1. LEN
  2. LEFT$
  3. RIGHT$
  4. MID$
  5. POS$

In addition you should learn the meanings of the following terms:

Concatenation   Null string
Substring   Text editing
Word
processing

In the earlier chapters we have used strings and string variables whenever we needed to, so you are already familiar with some simple string processing. In this chapter we will concentrate on string processing and describe some of the advanced techniques that can be used with strings to solve some interesting problems. Except for Fig. 8.2, the programs in this chapter were executed on a TRS-80.

ELEMENTARY STRING PROCESSING

Before we get to the advanced techniques, let's look at two programs that manipulate strings but that use only those techniques you already know.

Automatic Song Writer

As the first simple string-processing problem let's discuss the program in Fig. 8.1, which might be called an automatic song writer. I have created four lines, as shown in the DATA statements, which could be

```
10 REM AUTOMATIC SONG WRITER
20 REM PROGRAMMER. M TROMBETTA
30 DIM N$(4)
40 REM READ LYRICS INTO N$
50 FOR I = 1 TO 4
60    READ N$(I)
70 NEXT I
80 REM RANDOMLY PRINT FOUR LINES
90 RANDOM
100 FOR I = 1 TO 4
105 REM J IS A RANDOM INTEGER BETWEEN 1 AND 4
110    LET J = 1 + INT (4 * RND (0))
120    PRINT N$(J)
130    PRINT "LA DE DA DE DA DE DA"
140 NEXT I
150 DATA "I LOVE ONLY YOU"
160 DATA "I'LL ALWAYS BE TRUE"
170 DATA "WITHOUT YOU I'M BLUE"
180 DATA "SAY YOU LOVE ME TOO"
190 END
```

This is TRS - 80's version of the RANDOMIZE statement.

In the TRS-80 the RND function requires an argument.

```
RUN

I LOVE ONLY YOU
LA DE DA DE DA DE DA
WITHOUT YOU I'M BLUE
LA DE DA DE DA DE DA
WITHOUT YOU I'M BLUE
LA DE DA DE DA DE DA
I LOVE ONLY YOU
LA DE DA DE DA DE DA
READY
```

Fig. 8.1. Automatic song writer.

used as the lyrics for a song. These four lines are read into the N$ array in the FOR-NEXT loop in lines 50–70.

In the second FOR-NEXT loop in lines 100–140, four of members of N$ are randomly chosen to be printed. In line 110 J is calculated to be a random integer between 1 and 4. (If you don't understand line 110, review the discussion of the INT and RND functions in Chapter 5.) The Jth member of N$ is printed and is followed by the brilliant instrumental line shown in line 130.

Since the members of N$ printed are chosen randomly, we get a different song each time we run the program. With four different lines to choose from we can generate 4^4, or 256 different songs. If you could think of two more possible lines (how about "I love you like an old shoe"), there would be a total of 6^6, or 46,656 different songs. Surely one of them would be bound to become a hit.

Personal Form Letters

We have all received advertising letters that try to sell us something by making it seem as if the letter were written personally to us. The personal touch is added by including our name, or perhaps our home town, in the body of the letter. Computers are usually used to generate such "personal" form letters.

A BASIC program that writes personal form letters is shown in Fig. 8.2. This program happens to write a letter that a BASIC instructor might want to send, but the programs that write the letters used to sell magazine subscriptions or Florida real estate are not very different. In a program used commercially the personal data would be obtained from a file rather than from an INPUT statement. Since the program uses familiar techniques, it should be easy to understand.

Exercises

8.1 Sometimes parents have a hard time choosing a name for a new baby. It might be helpful to let the computer choose a name randomly. Write a program that will accept a value for N and N names. Then have the program randomly select and print one of the names.

8.2 As the output in Fig. 8.1 shows, the program may print the same line more than once. In fact, it could print the same line four times! Modify the program in Fig. 8.1 so that, in each execution, each line is printed only once. The order in which the lines are printed should still be chosen randomly. (*Hint*: This problem is a little harder than you might at first think.)

8.3 Why does the program in Fig. 8.2 require the student's sex to be entered?

8.4 Write a program that will write a personal form letter. The program can write any letter you like. Some suggestions are a love letter, a politican's reelection letter, or a used-car dealer's sales letter.

String Functions

The programs in Figs. 8.1 and 8.2 illustrate rather simple string processing. To solve more complicated problems we must learn how to use the string-processing functions that BASIC provides. Although almost all versions of BASIC provide these functions, there is unfortunately a wide variation in the way these functions are used in different BASICs. I will show you how functions are used in TRS-80 Level II BASIC. Your instructor will tell you the functions used in your version of BASIC, and you should enter them in the space provided on the inside front cover

```
10 REM PERSONAL FORM LETTER
20 REM PROGRAMMER. M. TROMBETTA
30 PRINT "ENTER STUDENT'S FIRST NAME, LAST NAME AND SEX (M/F)"
40 INPUT F$,L$,S$
50 IF S$ = "M" THEN 90
60 LET C$ = "DAUGHTER"
70 LET P$ = "HER"
80 GO TO 110
90 LET C$ = "SON"
100 LET P$ = "HIS"
110 PRINT
120 PRINT
130 PRINT "DEAR MR. AND MRS. ";L$;","
140 PRINT "    I'M SORRY TO TELL YOU THAT YOUR ";C$;", ";F$;","
150 PRINT "HAS NOT BEEN DOING ";P$;" BASIC HOMEWORK.  MAY I"
160 PRINT "SUGGEST THAT YOU NOT ALLOW ";F$;" TO WATCH TV FOR A WEEK."
170 PRINT "                          YOURS TRULY, "
180 PRINT "                          CHARLES BABBAGE"
190 PRINT
200 PRINT
210 GO TO 30
220 END

RUN

FIG8#2      15:51    02/25/80

ENTER STUDENT'S FIRST NAME, LAST NAME AND SEX (M/F)
?ADA,LOVELACE,F


DEAR MR. AND MRS. LOVELACE,
     I'M SORRY TO TELL YOU THAT YOUR DAUGHTER, ADA,
HAS NOT BEEN DOING HER BASIC HOMEWORK.  MAY I
SUGGEST THAT YOU NOT ALLOW ADA TO WATCH TV FOR A WEEK.
                          YOURS TRULY,
                          CHARLES BABBAGE


ENTER STUDENT'S FIRST NAME, LAST NAME AND SEX (M/F)
?HERMAN,HOLLERITH,M


DEAR MR. AND MRS. HOLLERITH,
     I'M SORRY TO TELL YOU THAT YOUR SON, HERMAN,
HAS NOT BEEN DOING HIS BASIC HOMEWORK.  MAY I
SUGGEST THAT YOU NOT ALLOW HERMAN TO WATCH TV FOR A WEEK.
                          YOURS TRULY,
                          CHARLES BABBAGE


ENTER STUDENT'S FIRST NAME, LAST NAME AND SEX (M/F)
?

STOP.
RAN 0.0 SEC.
```

Fig. 8.2. A program that prints a "personal" form letter.

of this book. Fortunately, the fundamental principles apply to all versions of BASIC.

The LEN Function

The first function we will discuss is the LEN function. The LEN function is used as follows:

LET P = LEN (A$)

LEN stands for "length," and this statement assigns to the variable P the length of the string variable A$. The length of a string variable is just the number of characters it contains. You recall from the discussion of functions in Chapter 5 that A$ is called the argument of the LEN function. We say that the LEN function "returns" the length of its argument. If A$ were assigned a value using the statement

LET A$ = "MONDAY"

then P would be 6 because there are 6 characters in MONDAY. (Recall that the quotation marks are not part of the string assigned to A$.) As a second example, if A$ were assigned a value using the statement

LET A$ = "HELLO, I MUST BE GOING"

then P would be 22, because the comma and the spaces count as characters.

The format of the LEN function is

LET variable = LEN (string-variable)

Notice that the argument of the LEN function is a string variable and that, since the LEN function returns a number, the variable on the left side of the equal sign is a numeric variable.

The LEFT$ Function

Three functions—LEFT$, RIGHT$, and MID$—are used to extract parts of a string. When we extract part of a string, we form what is known as a **substring.** Let's consider first the LEFT$ function.

The LEFT$ function is used as follows:

LET B$ = LEFT$ (A$, 3)

This statement causes 3 characters of A$, starting from the left (that's how the function gets its name) to be assigned to B$. So if A$ were equal to ORANGE, B$ would be equal to ORA.

The format of the LEFT$ function is

LET string-variable = LEFT$ (string, number-characters)

This format takes a little explanation. The LEFT$ function requires two arguments, and they must be separated by a comma as shown. The first argument must be a string or a string variable; it is the string from which a substring is to be extracted. The second argument, which must be a number, a numeric variable, or an expression, specifies the number of characters of the first argument that are to be extracted. Remember that the extraction always starts with the left-most character. Since LEFT$ returns a string, the variable on the left of the equal sign must be a string variable.

Many (but unfortunately not all) versions of BASIC use a convention that can help you remember how different functions work. The convention is that any function that returns a string should have a $ as the last character of its name. Using this convention you can see at a glance that LEFT$ returns a string and that LEN returns a number.

Let's get a better feel for how the LEFT$ function works by examining the simple program in Fig. 8.3. We start by setting A$ equal to HIPPOPOTAMUS and L equal to the length of A$. Then, in the FOR-NEXT loop when J is 1, we extract and print the first letter of A$. Then when J is 2, we extract and print the first 2 letters of A$. This continues until finally when J is equal to L, we extract and print all the characters of A$.

The RIGHT$ Function

The RIGHT$ function is similar to the LEFT$ function except that it extracts characters starting from the right. So if A$ were equal to ORANGE, the statement

LET B$ = RIGHT$ (A$, 3)

would cause B$ to be assigned the string "NGE."

The format of the RIGHT$ function is

LET string-variable = RIGHT$ (string, number-characters)

This format is identical to the format of the LEFT$ function; the only difference between the two functions is that RIGHT$ extracts characters starting from the right. Notice that, because the last character in the name of the RIGHT$ function is a $, we know it returns a string.

The RIGHT$ function is used in a program in Fig. 8.4. This program is very similar to the program in Fig. 8.3. In both cases we extract and print first one character from A$, then two characters, and so on until finally all of A$ is printed.

```
10 REM DEMONSTRATING THE LEFT$ FUNCTION
20 LET A$ = "HIPPOPOTAMUS"
30 LET L = LEN (A$)
40 FOR J = 1 TO L
50    LET B$ = LEFT$ (A$,J)
60    PRINT B$
70 NEXT J
80 END


RUN

H
HI
HIP
HIPP
HIPPO
HIPPOP
HIPPOPO
HIPPOPOT
HIPPOPOTA
HIPPOPOTAM
HIPPOPOTAMU
HIPPOPOTAMUS

READY
```

Fig. 8.3. Program to demonstrate the LEFT$ function.

```
10 REM DEMONSTRATING THE RIGHT$ FUNCTION
20 LET A$ = "HIPPOPOTAMUS"
30 LET L = LEN (A$)
40 FOR J = 1 TO L
50    LET B$ = RIGHT$ (A$,J)
60    PRINT B$
70 NEXT J
80 END


RUN

S
US
MUS
AMUS
TAMUS
OTAMUS
POTAMUS
OPOTAMUS
POPOTAMUS
PPOPOTAMUS
IPPOPOTAMUS
HIPPOPOTAMUS

READY
```

Fig. 8.4. Program to demonstrate the RIGHT$ function.

The MID$ Function

The most powerful string-extraction function is the MID$ function. The format of the MID$ function is

MID$ (string, starting position, number of characters)

Notice that the MID$ function requires three arguments and that the three arguments are separated by commas. As with the LEFT$ and RIGHT$ functions the first argument must be a string or string variable and is the string from which a substring is to be extracted. The remaining two arguments must be numbers, numeric variables, or expressions. The first of these, starting position, specifies the character at which string extraction is to begin. The second numeric variable, number of characters, specifies the number of characters that will be extracted.

With this background let's examine the following statement:

LET B$ = MID$ (A$, 2, 3)

Assume that A$ is equal to ORANGE. The starting-position argument is 2, so we will start string extraction at the second character of A$, which is R. The number of characters argument is 3, so we will extract 3 characters. Therefore the characters RAN are assigned to B$. What characters would be assigned to B$ if the statement were written

LET B$ = MID$ (A$, 3, 2)

The answer is given at the end of the chapter.

A program that demonstrates the use of the MID$ function is shown in Fig. 8.5. The length of A$ is 12. The final value on the FOR-NEXT loop is set to half of this, or 6. Inside the FOR-NEXT loop the starting value for string extraction, S, is calculated as 7 − J, and the number of characters to be extracted, N, is calculated as 2 ∗ J. When J = 1, S = 6, and N = 2, so we extract and print the sixth and seventh characters of A$. When J = 2, S = 5, and N = 4, so we extract and print the fifth through the eighth characters of A$. Finally, when J = 6, all of A$ is extracted and printed.

I said earlier that the MID$ function is the most powerful string-extraction function. This is true because MID$ can be used to perform the same functions as LEFT$ and RIGHT$. If MID$ is used with a starting-position value of 1, it functions exactly like the LEFT$ function. In other words the following two statements are equivalent:

LET B$ = LEFT$ (A$, N)

and

LET B$ = MID$ (A$, 1, N)

```
10 REM DEMONSTRATING THE MID$ FUNCTION
20 LET A$ = "HIPPOPOTAMUS"
30 FOR J = 1 TO 6
40    LET S = 7 - J
50    LET N = 2 * J
60    LET B$ = MID$ (A$,S,N)
70    PRINT B$
80 NEXT J
90 END


RUN

PO
OPOT
POPOTA
PPOPOTAM
IPPOPOTAMU
HIPPOPOTAMUS

READY
```

Fig. 8.5. Program to demonstrate the MID$ function.

Similarly, MID$ can be used to perform the same function as the RIGHT$ function, but this is a little more complicated. If L is the length of A$, then the following two statements are equivalent:

LET B$ = RIGHT$ (A$, N)

and

LET B$ = MID$ (A$, L − N + 1, N)

Exercises

8.5 What is the value of B$ after the following statements are executed:

LET B$ = LEFT$ ("ALABAMA", 3)

LET B$ = RIGHT$ ("ALABAMA", 3)

8.6 What is the value assigned to L in Fig. 8.3?

8.7 Modify the program in Fig. 8.3 so that the results are printed in reverse order. The output should be

HIPPOPOTAMUS

HIPPOPOTAMU

HIPPOPOTAM

.

.

.

H

(*Hint*: It is only necessary to change line 40.)

8.8 Suppose that line 20 in Fig. 8.4 were changed to

20 LET A$ = "GIRAFFE"

Considering the fact that HIPPOPOTAMUS has 12 letters, and GIRAFFE has only 7 letters, determine whether the program in Fig. 8.4 would work properly.

8.9 Convince yourself that the following two statements are equivalent:

LET B$ = RIGHT$ (A$, N)

and

LET B$ = MID$ (A$, L − N + 1, N)

What value will they each assign to B$ if A$ is equal to WYOMING and N is equal to 3? (L is equal to the length of A$.)

8.10 Revise the program in Fig. 8.5 so that it will work properly when A$ is equal to any string whose length is an even number.

8.11 The output produced by the program in Fig. 8.5 would be much more impressive if it formed a triangle:

PO

OPOT

POPOTA

PPOPOTAM

IPPOPOTAMU

HIPPOPOTAMUS

Write a program that will generate this output. (*Hint*: One way to do this is to change line 70 to

70 PRINT P$; B$

P$ is a padding string of blanks that is used to force B$ to start printing at the right spot. Note that P$ must be assigned the correct number of blanks.)

USING STRING FUNCTIONS

Now that you have learned how these string functions work, it is time to use them to solve some problems. The first problem to consider involves reading a name given in the format

first name space last name

such as GEORGE WASHINGTON,
and printing it in the format

last name comma space first name

such as WASHINGTON, GEORGE.
The variable names we will use are

Input variable

Name   N$

Internal variables

Length of N$ L

Subscript   J

A character
   from N$ C$

Output variables

First name   F$

Last name   L$

The basic algorithm we will use is

1. Read N$ and set L equal to the length of N$

2. Search N$ one character at a time and look for a blank.

3. If no blank is found, print a message.

4. If a blank is found, extract the first name and last name and print them.

The only parts of this algorithm that require explanation are steps 2 and 4. The flowchart in Fig. 8.6 shows how these steps are carried out.

We perform a sequential search, the logic of which is identical to the sequential search we studied in Chapter 6. In a FOR-NEXT loop we extract and examine one character after another from N$ as we search for one that is a blank. The index J of the FOR-NEXT loop varies from 1 to the length of N$. Notice the way the MID$ function is used:

LET C$ = MID$ (N$, J, 1)

The third argument, the number-of-characters argument, is 1. The second argument, the starting-position argument, is J. Therefore when J = 1, C$ will be equal to the first character of N$; when J = 2, C$ will be equal to the second character of N$, and so on.

The character C$ is tested to see whether it is blank. If it is not a blank, we simply go on to extract the next character from N$. If

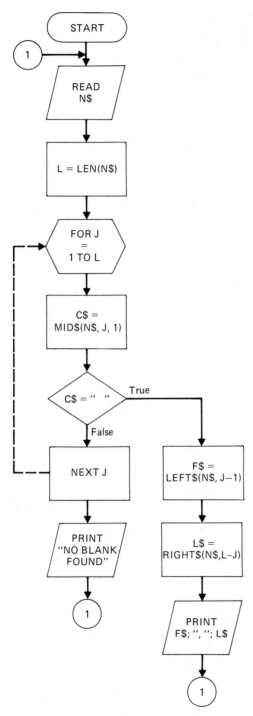

Fig. 8.6. Flowchart for rearranging names.

the search is unsuccessful and we never find a blank, we print a message and go on to read the next name. When we do find a blank, we know we have found the divider between the first and second names, so we branch out of the FOR-NEXT loop to the statements that will extract the first and last names from N\$.

The first name is extracted from N\$ by the statement

LET F\$ = LEFT\$ (N\$, J − 1)

How does this statement work? Recall that, when we execute this statement, J is equal to the position of the blank in N\$. We can say that J points to the blank. For example, if N\$ were equal to GEORGE WASHINGTON, J would be equal to 7. Then the above statement would assign the J − 1, or 7 − 1, or 6 left-most characters of N\$—that is, we assign GEORGE to F\$—which is exactly what we want.

The last name is extracted from N\$ by the statement

LET L\$ = RIGHT\$ (N\$, L − J)

Again assuming that N\$ were equal to GEORGE WASHINGTON, J would be equal to 7, and L, which is the length of N\$, would be equal to 17. This statement would therefore assign the L − J, or 17 − 7, or 10 right-most characters of N\$—that is, we assign WASHINGTON to L\$—which again is exactly what we want.

Finally, we can print the names in the format we want by the statement

PRINT F\$; ", "; N\$

The program, which follows directly from the flowchart, is shown in Fig. 8.7. You should have no trouble understanding it.

I have explained this program at some length, because searching and substring extracting are techniques we will use many times in this chapter. You should understand them thoroughly before you go on.

Exercises

8.12 Show how you would modify the program in Fig. 8.7 so that a space is not printed after the comma.

8.13 Suppose we are given data in the format

name comma space telephone number

for example:

MARY, 576-1342

```
10  REM REARRANGING NAMES
20  REM PROGRAMMER. M TROMBETTA
30  READ N$
40  LET L = LEN (N$)
50  REM SEARCH FOR A BLANK
60  FOR J = 1 TO L
70    LET C$ = MID$ (N$,J,1)
80    IF C$ = " " THEN 130
90  NEXT J
100 REM NO BLANK FOUND, PRINT ERROR MESSAGE
110 PRINT "NO BLANK IN NAME "; N$
120 GO TO 30
130 REM BLANK FOUND, EXTRACT FIRST AND LAST NAMES
140 LET F$ = LEFT$ (N$,J-1)
150 LET L$ = RIGHT$ (N$,L-J)
160 PRINT L$;", ";F$
170 GO TO 30
180 DATA "GEORGE WASHINGTON"
190 DATA "THOMAS JEFFERSON"
200 DATA "ABRAHAMLINCOLN"
210 END


RUN

WASHINGTON, GEORGE
JEFFERSON, THOMAS
NO BLANK IN NAME ABRAHAMLINCOLN
?OD ERROR IN 30

READY
```

Fig. 8.7. Program to rearrange names.

Write a program that prints the data in the order

phone number space name

for example:

576-1342 MARY

Notice that the comma has been eliminated.

CONCATENATION

So far all we have learned to do with strings is to take them apart. It is also possible to put strings together. The technical word for putting strings together is, believe it or not, **concatenation**.

To understand concatenation, consider the following BASIC statements:

```
10 LET A$ = "WATER"

20 LET B$ = "MELON"

30 LET F$ = A$ + B$
```

In line 30 the plus sign, +, indicates that A$ and B$ are to be concatenated, or put together, and the result assigned to F$. After line 30 is executed, F$ will contain WATERMELON. Notice that the two strings are just put together end to end; no blank is inserted between them. In some versions of BASIC the ampersand, &, is used to indicate concatenation. You should write the symbol used in your BASIC on the inside front cover of this book.

Strings as well as string variables may be concatenated, and as many strings and string variables as you like may be concatenated in a single expression. So we can expand our example to the following statements:

```
10 LET A$ = "WATER"

20 LET B$ = "MELON"

30 LET C$ = "SWEET"

40 LET F$ = "RIPE " + C$ + " " + A$ + B$
```

After line 40 is executed, F$ will contain RIPE SWEET WATERMELON. Notice that to get a space between RIPE and SWEET I included a space at the end of RIPE, and to get a space between SWEET and WATERMELON I concatenated a string that consists of a single space.

The Pig Latin Problem

Now that we know how to form substrings and how to concatenate, we can take strings apart and put them back together any way we like. As an example, I would like to develop a program that takes an English sentence and prints it in pig latin. Do you remember how to change an English word into pig latin? You simply move the first letter of the word to the end of the word and then add "ay." So pig latin becomes igpay atinlay.

We will use the following variables:

Input variable

Original English text   E$

Internal variables

Length of E$ L

A character from E$	C$
A subscript	J
A pointer	S

Output variable

Pig latin text	P$

How the pointer variable S is used will be made clear when we examine the program.

The algorithm we will use is

1. Read E$ and set L equal to the length of E$.

2. Search E$ one character at a time, looking for a blank.

3. When a blank is found, convert the current word to pig latin and add it to P$.

4. Repeat for all the words in E$.

The logic of this program is simple enough so that we do not need a flowchart to explain it. Instead let's discuss the program, shown in Fig. 8.8. The first thing we do in line 40 is to set P$ equal to "". Two quotation marks right next to each other is know as the **null string**. It is the string equivalent of zero. We must start P$ equal to the null string because in line 170, we will use P$ as a string accumulator. Just as numeric accumulators must be given an initial value of zero, so string accumulators must be given an initial value equal to the null string.

We next read E$ and then in line 70, concatenate a blank on the end of E$. The reason we do this is that, when we search E$, a blank will be the indication that we have reached the end of a word. But initially there is no blank at the end of the last word in E$. We could do something special to handle the last word, but the simplest thing to do is to concatenate a blank to the end of E$. This allows us to treat the last word as all the other words were treated.

The next significant step is line 100, where we set S to 1. S is equal to the position in E$ of the first letter of the current word. In other words S points to the start of the current word. Initially the current word is the first word, and the first letter of the first word is in position one. Therefore we initially assign S the value 1. The reason we need S is that, when we convert the current word to pig latin, we must know where in E$ the current word starts. S tells us where it starts.

In the FOR-NEXT loop each character in E$ is extracted and examined. Line 130 functions exactly like line 70 in Fig. 8.7. If the current

```
10 REM CONVERT ENGLISH TO PIG LATIN
20 REM PROGRAMMER. M TROMBETTA
30 REM INITIALIZE PIG LATIN STRING
40 LET P$ = ""
45 REM READ AND PRINT ENGLISH STRING
50 READ E$
55 PRINT "ENGLISH    ";E$
60 REM ADD A BLANK AT THE END OF E$
70 LET E$ = E$ + " "
80 LET L = LEN (E$)
90 REM SET START OF CURRENT WORD TO 1
100 LET S = 1
110 REM SEARCH E$ FOR BLANKS
120 FOR J = 1 TO L
130    LET C$ = MID$ (E$,J,1)
140    IF C$ <> " " THEN 200
150 REM BLANK FOUND AT POSITION J. CONVERT PREVIOUS WORD
160 REM TO PIG LATIN AND CONCATENATE IT TO P$
170    LET P$ = P$ + MID$ (E$,S+1,J-S-1) + MID$ (E$,S,1) + "AY "
180 REM UPDATE START OF CURRENT WORD
190    LET S = J + 1
200 NEXT J
210 REM E$ COMPLETELY TRANSLATED, PRINT IT
220 PRINT "PIG LATIN ";P$
230 DATA "EITHER HE IS DEAD OR MY WATCH STOPPED"
240 END


RUN

ENGLISH    EITHER HE IS DEAD OR MY WATCH STOPPED
PIG LATIN ITHEREAY EHAY SIAY EADDAY ROAY YMAY ATCHWAY TOPPEDSAY

READY
```

Fig. 8.8. Program to convert English to pig latin.

character, C\$, is not equal to a blank, we bypass that character. If it is equal to a blank, we know we have reached the end of the current word. We must now convert that word to pig latin and concatenate it to P\$. All that is done in line 170.

To understand how line 170 works, let's examine it when it operates on the data given in Fig. 8.8. Remember that initially S is equal to 1. When we find the first blank, J is equal to 7. Then the first use of MID\$ becomes

$$MID\$ (E\$, S + 1, J - S - 1) = MID\$ (E\$, 2, 5)$$

This refers to 5 letters from E\$, starting in postition 2, which are the letters ITHER. Similarly, the second use of MID\$ in line 170 becomes

$$MID\$ (E\$, S, 1) = MID\$ (E\$, 1, 1)$$

This refers to one letter from E$, starting in position one, which is the letter "E." At this point line 170 is equivalent to

170 LET P$ = P$ + "ITHER" + "E" + "AY "

Since P$ was initially set equal to the null string, after line 170 is executed, P$ will contain ITHEREAY, which is the translation of the word "either" into pig latin. Notice the blank at the end of the string AY. This provides the space between words in P$.

We then calculate a new value of S equal to J + 1, or 8. We see that, as it should, S is pointing to the start of the next word. The loop then continues, searching for the next blank. By the time we fall through the FOR-NEXT loop, E$ has been completely translated, and all we have to do is print P$.

I would not want you to get the idea that line 170 sprang into my head as one sudden inspiration. I didn't see the correct version of the first MID$ function immediately. I was not sure whether the starting position argument should be S, or S − 1, or S + 1. Similarly, I knew that the number of characters argument would include J − S because J pointed to the end of the word and S pointed to the start, but I was not sure whether it would be J − S + 1 or J − S − 1 or maybe even something different. I determined the correct expressions in both cases exactly the same way you should: I invented some English text, found the values of S and J when the first blank was found, and then adjusted the two arguments until I got the MID$ function to do what I wanted it to do. Next I determined the values of S and J when the second blank was found and checked that the expressions I had determined also worked for the second word. You should follow the same procedure in your programs.

Exercises

8.14 To convince yourself that you really understand how the program in Fig. 8.8 works, trace line 170 when the second blank is found.

8.15 Write a program to convert pig latin into English.

8.16 Write a program to read a phrase and print it backwards. If your phase is

HAPPY BIRTHDAY

your program should produce

YADHTRIB YPPAH

TEXT EDITING

The POS Function

The POS function is very useful, but it is not available in all versions of BASIC. Many BASICs however, have functions equivalent to the POS function but with different names. Again your instructor will tell you the name of the function used in your BASIC, and you should write it on the inside front cover of this book.

The POS function searches for the appearance of one string in another. It is used as follows:

LET J = POS (A$, B$, N)

The first argument, A$, is the string to be searched. The second argument, B$, is the string we are searching for. The third argument, N, is the position in A$ where the search is to begin. If B$ is found in A$, J is set to the position in A$ where B$ starts. If B$ is not found in A$, J is set to zero. Strings may be used in place of A$ and B$, and a number or an expression may be used in place of N.

This may all sound very confusing, but the POS function is really quite simple, as some examples will demonstrate. Suppose A$ equals CONCATENATION. Now consider the statement

LET J = POS (A$, "T", 1)

The statement causes A$ to be searched, starting from position 1, for the string "T." Since T appears in position 6 of A$, J is set equal to 6. Notice that the second T, in position 10, is ignored. POS stops searching as soon as it finds a T.

Consider next the statement

LET J = POS (A$, "T", 8)

This statement causes A$ to be searched, starting from position 8, for the string T. Since T appears in position 10, which is after the starting position, J is set to 10. Notice that J is the position of the T measured from the start of A$, not from the starting position of the search. Finally consider the statement

LET J = POS (A$, "T", 11)

This sets J equal to zero, because no T appears in A$ after starting position 11.

We can also search for the appearance of strings of more than one character. The statement

LET J = POS (A$, "CAT", 1)

would set J equal to 4. Notice that J is set equal to the position in A$ where CAT starts. On the other hand the statement

LET J = POS (A$, "DOG", 1)

would set J equal to zero.

Not all versions of BASIC have a POS function because by using the MID$ and LEN functions we can write a subroutine to do what the POS function does. This should not surprise us, for in our previous problems we searched a string for the appearance of a blank.

The INSTRING Subroutine

The BASIC for the TRS-80 does not have a POS function. The TRS-80 manual suggests using the following subroutine, which they call the INSTRING subroutine, in place of the POS function.[1]

1000 FOR J = N TO LEN (A$) − LEN (B$) + 1

1010   IF B$ = MID$ (A$, J, LEN (B$)) THEN 1040

1020 NEXT J

1030 LET J = 0

1040 RETURN

This subroutine assigns to J exactly the same values that would be assigned by the statement

LET J = POS (A$, B$, N)

The logic of this subroutine is so similar to the logic we used in our problems when we were searching for blanks that it should be pretty easy to understand.

In line 1000 the FOR-NEXT loop starts at N, not 1, because we want to search A$ starting at position N. Also the final value in the FOR-NEXT loop is not LEN (A$), as we used when we searched for a blank, but rather LEN (A$) − LEN (B$) + 1. Notice that if LEN (B$) is equal to 1, as it was when we searched for a blank, then the final value of the FOR-NEXT loop is indeed LEN (A$), just as we used. If, however, LEN (B$) is greater than 1, then the final value should be as given in line 1000.

To see why, let's assume that A$ has a length of 10, and B$ has a length of 3. According to line 1000 the final value of J will be 10 −

---

1. I have modified the subroutine slightly to conform to our style.

3 + 1, or 8. When J is equal to 8, the MID$ function will extract from
A$ the substring at positions 8, 9, and 10. That substring is clearly the
last three-character substring we can extract from A$. If by mistake we
allowed J to become 9, we would try to extract the substring at positions
9, 10, and 11. This would be wrong, since the length of A$ is only 10.

In line 1010 the MID$ function is written to extract from A$ a
substring whose length is equal to the length of B$. Since we are trying
to find a substring equal to B$, the substring must clearly have the
same length as B$.

As the first example of a program with the POS function I would
like to solve a **text-editing** problem. Text editing refers to the use of
computers to simplify making corrections to a text, where the text may
be a computer program, a report, or a poem. In business the use of
computers in this way is called **word processing**.

In a real text-editing or word-processing application the original
text would be saved in a file. If we stored our text on file, however, it
would just make our example harder to understand, so I will let the text
we want to edit be contained in a single DATA statement.

Assume an author has written a screen play, and as he rereads it,
the line "Play it again, George" seems not to have exactly the right
tone. If the author had available the text-editing program shown in Fig.
8.9, changing that line would be easy.

The output in Fig. 8.9 shows that the program first prints the
original text and then requests the user to enter the bad string, which
is to be replaced, and the replacement string. The replacement is made,
and the modified text is printed. Notice that the bad string and the
modified string do not have to have the same length. Let's look at the
program to see how it works.

The variables used in the program are

Input variables

Original text	O$
Bad string	B$
Replacement string	R$

Internal variables

Length of O$	L1
Length of B$	L2
Pointer to start of B$ in O$	J

```
10 REM TEXT-EDITING PROGRAM
20 REM PROGRAMMER. M TROMBETTA
30 REM READ AND PRINT ORIGINAL TEXT
40 READ O$
45 PRINT "ORIGINAL TEXT:    ";O$
50 PRINT "ENTER BAD AND REPLACEMENT STRINGS"
60 INPUT B$,R$
70 LET L1 = LEN (O$)
80 LET L2 = LEN (B$)
85 REM
90 REM FIND B$ IN O$
100 GOSUB 1000
110 IF J = 0 THEN 160
120 REM B$ WAS FOUND. REPLACE IT WITH R$
130 LET N$ = LEFT$ (O$,J-1) + R$ + MID$ (O$,J+L2,L1+1-J-L2)
140 PRINT "MODIFIED TEXT:    ";N$
150 STOP
160 PRINT B$;"  NOT FOUND"
170 GO TO 60
180 DATA "PLAY IT AGAIN, GEORGE"
1000 FOR J = 1 TO L1 - L2 + 1
1010    IF B$ = MID$ (O$,J,L2) THEN 1040
1020 NEXT J
1030 LET J = 0
1040 RETURN
1050 END


RUN

ORIGINAL TEXT:    PLAY IT AGAIN, GEORGE
ENTER BAD AND REPLACEMENT STRINGS
? GEORGE,SAM
MODIFIED TEXT:    PLAY IT AGAIN, SAM
BREAK IN 150

READY
```

Fig. 8.9. Text-editing program.

Output variable

Modified text   N$

After reading and printing O$ and accepting B$ and R$, the program searches for B$ in O$. The program in Fig. 8.9 was run on a TRS-80, which as I said earlier, does not have a POS function. I therefore wrote an INSTRING subroutine, which is shown in lines 1000–1040. This subroutine is executed from line 100:

100 GOSUB 1000

If your version of BASIC does have a POS function, you would eliminate lines 1000–1040, and replace line 100 by

100 LET J = POS (O$, B$, 1)

I want to emphasize that these are the only changes you would have to make to the program.

If on return from either the POS function or the INSTRING subroutine J is equal to zero, it means that B$ is not contained in O$. If J is not zero, it means that B$ was found in O$, and J points to the character in O$ where B$ starts. It remains only to delete B$ from O$ and insert R$ in its place. Both these functions are done by line 130. Line 130 is not exactly a simple statement, but by now, especially after our discussion of line 170 in the pig latin program in Fig. 8.8, you should be able to figure out how it works for yourself.

Exercises

8.17 Determine the value of J after each of the following statements is executed

   a) LET J = POS ("MATRIMONY", "M", 1)

   b) LET J = POS ("MATRIMONY", "M", 4)

   c) LET J = POS ("MATRIMONY", "M", 7)

   d) LET J = POS ("MATRIMONY", "MONEY", 1),

   e) LET J = POS ("MATRIMONY", "MAT", 1)

8.18 To make sure that you really understand how it works, trace the execution of line 130 in Fig. 8.9 with the data given in the program.

8.19 Suppose you wanted to change the original text in Fig. 8.9 to PLAY IT SOME MORE, GEORGE. What would you enter for B$ and R$?

8.20 Try to think of a way to use the program in Fig. 8.9 to delete a string but not to replace it with anything. For example we might want to change the original text to PLAY IT AGAIN.

8.21 There is one problem with the program in Fig. 8.9. If B$ starts at the first character in O$, J will be equal to 1. Then in line 130 the second argument of the LEFT$ function, which is J − 1, would be zero. We really do want to extract the left-most zero characters from O$, but in some versions of BASIC a zero argument in the LEFT$ function would be interpreted as an error. Modify the program to avoid this problem.

8.22 The program in Fig. 8.9 changes only the first occurrence of B$. Modify the program to change all the occurrences of B$. For example, suppose a famous movie star was originally named Rin-Aluminum-Aluminum. If we tried to change this name by using the program in Fig. 8.9, with B$ equal to Aluminum and R$ equal to Tin, the name would be changed to Rin-Tin-Aluminum. That's an improvement, but not much. Modify the program so that the name would be changed to Rin-Tin-Tin.

MAKING A CODE

Some years ago it was reported that within the federal government the agency that made the greatest use of computers was, perhaps surprisingly, the CIA. Most foreign governments use computer programs to put their messages into code, and the CIA uses programs to break these codes. The programs used by governments are quite sophisticated, but it is possible to write a rather simple BASIC program to encode a message. The code would not stump the CIA, but at least it should baffle your friends.

The program in Fig. 8.10 uses a simple substitution code, in which every letter in the original English message is replaced by a different letter in the coded message. The variables used are

Input variable	
English message	E$
Internal variables	
Alphabet string	A$
Translating string	T$
Current character	L$
Pointer	J
Length of E$	L
Subscript	I
Output variable	
Coded text	C$

The translation string, T$, causes letters in the English message to be replaced by different letters in the coded message. In the program in Fig. 8.10, I have arbitrarily chosen T$ to be the alphabet in backwards order. This choice of T$ will cause an A in the original English message to be changed to a Z in the coded message, a B to be changed to a Y, a C to an X, and so on, with a Z being changed to an A. You should understand, however, that the letters in T$ can be in any order. The only requirement is that T$ contain every letter exactly once.

How does the encoding actually work? In the FOR-NEXT loop the characters in E$ are extracted one at a time and assigned to L$. Then A$ is searched for L$. Once again I have used an INSTRING subroutine,

```
10 REM ENCODING A MESSAGE
20 REM PROGRAMMER, M TROMBETTA
30 REM INITIALIZE ALPHABET, TRANSLATING AND CODE STRINGS
40 LET A$ = "ABCDEFGHIJKLMNOPQRSTUVWXYZ"
50 LET T$ = "ZYXWVUTSRQPONMLKJIHGFEDCBA"
60 LET C$ = ""
70 PRINT "ENTER ENGLISH MESSAGE"
80 INPUT E$
90 LET L = LEN (E$)
100 REM TRANSLATE ONE LETTER AT A TIME
110 FOR I = 1 TO L
120    LET L$ = MID$ (E$,I,1)
130    GOSUB 1000
140    IF J = 0 THEN 170
150    LET C$ = C$ + MID$ (T$,J,1)
160    GO TO 190
170 REM CURRENT CHARACTER NOT IN A$, ADD IT TO C$ UNCHANGED
180    LET C$ = C$ + MID$ (E$,I,1)
190 NEXT I
200 PRINT "CODED MESSAGE:    ";C$
210 STOP
1000 FOR J = 1 TO 26
1010    IF L$ = MID$ (A$,J,1) THEN 1040
1020 NEXT J
1030 LET J = 0
1040 RETURN
1050 END


RUN

ENTER ENGLISH MESSAGE
? ONE IF BY LAND TWO IF BY SEA
CODED MESSAGE:    LMV RU YB OZMW GDL RU YB HVZ

BREAK IN 210

READY
```

Fig. 8.10. Program to encode a message.

but if you have a POS function in your version of BASIC line 130 could
be written

LET J = POS (A$, L$, 1)

and lines 1000 through 1040 would be eliminated. If J is equal to zero,
it means that L$ does not appear in A$ (it might be a space or punc-
tuation mark). In that case L$ is just concatenated to C$. If J is not
zero, it points to the position in A$ where L$ appears. Line 150 causes
the corresponding character from T$ to be concatenated to C$.

To see exactly how this works, assume that L$ is equal to E. When
A$ is searched for L$, J will be set to 5, because E is the fifth character
in A$. Then in line 130 the fifth character of T$, V, will be concatenated

to C$. In this way the E in the original English message is changed to a V in the coded message.

Exercises

8.23 A particularly simple type of substitution code is known as a Caesar code, after Julius Caesar who supposedly used it. In the terms of our program, the T$ string is in normal alphabetical order, but it is shifted to the left by an arbitrary number of letters. The letters that are pushed out of the front end of T$ are added to the back. For example, if we shifted T$ by four letters, it would be

LET T$ = "EFGHIJKLMNOPQRSTUVWXYZABCD"

With this T$ every letter in the original English message is replaced by the letter four letters after it in the alphabet. (We understand that, for example, the letter four letters "after" Z is D.) Since the shift can be any number from 1 to 25 characters, there are 25 different Caesar codes.

Suppose you have found a coded message that was encoded with one of the Caesar codes, but of course, you don't know which one. Write a program that will decode the message by systematically trying all 25 Caesar codes. Try your program on the following message:

JVUNYHABSHAPVUZ, FVB JHU HWWSF AV AOL JPH MVY H QVI

8.24 Write a program that will read a text and will count and print the number of times each letter is used. To make the program interesting, you might like to have several DATA statements of text. In that case you can use a DATA statement containing the word END as trailer data. If you examine Lincoln's Gettysburgh Address, you will find that it contains no J's, K's, or Q's. *Hint:* It will be useful to set up an alphabet string A$, like the one used in Fig. 8.10. In addition you should set up a counter array C with 26 members, corresponding to the 26 letters. Whenever you find a letter, you should add one to the corresponding member of C.

SUMMARY

In this chapter you have learned

■   How to use the LEN function to determine the length of a string

- How to extract substrings using the LEFT$, RIGHT$, and MID$ functions
- How to use an example to help determine the arguments for the LEFT$, RIGHT$, and MID$ functions
- How to concatenate strings
- How to search a string for the occurrence of another string using either the POS function or the INSTRING subroutine
- The answer to question in this chapter: B$ is assigned the characters "AN"

glossary

Accumulator. A variable used to accumulate the values of another variable.

Algorithm. A sequence of steps that can be followed by a computer to solve a problem.

Argument. A constant, variable, or expression given to a function and used by the function to determine a result.

Array. A collection of storage locations that have the same name. To specify a particular member of a one-dimensional array requires one subscript, and to specify a particular member of a two-dimensional array requires two subscripts.

Branching statement. A statement that causes a change in the normal sequence of execution by causing the computer to branch to, or execute, a specific line rather than the line with the next-

higher line number. An unconditional branching statement causes the branch to be taken whenever it is executed, but a conditional branching statement causes the branch to be taken only when a given condition is true.

Central processing unit. See **CPU.**

Command. An order to the computer to perform some function immediately.

Compiler. A program that must be used to translate a program written in a language like BASIC into machine language before the BASIC program may be executed.

Concatenation. Adding together strings or string variables.

Condition. In a simple condition a variable is compared with another variable or with a constant. In a compound condition two or more simple conditions are joined by the words AND or OR.

Control break. A change in the value of a control variable, which means that some special processing, such as printing subtotals, should be performed.

Conversational computing. A method of computing in which the computer gives answers immediately.

Counter. A variable used to count. A counter might be used to count the number of times a loop is executed.

Counter-controlled loop. A loop that has a counter controlling the number of times it is executed.

CPU. Central processing unit. The computer component in which arithmetic and logical operations are performed.

Debugging. Removing errors (bugs) from a program.

Documenting. Adding comments to a program to explain what the program does and how it does it.

End-of-file mark. A special magnetic signal that is automatically written by the computer at the end of a file stored on magnetic tape or disk.

Exponentiation. Raising to a power.

Expression. A combination of variables, constants, and arithmetic or string operational symbols that can be evaluated to produce a numeric or string value.

Field. An area reserved in a record to store an item of data.

File. A collection of related records. In a sequential file the records must be processed sequentially. In a direct file the records may be processed in any order.

Flag. A variable introduced into a program for the sole purpose of controlling the execution of the program, based on whether some condition is true or false.

Flowchart. A picture of an algorithm showing the logical structure of the algorithm very clearly.

Function. A subroutine supplied by BASIC that performs a commonly required programming task.

Independent loops. FOR-NEXT loops that do not intersect (See Fig. 5.13).

Input unit. The component of a computer system that sends data and instructions from the outside world to the computer.

Key. A field in a record used as the identifying field.

Logic error. An error in a program that causes the program to calculate the wrong answer.

Loop. A series of instructions that is executed repeatedly.

Master data. Data showing the

current status of a business or activity. When master data are organized into a file, it is called a master file.

Nested loops. FOR-NEXT loops in which an inner loop is completely enclosed in an outer loop. (See Fig. 5.13).

Null string. A string containing no characters.

On-line. Connected to a computer.

Output unit. The component of a computer system that sends the computer's answers to the outside world.

Primary storage. The computer component in which data and instructions being processed are stored.

Program. A set of instructions that a computer is to follow to solve a problem.

Prompt. A message printed by a program to tell a user what to do next.

Record. A group of related fields that refer to one item.

Relational symbol. One of the following six symbols: $=$, $<$, $>$, $<=$, $>=$, or $<>$.

Round-off error. A small numeric error that occurs in computer-calculated answers because of the way in which computers store numbers.

Rules of precedence. The order in which the computer evaluates expressions. The order is

0. Evaluation of expressions inside parentheses.
1. Exponentiation.
2. Multiplication and division.
3. Addition and subtraction.

Secondary storage. Storage outside the computer itself, where data and programs may be stored permanently. The devices used for secondary storage include magnetic tape and disks.

Sign-on. The procedure for connecting a terminal to a computer.

String. A group of letters, numbers, or special characters.

Subroutine. A group of statements that perform some calculation or function.

Subscript. A constant, variable, or expression that indicates which member of an array is being used.

Substring. Part of a string.

Syntax error. An error that violates the rules of BASIC.

Terminal. Any device that can be used to send data to and receive responses from a computer. All terminals have a keyboard for entering data. In CRT terminals the computer's responses are displayed on a TV screen, while on a hard-copy terminal the computer's responses are printed on paper.

Text editing. Using a computer to make corrections to a text.

Timesharing. A method of using a computer in which two or more users can execute programs at the same time.

Tracing. Executing a program by hand, line by line, and keeping track of the changing values of the variables.

Trailer data. Extra data added after all the real data to signal that all the real data have been read.

Transaction data. Data that indicate changes to be made to master data. When transaction data are organized in a file, it is called a transaction file.

Uninitialized variable. A variable that is used before it is assigned a value.

Variable. A quantity whose value may change when a program is executed. An ordinary, or numeric, variable may have a value that is a number, while a string variable may have a value that is a string.

Word processing. See **text editing.**

index

summary of
BASIC statements,
functions, and commands

For quick reference those BASIC statements, functions, and commands that are the same in most versions of BASIC are listed here. Those statements, functions, and commands that are different in different versions of BASIC are listed on the inside front cover.

BASIC STATEMENTS (Statements must begin with a line number.)

General Format	Example
DIM variable (number), variable (number)*	**DIM A(10),N$(8)**
or	
DIM variable (number, number)*	**DIM C(12,15)**
END	**END**

    ⎡ **FOR** variable = S TO F **STEP** step   ⎡ **FOR J = 1 TO W STEP R**
    │   where S = the starting value;   │ •
    │   F = the final value;   │ •
    │   step = the step size.   │ •
    ⎣ **NEXT** variable   ⎣ **NEXT J**

General Format	Example
GO TO line number	**GO TO 10**
GOSUB line number	**GOSUB 500**
IF condition **THEN** line number	**IF A < B THEN 60**
INPUT variable, variable, variable*	**INPUT P,S,M**
LET variable = expression	**LET V = R − S**
(Many **BASIC**s allow the word **LET** to be omitted.)	
PRINT variable,variable,variable*	**PRINT F,H,C$**
or	
PRINT "string,"variable*	**PRINT "TOTAL",T**
(Semicolons may be used in place of commas.)	

---

* You can list as many variables or values as you like.